W9-AHA-770

STEVE LYONS

PSYCHO*analysis*

By
Steve Lyons

SAGAMORE PUBLISHING
Champaign, IL

Production Manager: Susan M. McKinney
Editor: Mary Jane Harshbarger
Dustjacket and photo insert design: Michelle R. Dressen
Proofreader: Phyllis L. Bannon

ISBN: 1-57167-013-0
Library of Congress Catalog Card Number: 95-69132

Printed in the United States

To my mother, who encouraged me to have a dream,
and to my father, who gave me the strength to pursue it.

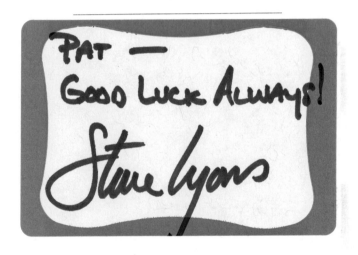

CONTENTS

ACKNOWLEDGMENTS

A special thanks to Tom Demakis, my agent and forever my friend, whose guidance and dependability have always gone unsurpassed. To David Greenbaum, for his long hours of typing and editing, and to Christina Hahn for assisting him. To Ann Russell, for beginning the whole process. To Homemakers Furniture Stores, and particularly Gloria Michael, for letting us shoot the cover photo in their store. To Pete Powers and Grandstand Sports Memorabilia Store for providing the uniforms for the cover shot. To photographers Wally Wright, Sharon Smith, and LauriAnn Mardo-Zayat. To Stephen King, for doing me the great honor of writing the foreword for this book. Words cannot express my gratitude. To Christa Schiffmann, my financee, for convincing me to write this — and for putting up with me while I did. To the visiting dugout benches in every major league ball park — I've sat on them all. And finally, thanks to my family, friends, coaches, and all the fans who helped make baseball the greatest experience of my life.

INTRODUCTION

I will be the first to tell you that I was not the greatest ballplayer to ever don a major league uniform. In fact, I was an average major leaguer.

There were many people in my life and throughout my career who concerned themselves with reminding me of my shortcomings. Nay-sayers who had nothing better to do than to tear me down. What they didn't know was that they became part of my inspiration and desire to succeed. I think many people can relate their own life's experiences to those of my career much more easily that they can to a superstar's.

We live our lives trying to muster up enough courage to strive for greatness. The fame and fortune of being the best is a dream that lives within us all. But what we must realize is that *doing* our best is far more important than *being* the best.

I know I was the best ballplayer I could be. I showed up on time, day in, day out, with a desire to win. I played hurt, I played hard, and the effort I gave for 13 years, nine in the major leagues, was second to none. I busted my tail every day to play a game I loved.

Nobody had more fun playing the game than I did. My emotions were there for all to see. Sometimes I was mad, sometimes silly, but nobody said you shouldn't act like a kid in the middle of a ballfield.

My contribution to baseball was every bit as important as any of the hall of fame players, because, just like in life, there are a lot more guys like me than there'll ever be of them. We are the dependable, the reliable, the steady masses that really make the machine work.

What follows is my perspective on what happens in and around baseball. The game is serious, it's sad, it's funny, it's unfair. It's what happens before, during, and after each pitch is thrown. But most of all it's a game—never forget that.

FOREWORD

At some point between the time when baseball crapped out in August of 1994 and the time when it finally crapped back in during April of 1995, Steve Lyons wrote a book, which he calls Psycho*analysis*. Great title. And, if you happened to go through most of your baseball career nicknamed Psycho, maybe the only title.

I had admired Steve Lyons a great deal during his Red Sox years (he played for the Sox four times, which may be a record—you could look it up, as Casey would say); he seemed to me to be an island of hardworking, blue-collar sanity at a time when many of the higher-paid Red Sox players were lazy and complaining, the baseball equivalents of gasbag floats in the Macy's Turkey Day Parade.

I admire him as much as a writer and raconteur as I did as a player, and for many of the same reasons. There is nothing very slick about Psycho*analysis*; it doesn't have that smarmy, ghost-written-by-a-sports-reporter-with-extra-bills-to-pay feel to it that so many baseball bios seem to have. It's no more calculated than Steve's baserunning techniques (according to legend, he once responded, "Run 'till you're out" when asked for his baserunning philosophy), and that alone is enough to set it apart from most of the competition. Steve Lyons, who many Fenway bleacher-creatures honored by dressing in shower curtains and wielding rubber knives (at least I hope they were rubber), was never a cookie-cutter baseball player, and he has not written a cookie-cutter book.

Was he, as a player, unique enough to be interesting, or to offer a fresh perspective on a game so many Americans love? I think the answer to those question is a big ten-four, because Lyons epitomizes what may be best in sport: a player who is not great, but who was at times elevated (crazed, some might believe) by his love of the game and his determination to play it well. He states repeatedly in Psycho*analysis* that he was an average player; that is how he starts off, right in the introduction. "I will be the first to tell you I was not the greatest player to ever don a major league uniform," Lyons begins. "In fact, I was an average major leaguer." The fact that that makes him better at the game than 99.99% of the planet's population doesn't matter, and Lyons knows it.

Running in tandem with this self view, which isn't modesty, but a simple and honest assessment, is Lyons's clear desire, all through his career, to be the best player he could be. He drafts his own baseball balance sheet with admirable brevity and insight:

Can he hit? *A little.*
Can he field? *Anywhere.*
Can he run? *Not bad for a white guy.*
Can he bunt? *Yes.*
Can he throw? *Yes.*
Can he hit with power? *No.*
Does he stay healthy? *Always.*
Does he play hard? *Yes.*
Is he coachable? *Yes.*

If your idea of a great baseball book is one that starts at point A (probably with the kid's first Little League hit) and ends at point Z (the ex-player's first endorsement for Grecian Hair Formula or Ballpark Franks), you're going to be disappointed here. Lyons's book is anecdotal, jumping from one story to the next, and sometimes backward and forward in time, as well. But if you stick with it, you'll discover that the format is uniquely suited to Lyons's style, and he covers—if you'll pardon an entirely appropriate pun—all the bases. You get to share the excitement of finding out that you're the #1 draft pick in spite of your paltry OSU batting average (.246) on one end; on the other you get to share the weirdness of selling hot dogs at the local golf club for three bucks an hour after retiring, sometimes to the same people you played with or for. And along the winding road between, the inside dope on what major leaguers talk about (Lyons once heard catcher Ernie Whitt bellow "Shit!" from behind him just before he, Lyons, drove one out of the park— guess Whitt didn't think much of the pitch, but Steve sure liked it), what the crowd sounds like when you're on the field, how the hidden ball trick really works, plus how Lyons and pitcher Joe Hesketh modified a Bosox "Crunch Bunch" tee-shirt to reflect Jack Clark's —shall we say volatile? Let's!— volatile personality.

Why would I write a foreword to a book like this, or follow a player like Steve Lyons in the first place? I followed him, I suppose, because I see a little of myself in him, someone whose success has been due, in the end, more to hard work than actual talent . . . and who has seen (as Lyons has) people with more talent fall by the wayside, as a result of self-indulgence, conceit, or just plain laziness. I am also fascinated by how someone who works his ass off can end up with a nickname suggesting he is a lunatic. It says something about what has happened to the American work ethic, maybe . . . and maybe it's something not so nice. I followed him because in the years when the Red Sox were pretty much asleep, Steve Lyons never even dozed. He played where he was asked to play, and he sat on the bench—the hardest position of all to play with good grace, as anyone who knows the game will tell you—when there was no place for him out on the grass. He played every position on the field during his major league career, including pitcher. When he was cut from the Cubs in 1993, he was prepping to become the team's backup catcher . . . and he wasn't cut for lack of ability at the position, but because management didn't think he could hit (he had a cracked bone in one hand during most of that spring training).

And I believe there is more to be gained from Steve Lyons's book than simple entertainment—although God knows, there's plenty of that. In some very important ways, Steve Lyons's retirement from baseball in the fall of '93 came at a good time for a scrap-iron player such as he was: '94 was the year when greed— the ultimate ascendancy of bucks over baseball—finally came to the fore in what Steve Lyons calls the Grand Game. It was a shameful shutdown fostered by hungry agents, pampered players, and owners so headstrong that most of them would make angry billygoats look like U.N. diplomats. Players like Steve Lyons, who did it until it got done because that's the way they were made, have not been much in demand lately. "Run 'til you're out" as a philosophy has been replaced by "Negotiate until no one cares."

Steve Lyons's book describes a different kind of baseball than that: it's the story of a hard-working (and occasionally ill-used) player who never lost his love of the game ... or (lucky for him) his sense of humor. It doesn't tell everything; there's not much in the way of sin, sex, and scandal (what a relief) but it tells enough to make me absolutely positive of one thing: if Steve Lyons is a psycho, I want to be one, too.

Stephen King
Bangor, Maine
May, 1995

Beginning of a Dream

Every so often, these huge waves of nostalgia pass over me, bringing back memories and emotions from my childhood that I thought I'd forgotten. Memories are a beautiful and powerful part of our lives, and I think it's true that our memories of events are always better or worse than the actual event.

In 1993, while I was playing with the Boston Red Sox, we were riding the bus back to Fenway after an all-night flight back from the west coast. We passed by a little league park and saw some kids playing baseball. It looked the same way it used to when I was a kid. One family was there with mom, dad, and sis shagging balls with a couple of neighborhood friends. There were no bases, a couple of balls, and a couple of bats. Nobody was watching or cared about who did what—it was just baseball, taught by the older to the younger, for the purpose of enjoyment. It was the American pastime being handed down to the next generation by some dad who cared enough not to let it die. As I watched, I thought about how long it had been since I had actually seen a little league game. I remembered how important those games were to us.

The excitement of the day when the uniforms were handed out, wondering if I'd get my favorite number. Racing to the ballpark early, hoping someone else might be there too—just so we could play catch. Trying to break in that new glove to form the perfect pocket inside my pint-sized hand, and reminding myself over and over the lessons I'd learned—look like a ballplayer, keep your eye on the ball, keep your head up and ready—then you'll never have to put it down.

I was in little league. That transition world where boys try to act like men—but crying is still O.K. if you lose. We played with our hearts. We wore size 4 cleats, couldn't keep our socks up, and we had freckles, but we had a love for the game, a dream. And for me it was a dream that lasted for 30 years.

"Good-Bye"

Where in these pages do I explain my father's influence? He must know that he was the driving force in my early years. He taught me what it meant to be a winner, even if I didn't win. He showed me what it meant to compete and be proud of my efforts. He demanded excellence, common sense, and humility all at once. He was my biggest fan and my harshest critic. He usually pointed out my shortcomings; I could have done this or should have done that. And at the end of our discussions, he'd usually say, "nice game." I always heard his voice above all others. The roar of the crowd in a high school basketball game was always just a muffled blur, except for Dad. Every time I touched the ball he'd yell, "Shoot it, take him to the hoop." Like there wasn't another player on the court.

I don't remember the first time I ever beat him in a game of "h-o-r-s-e" on the basketball court, but I know how long I practiced until I could.

Richard Lyons was a working man, an insurance salesman. We didn't have a lot of money so we didn't spend our vacations flying across the country to visit family or going to Disneyland. In fact, I can only remember one vacation when I was growing up. A three-day stay on the Oregon Coast, 60 miles from home, where we rented a cottage on the beach. With seven stitches in my head from the removal of a cyst, I begged my Dad to hit fly balls to me on the beach. And aside from my grandmother visiting, that's the only thing I remember about the vacation.

You see, even though my father grew up as a second baseman, he loved to hit fly balls. I caught fly after fly off my Dad's fungo bat. He used to try to get me motivated by setting up game situations and taunting me. "You'll never get this one," he'd say. And the one thing he'd say that made me try harder than anything was "good-bye." Sometimes he would accidentally hit a ball that even he knew was way out of reach — too far over my head and nowhere near catchable. And of course he'd yell "good-bye," which meant that I'd eventually have to chase it down.

But on this day, I heard the crack of the bat, realized the ball was deep over my head, and knew it would take an all-out effort to catch it. I turned and ran, my back to the ball as I had been taught, as all good outfielders do. As I ran, I heard those words of doom: "good-bye." As he reached down to get another ball to hit, I struggled through the sandy beach reaching for that unreachable fly ball.

After running for what seemed like a 1/2 mile down the beach, I let my instincts take over and dove headlong into the sand for the baseball. It wasn't a real game. It didn't mean anything in the total realm of life. It was just me and my Dad playing ball. As I skidded through the sand, I tried to shield my eyes from the spraying dust as well as I could. Lying there, I opened my glove to one of the most exciting times of my life. Nestled in the web of my Wilson A2000 was a dirty white ball, the one that had "good-bye" written all over it. In some small way, as a nine year old on the beach in Oregon, I had beaten my father and seen a glimpse of my future.

The draft and my first nine days

I remember the day I was drafted as if it were yesterday. My parents, who were living in California, had come up to Corvallis, Oregon to be with me at Oregon State University for two reasons: my 21st birthday and the major league baseball amateur draft, which was the same week.

I wasn't sure which round I would be drafted. I had only hit .246 that year as a shortstop converted from the outfield — sort of a fish out of water with some potential. But I had heard from seemingly reliable sources that I might get drafted as high as the third round. What an experience for any kid to go through — for weeks before the draft I got phone calls from scouts representing major league ball clubs asking me about how much money it would take to sign me? Did I want to play pro ball? What position was I best at?

Having a five-minute conversation speculating on what round I'd get drafted and how much money between $50,000 and $200,000 I was worth, made studying for my upcoming finals very difficult. The strangest call came from a Yankee scout who said, "If you are a #1 draft pick, how much money would it take to sign you?" I told him that I wasn't interested in setting my market value on a hypothetical question. "Draft me #1 and we'll talk money," I said.

"Surely," he said, "you must have an idea of what it's worth to you to be a #1 pick. Can we assume that it would take at least $100,000?"

"Somewhere around there probably," I responded, "but I don't want to be held to any number I say now, or scare any team away with any number I say now. Let's just see how the draft goes."

"Well," he said, "we don't have a #1 pick this year. In fact we don't draft until late in the second round, but you understand we like to have an idea of what it's going to take to sign our players. It looks like it's coming down to a choice between you and a third baseman at Stanford — so we just want to know what we're dealing with."

I said, "Thanks," and he hung up. When draft day did arrive, in June of 1981, we woke up early and sat by the phone. Only the first two rounds were held that day, with the rest the next day. The best indication I had was that if I was still available, I'd be taken in the third round by the Phillies. But I told all my friends not to call me that day so the phone lines would be open — just in case something happened. The draft started at 9 a.m. in Oregon — but by 1 p.m. my phone still hadn't rung. We knew it wouldn't take more than four hours to draft two rounds, so we all were a little disappointed. But we still had hope something would happen that day. At the same time, it was my birthday, we had some shopping to do, and I wanted to crush my dad in a game of racquetball on campus. My mom stayed home just in case.

At about 6 p.m. we were getting ready to get some dinner and the phone rang — by now we had already had a couple false alarms: a couple of friends couldn't wait to hear, so they had called to find out if I had heard anything. Both times, my heart jumped into my throat in anticipation, only to be let down by the familiar voice of a friend. This time it was my girlfriend calling, "Have you heard anything?" she said. By now I was tired of hiding my disappointment of not going in the first or second round and defensive about having to explain why. I lashed out at her, saying I asked her not to call and that she would have been the first to know if I had heard anything at all. She stopped me and said, "You don't understand, turn on the news. They're talking about it right now. You got drafted by Boston in the first round."

I knew she wouldn't joke about something this important to me, but I was still a bit skeptical. Perhaps she got her information wrong. This wasn't just a first-round selection, this was the Red Sox, my favorite team! No way could this all be happening at the same time. My Dad was from Boston, so I grew up hearing about Ted Williams and Carl Yastrzemski, and every Saturday I was mad if the Red Sox weren't the featured game on national television. Growing up 3,000 miles away in Oregon didn't help, but nevertheless the Red Sox, now, truly were my team!

We quickly called the *Oregonian* newspaper to get them to check the wire service, and sure enough, the Boston Red Sox, using the 19th pick in the first round chose Stephen Lyons, Oregon State University.

Unfortunately, 1981 became one of the cheapest years in recent history as far as signing bonuses were concerned. Mike Moore set the tone by signing a $100,000 bonus. He was the first pick in the nation and generally his bonus reflects what everybody else would get. In 1980, Darryl Strawberry was #1 — He got $250,000. I ended a three-week negotiation, which was frightening and sometimes bitter, by signing a $55,000 bonus and left the next day for "A" ball. As for the Yankees, they drafted a third baseman from Stanford — his name was John Elway. He got $120,000 for one summer of "A" ball and opted for the Denver Broncos football team the next year.

A lot of questions were raised about me being a first-round selection. I had a three-year career average at OSU of .245, and I was the only non-pitcher in the first three rounds that didn't hit over .300. Even some of the other players used me in their negotiations. Mike Sodders led Arizona State to the College World Series, was series MVP, and had spectacular regular season stats. But he was the twelfth overall selection by the thrifty Minnesota Twins. They were stuck on a $25,000 bonus. Sodders was quoted as saying, "How can I do everything I did in college this year and sign for half as much as Steve Lyons?"

The Red Sox even issued a press release that said I was hurt for most of the season, and that's why my numbers weren't that impressive. But I never was hurt, the organization was just scared to say they were taking a chance on a guy with potential ability. I had a great year playing in the summer collegiate league in Dodge City, Kansas, hitting .370, 20 homers and 77 RBIs. That was all the scouts needed to see. They knew that coming back to Oregon State, playing only three games per week in the rain, there was no way I'd put up those kind of statistics again. But they also thought if I could do it once, I could do it again — so they drafted me number one.

Mike Sodders never made it past "AA," even with all the success he had at ASU. I guess at least in this case, the scouts knew what they were doing.

I signed with Boston and was sent to "A" ball Winston-Salem, in the Carolina League. I had been on an airplane twice in my life, and I was excited and scared all at the same time, but most of all, I was now a *professional* baseball player.

I took a red-eye flight from Oregon to Winston-Salem, North Carolina, arrived at 10 the next morning and watched the team get beat 18-2. The next morning, the bus left at 6 a.m. for an eight-day road trip — first stop, Haggerstown, Maryland, eight hours away. Eight hours, that is, if you're taking a normal bus. Our bus, built in 1956, was barely in working order.

A half an hour into the trip, the gearbox locked up — while we were in second gear. Twelve hours later, we limped into Haggerstown and went straight to the ballpark for the game scheduled to start in 30 minutes.

The public address announcer was an idiot. He gave everyone's life history when announcing their plate appearance. We had a few guys on our team who had interesting ties to the organization, but when they came up to the plate was not the time to hear about it.

I was hitting fifth that day, and this is what I heard before me: "The number-three hitter in the line-up, number 26 Jeff Hunter, first baseman and brother of manager Buddy Hunter. . . . The clean-up hitter for the Red Sox, number 24 and catching, Marc Sullivan. Sullivan is the son of Boston Red Sox owner Haywood Sullivan. . . . and now hitting, the centerfielder, wearing number 19, the Red Sox first-round draft pick, 19th selection overall in this year's amateur draft, out of Oregon State University, Steve Lyons." I couldn't believe how ridiculous it sounded, and I know Sully and Hunter didn't care for their introductions either. In my first "professional" at-bat, I tapped the second pitch lightly back to the pitcher for an easy out — hardly a great beginning. We lost three straight in Haggerstown, but I was getting acclimated to what pro baseball is all about and starting to get to know my teammates a little better. The long bus rides made it easier to learn more about each guy.

The thing that surprised me most was how everybody ridiculed each other, both seriously and jokingly. We had a pretty good mix of players, so there were some built-in tensions. There were blacks, whites, northerners, southerners, South Americans, Puerto Ricans, and Californians. Then there was me, the kid from Oregon. Hell, I'd only seen a couple of black guys in my whole life and never met anyone whose primary language was Spanish. But these guys had already played together for a couple of months, and they knew each other well. They were calling each other some of the most racial slang names you could come up with, but just joking around. It was a privilege I certainly hadn't earned, and it was certainly not something a new guy should try.

My first two roommates were black. Gus Burgess and Eddie Lee knew I didn't have a place to live, and they asked if I wanted to move in with them. I jumped at the chance. Growing up in Oregon, an area populated mainly by whites, I hadn't had many experiences with other races. The color of someone's skin never meant anything to me, but at the same time, it was impossible for me not to see color. I wanted the chance to learn about a race different from my own. So Gus, Eddie, and I were roomies, and I learned what I already thought was true, there really wasn't any difference.

Everyone became friends quickly. We played stupid games on the bus rides to pass the time. We always picked one guy and piled on him all at once. After leaving Haggerstown, Jackie Gutierrez was the target. Jackie used to sit all the way in the back of the bus on a little loft against the window. There was no seat there, but he could almost lay down, and it was really the prime spot on the whole bus. George Mecerod gave the word, and half the team charged the back of the bus. George was the first one to get there and tackled Jackie hard against the window. The window shattered out the back of the bus, and Mecerod was holding Gutierrez by his ankles trying not to drop him. The rest of us frantically grabbed at Jackie trying to pull him back inside the bus, while everybody else was screaming for the driver to stop. We got Guti back inside, but it was a scare. Looking back, all of us were thankful that nothing worse happened.

Of course we got beat that night, and on the ride back to our hotel, Lee Pruitt had something to say. Pruitt was definitely a veteran of "A" ball. At 25 he was already too old to be playing "A" ball, but he was a leader for the younger players, and he was a "gamer." He said "I'm so sick and tired of you gutless pitchers blowing leads late in the game. We bust our ass every night only to get beat 9-8 and 10-7. Pull your head out of your asses and start playing." Then he sat down. I was scared, and I don't even pitch. I'd never heard players get on each other face to face. Growing up, those speeches came from the coaches, and if anything else was said, it was behind the guy's back!

The next morning we woke up to find out our bus driver had died in his sleep. And of course we lost again. The next stop was Alexandria, Virginia. There I began to see how minor league facilities can start wearing on you. Our locker room was a grade school classroom next to the ball park. After losing again, we went to a Howard Johnson's to get something to eat. Right after ordering, I noticed a very tall woman waiting in line to pay her bill. She was way overdressed for Ho Jo's. High heels, blue party dress and excessive make up. After further inspection, it became obvious this woman was actually a man. The news spread quickly through the 15 or so players in the restaurant, and soon our friend was the center of attention and he knew it. He pranced out of the restaurant, blowing kisses to some of the guys. Everybody was laughing except my "on-the-road" roommate Ronnie Hill. He was white as a sheet. He was from St. George, Utah, where, obviously, he had never experienced anything that strange before.

"You mean that's really a guy? No way," he said. Ronnie didn't touch his dinner and went straight back to our room. For the next two days we spent in Alexandria, he didn't step foot out of our room except to go to the games. Hill got released the next year.

In 1993, after my release from the Cubs, I was sitting at a black jack table in Las Vegas. I struck up a conversation with the other guys at the table. After finding out they were all from St.

George, I thought for a moment and said, "I used to know somebody from there, Hill, Ron Hill, I think." They all kind of laughed and said, "He's sitting right next to you." After 12 years, we didn't recognize each other, but we both remembered that night in Alexandria. (Ron Hill is now a golf pro at a course back in St. George.)

Though our road trip still wasn't over, we made a four-hour ride to attend the funeral of our bus driver in our uniforms. The wife of the driver said he loved driving the bus for us so much, that wearing our uniforms to the service would be special for her. We then went back to Salem, Virginia where we lost three straight. On our final ride home, we were cold and sick, and with no rear window in the back of the bus, it sucked in the cold night air and the exhaust fumes. Most of us were trying to sleep — made easier by the fumes. Suddenly Tony Stephens stood up and panicked — he couldn't see anybody! The bus was engulfed with smoke. "Fire!" he yelled, waking people up and screaming for our owner and now bus driver to pull over. Screaming and yelling, we all streaked to the front of the bus, jumping out by twos and threes — totally overtaken by fear and panic. On the side of the freeway we were all counting heads to make sure everybody was off, "check your roomie" everyone said. But someone was missing. Finally someone yelled, "Guti!" Jackie Gutierrez was still sleeping in the back of the bus. Someone ran back on and pulled him out, half asleep. When he realized what was happening he sprinted 100 yards out into a field away from the bus.

We all opened the luggage compartment and threw all our bags out to see where the fire was coming from. Lying up against some exposed wires was our bat bag, and the bats were smoking and beginning to burn. After pulling everything out we noticed that both bats were Frankie Gill's, our second baseman. Frankie was about 5'6" 140 lbs., and he had trouble ordering bats light enough for him to swing. So he actually went to K-Mart and bought a couple of "Pete Rose" autographed models. He wasn't having a great year, but after he bought those bats he started hitting. And now they were burned and unusable.

That night turned out to be less serious than we originally thought, but the look in everybody's eyes as we got back on that bus said we realized what could have happened. But as we pulled back onto the freeway somebody yelled out, "Hey Frankie, that's the first time your bats have been hot all year."

It was my first nine days in pro ball. We lost nine straight games, our bus caught fire, our driver died, and I'd seen people act towards each other in ways I'd never seen before. We almost dropped our shortstop out the back window, and I was hitting about .220. I was cold, tired, and hungry, and I began to realize just how long the road to the big leagues was going to be.

Winter ball

I'd say at least 70 percent of the players in the major leagues have played winter ball at one time or another. Some cringe at the thought of it, others thought it was fun and play year after year. There are two reasons to play. The first is to keep playing baseball. The "A" and "AA" ballplayers go to continue the educational process of learning the game itself. The way you get better at baseball is to play. It's no great secret, and it's just like anything else; if you want to be a good golfer, you practice golf shots, if you're a typist, you learn the keys and work on your speed and accuracy by typing. It's not surprising then, that players go to foreign countries to play in winter leagues to hone their skills.

The second reason for playing winter ball is the money. Contrary to most people's views, minor league ball players do not make good money. In the winter of 1982, I had just finished my first season in "AA" Bristol, Connecticut for the Red Sox. I made $1,000 per month. I knew I couldn't afford to drive cross-country back to Oregon to live for the winter with no prospects for off-season work, so I was hoping for the chance to play in one of the winter leagues.

A lot of baseball organizations have working agreements with the winter league teams. They send most of their prospects to the same team so that they can play together and get to know each other both on and off the field. The Red Sox didn't operate that way. Their attitude was: If you want to play winter ball, you can, but we don't care one way or the other, so we're not going to make a big effort to get you down there. So with the help of my agent, Tom Demakis, I landed a job in Columbia, South America, for 1,000 tax-free dollars, lodging, and meal money. What followed was the most educational four months of my baseball career.

My wife Lynn, my daughter Kristen and I arrived in early October to a climate that was more humid than Boston in the middle of August. Our first workout was cut short because of a torrential downpour unlike any I'd ever seen. A team bus transported us to and from the apartment building we lived in, and we all had to keep our feet up because of the rushing water *inside* the bus. It looked as if half the town was streaming down the streets: huge tree branches, small vehicles, people, you name it and it was floating down the rivers that used to be the streets of Baranquilla. I knew then that this winter ball season would be the ultimate culture shock and a true test of my will to play baseball.

At the time, Barranquilla was a city of about 800,000 people, 700,000 of which were at or below the poverty level. We lived in a two-bedroom apartment with another couple on the team for three weeks before getting our own apartment. I slept on twin beds pulled together, with my wife and four-year-old daughter, Kristen. Sleeping in Columbia was altogether different. Our apartment building (where all the players lived) was at the only intersection in town with a traffic signal. But traffic lights were just suggestions to the drivers in town. It quickly became obvious that if a driver didn't want to stop for a red light, he simply gave a blast on his horn and kept going. The automobile horn took on a language all its own. They used it for everything: to say hello, good-bye, get out of the way, hurry up, do you need a ride? and look out here I come. The noise level on the streets was incredible. This "horn party" would last until about 4 a.m. and then pick up again around 6 a.m. for the morning rush. We spent most of our days and evenings after games on our sixth-floor balcony watching the action in the streets.

When we finally got our own apartment we thought things would get a little better. Kristen would have her own room, we'd have some privacy and not feel so cramped with five people in one apartment. We were wrong. We had no hot water, our stove took 45 minutes to boil water, our refrigerator barely kept things above room temperature, and our freezer didn't work at all! We kept telling ourselves that this was not a vacation; we were here to further my career in baseball, so I could become a better player.

Across the street was the grocery store where we tried to shop. Let's face it, we weren't at home and they do things a little differently down there. We were amazed at how many things came unpackaged, from meat to blocks of sugar. It was not uncommon to see a trail of ants leading from the sugar aisle all the way out of the store. We learned, by trial and error, what we could tolerate and what we couldn't. They did have a few items familiar to us Americans. For instance, Captain Crunch cereal and peanut butter. Never, however, would you find one that was less than six months past the suggested sales date.

The milk sold in the stores was goat milk, and since we had a four year old, I thought it was important that we all get used to drinking it. It was not homogenized or pasteurized and, after awhile, I couldn't stand the face Kristen made as I forced her to drink it. And that was the end of milk in the Casa de Lyons.

Wednesday was the store's garbage day. The poorest people would line up along the side of the store waiting for the rotten fruits and vegetables that would be tossed into a huge trash barrel outside. They'd cart off boxes, old newspapers, anything that looked as if it might have any shred of value to them. It was extremely depressing to observe. It taught me a lot about how good I had it already. I didn't grow up in a rich family, but I never went hungry. I don't even know what it really means to be hungry for food. I never had to worry about a roof over my head or new shoes come basketball season, and for that I'm unbelievably grateful to the U.S. and my parents.

I'd estimate that Barranquilla operated daily as a city at least 30 years behind the times. I was there exactly four months, and during that time I only saw one power tool. A water main broke in front of our building, and they used a jack-hammer to cut through the concrete to get to the leak. Directly across the street connected to the grocery store were two other buildings — a defunct five-and-dime and a bakery. They were stucco-type buildings connected in a primitive plaza-like setting. The five-and-dime went out of business before we arrived, and while we were there, somebody decided to tear it down.

For 37 straight days I watched as three men with two sledge hammers and one flatbed truck, literally hammered down the one-story building. The men would take turns hitting the walls while the odd man out had to pick up the boulders and throw them in the truck. It was a job that, with the right equipment and the right men, would have been completed before lunch here at home.

Playing baseball in Columbia was truly a new experience, mostly because of the fans. To those people it was the big leagues. They didn't have major league baseball to watch and support like in the U.S. This was it for them, and they treated it like serious business. These people didn't just bet on the game, they bet on every pitch! They'd bet on balls and strikes, individual players' statistics for the day, runs per inning. . . You name it, they'd bet it. You could literally see money changing hands between pitches.

Foul balls were like money to the kids in the stands. There were always fights over them. Anytime a kid had a new baseball to play with, he was the most popular kid on the block. These kids were used to playing ball with 20-year-old hand-me-down gloves (if they had one at all), clothes that Good Will would turn down, and shoes that their three brothers had worn before them. If you took the time to say hello to them or give them a worn-out batting glove, you were like a hero to them. The playing conditions they were used to were so bad, that I believe one of the main reasons you see so many Latin middle infielders in the big leagues today is because if they can catch a ground ball in the parking lot of the stadium, they sure as hell can catch one in Comiskey Park.

The players' families didn't enjoy the games too much. Nobody felt safe. The team owners had special, caged-in seating, which was guarded by Federales carrying M-16 rifles. (A Federale is the Colombian Military Police.) That atmosphere didn't lend itself to feeling safe and at ease. The Latin people couldn't contain their curiosity, so they would get up close against the caged-in families staring in amazement. The wives and children with blue eyes or blonde hair had to be extremely careful. The natives constantly tried to touch their hair and skin; not to be rude, but just because they were such a rarity in South America.

The women of South America all had dark hair, beautiful dark complexions, and bright red lipstick (at home, red lipstick had sort of taken a back seat to some of the softer shades, so it took me a while to get used to it. Remember, this was 1982). Never would you see a lady in public dressed casually. If she had a job, she was always in full dress and make-up. If you saw jeans at all, they were pressed and worn with a nicer blouse and heels. They all seemed to have been taught through their culture very alluring, lady-like qualities, even if you didn't find them attractive. They all acted as though they were quite aware of what being a woman meant and took a lot of pride in it.

Boredom became a big problem. There was very little to do in a country that was extremely poor and whose language was foreign to me. I tried to learn what I could from my Latin teammates. After a while, I could follow their conversations if I knew what they were talking about to begin with. But if I started in the middle of the conversation, I had no clue what was being said. I had the most common complaint of any foreigner: "They speak so quickly I can't keep up." I never got to the point where I could put an intelligent sentence together, but I could get my point across when I needed something, and I knew when somebody was calling me an asshole!

We played our games in either Barranquilla, where three teams were stationed, or Cartagena, where two teams played. We were the only team down there without a team nickname, so we made up our own, the "Rats." The drive between the two cities was only about 90 miles, but it routinely took three hours to make it to the game. All of the buses and cabs were so brightly colored, with fringe curtains hanging from the windows, tuck and roll upholstery, and dice hanging from the mirrors, you could easily spot any form of public transportation.

On the trip to one of our away games, I saw some of the most depressing sights. On the hillsides outside the city of Barranquilla lived thousands of people called "Squatters." Their makeshift homes were made of tree branches and cardboard boxes (I then understood why so many people were interested in the boxes at the grocery store). Lining the highway were power lines that supplied Barranquilla with its electrical power. Leading out of the transformers of those lines were literally thousands of individual lines. The squatters would tap into the power lines just to have a single lightbulb in their makeshift homes.

When I asked about these people, I was told that they had no rights to the land they were using. They were basically homeless and jobless. Tapping into the power lines was not only illegal, but very dangerous. Many people had electrocuted themselves trying to hook up the lines. But this source of electricity was all they had, and the authorities let them do it because those people had nothing to lose. They would rather die fighting to keep their power lines working than live without them. That experience also showed me the courage of those people and just what they could do if they were forced to do it.

Given the differences in culture, the fact that we were away from home, friends, and family for the holidays, and taking the risk of just burning out on baseball, I decided to go back to winter ball after my "AAA" season in 1984.

I had just had the best year of my career — a .267 batting average, 19 home runs, and the International league championship. But I didn't get called up to Boston for September, and I was very upset. I felt that for four years I had played my heart out for the Red Sox organization and thought it was time to be rewarded for what I had done. I guess I thought that if I went and played well at a higher league of competition (Puerto Rico), somebody would have to consider me as a major league player. Plus, once again, the money was considerably more than I earned at home. I made $12,000 in 1984 to play "AAA." In Puerto Rico I was to be paid $4,500 per month.

But what I began with good intentions turned out to be a disaster. Unlike the other winter leagues, in Puerto Rico you paid for everything — food, apartment, rental car. I needed $4,500 just to break even. I played at Arecibo and we got off to an awful start, winning just six of our first 22 games. I was hitting about .230 and had seven errors playing third base. That's not as bad as it sounds, considering our infield looked as if the grass was cut by cattle grazing after games.

My brother-in-law, Jim, came to visit for ten days and was involved in a head-on traffic accident. Nobody was seriously injured, but Jim did suffer a broken nose and black eyes. With all the legal hassles and expenses, it was 26 days before Jim got back home. And it got much worse. I was released shortly after the first month and had $500 deducted from my check for legal advice they gave Jim during his accident. What a bunch of bull! The team didn't do a thing to help Jim. He obtained his own lawyer and handled everything on his own. The winter leagues are full of horror stories of American players who didn't get paid the correct amounts for playing there. While I was with the "Rats" in Columbia, our team threatened to boycott the playoffs because of the proposed pay scale. Finally, we secured better pay for the games played, but were eventually beaten in the second round.

After being released by Arecibo, I was scared. I'd only been fired once in my life. I knew I wanted to prove my 1984 season wasn't a fluke, so I contacted my agent to get a job in one of the other leagues. Two days after being released in Puerto Rico, I flew to Venezuela to play for the "Navigators of Magallanes." This is where the winter ball fun began for me.

Valencia, Venezuela was one of the more affluent areas, about two hours from Caracas. All the players knew Caracas was a big-time city because it actually had a McDonald's. Venezuela was my first taste of what major league baseball was all about. Playing "AAA" ball in the U.S. never really drew very many fans — 6,000 or 7,000 people would be a great night for attendance. But down south, 20,000 to 25,000 people packed into the stadiums. Bands with drums, noise makers, and dancers in the stands. People would talk to you nonstop in Spanish, regardless of whether you understood them. Every game was an adventure, filled with adrenaline and anticipation. I really love that part of a baseball game, long before it ever starts —when the people are preparing themselves to go to the game in much the same way we prepare to play it. The special feeling you get just to be at the ball park, with the crowds, the vendors, and the awesome sight of a baseball diamond.

I didn't know it when I first got there, but I was playing for Venezuela's national team. We were their Dallas Cowboys. If you lived in a city that didn't have its own team, you were a Magallanes fan, and they knew their team.

Of course, by the time I got there, the season was a month old, and the first game I played was nationally televised in Caracas. I went 3 for 5 with a double and two RBIs. The next day we were on the road again in Aragua, and I hit two home runs. I was anxious to play a home game to see how our fans were, but that was still a couple of days away.

Next door to our apartment complex was a plaza where you could shop, get something to eat, and just kill time. I decided to do some exploring. Nobody had told me about the elementary school across the street. I was amazed at being mobbed by at least 75 kids wanting autographs. They were laughing and talking to me and pretending to swing a bat. I had been there two days, never played a home game, and these kids, eight to 12 years old, both boys and girls, all knew my name, who I was, and why I was there. It was an unbelievable feeling, one that comes so rarely, and one I'll never forget. That night I was hitting second in the lineup and when they announced my name, "Esteeb Lyons," the crowd stood and cheered for one full minute. I popped up, but it was still a great moment in my career.

The food in Venezuela was incredible. You could get four guys together, have steaks, baked potatoes, vegetables, salad, and a few beers for about $10. The money system is based on Boliviars or "Bs." When I was there in 1984, the exchange rate was about 12 "Bs" to the dollar. We received 120 "Bs" per day for meal money. The economy has fallen sharply in Venezuela since then, and the exchange rate now is about 45 "Bs" to the dollar. Every morning we'd have the same breakfast: scrambled eggs and ham, french fries, a doughnut, juice, and coffee for 19 "Bs"—about 40 cents in today's exchange.

All the fruits and vegetables looked stunted. Carrots were very thick and rarely longer than four or five inches. Oranges were usually the size of lemons. But what they lacked in size they made up for in flavor. On the streets, vendors would sell fruit drinks that were so good you'd find yourself craving them everyday. Truly, some of the most flavorful food I've ever eaten was in Venezuela.

One of the best things about winter ball are the players you meet. I spent six years in the Boston organization before being traded for the first time, and it got to the point where it felt like I knew everybody in the whole organization. Winter ball gives you the opportunity to play with guys from different organizations. This makes it more fun to play against them later on. You know a little more about a particular pitcher or what kind of hitter a guy is because he was your teammate in winter ball.

It was like another common bond between guys when you met up with them years later in the big leagues and you both stuck it out in one of the winter leagues. Also, some of the personalities made everything else seem bearable. For instance, I watched Charlie Kerfeld pound 70 beers in a two-day break for

Christmas. Partly because we were all partying, and partly to hide the pain we were all feeling about being out of the country, away from friends and family at Christmas time.

A lot of the guys on that team made it to the big leagues. Most of us bounced around, unable to establish ourselves as everyday players: Benny Distafano, Mark Bailey, Charlie Kerfeld, and myself; Chris Green and Jack Lazorko pitched in the big leagues. Joe Orsulak probably had the most success of all of us, playing for the Pirates, Orioles, and Mets. It was a new experience being out from under the robot-like strictness of the Boston minor leagues system.

Tommy Sandt was the manager from the Pittsburgh organization. At that time they were known to be the bad boys of baseball, with their nine different uniform combinations, long hair, and reputations for showing their individuality. It was as if their philosophy was taken from the pages of Al Davis, "Just win, baby."

Sandt had one rule — play hard. I knew I'd fit in the minute I heard that. I was amazed, however, when I showed up on my first day of batting practice in full uniform only to find everybody else in cleats, underwear, and an old sanitary sock tied around their head and nothing else. We won 10-2 that night, and I quickly fell in line with the pre-game uniform. (My tan needed work anyway.)

Our reputation as a scrappy team got us into more than our share of bench-clearing brawls, five to be exact, including three with the same team. Distafano was the ring master. His uniform top only had two buttons on it, because during the brawls he would rip his own shirt off and dive in the pile to smoke somebody, anybody. Everyone else spent most of their time pulling guys off of him by twos and threes. I was glad he was on our side.

It got so bad that we had Federales guarding our hotel when we played our last series before the playoffs against Zulia — our favorite team to fight with. We had to win one of the last two games, and when we won the first one, Sandt didn't even play the American players in the final game because of threats against us. We were advised not to leave the hotel except for the game, and our team bus was police escorted to the final game and out of town at game's end.

Staying out of trouble with the law was never a problem for me, but understanding their laws and the way they were enforced was a little more difficult. Someone once told us that in Columbia it wasn't illegal to shoot somebody, you just couldn't kill them without justification. How true that was I'm not sure, but I wasn't anxious to find out. While we were there, a ten-year-old boy was shot and killed on our street by one of the Federales. He had stolen a woman's purse and was running away with it. Some of these Federales looked no more than 16 years old, and they carried guns that were bigger than they were. They were a constant reminder of force, stationed on nearly every street corner.

They would stop our buses and search everybody on it during our trips from city to city for games. Nobody knew why or what they were looking for, but it was scary and dangerous. There were a couple of players in our living quarters in Columbia who started experimenting with cocaine. The average price was about $19 per gram compared to the $120 in the U.S. at the time (1982). I was never a drug user and have no idea what the costs are today. Everybody got by on the meal money allotted to them. Our expenses were paid, and most of us just sent our paychecks home. One player got so involved with cocaine that he couldn't leave the country with the rest of the team. We played our final game on a Thursday and we all left that Saturday. He had to wait until he could cash his paycheck on Monday to pay off a drug debt in order to leave the country. It's not my intention to defame anybody in this book, so he shall remain nameless. But I will say that he never did make it to the big leagues.

The people of both Columbia and Venezuela were good to us. They were just like any other fans. They wanted to get close to the players and wanted to feel like you were trying to win for "their" team. The language barrier was huge, but it was fun at times to break down those walls.

In Columbia, my wife, along with the other wives, tried to communicate with the maids that serviced our rooms daily. They'd give them make-up and lipsticks to try, leave them snacks that they'd made and tried to tell them the things that weren't necessary to do everyday. All of the American players left them some sort of weekly tip between $5-10. We found out later that our tip was more than they were actually paid to work there.

Just like we would learn enough Spanish to get by, I found it humorous that the would-be groupies found a way to learn enough English to get their point across. After games we would always be mobbed by crowds seeking autographs or by people just wanting to see blue eyes up close and touch for themselves white skin and light-colored hair. There were always a couple of girls who knew how to say "take me home." Nothing else, just "take me home." I always wondered who taught them to use that phrase exactly and if they really knew what they were saying. I guess that was as direct an approach as they could take!

There's usually a guy on every team who has played there a couple of winters. For whatever reason: the money was good, he didn't have anything better to do, or he just really enjoyed being there. On our team in Venezuela, it was Mike Anderson, nicknamed "Mongo," a left-handed pitcher in the Milwaukee organization. He looked like Alex Karras in the movie "Blazing Saddles." Hence, the nickname. He had spent two or three winters playing for Magallanes, and we ended up sharing an apartment. Since Lynn was seven months pregnant with our second child, Kori, she decided to go back home after I got released in Puerto Rico.

Mongo really loved being there. In fact, he built a baseball diamond for the elementary school kids near us. He took an empty lot next to the school and got permission to clean it out, map out the baselines, and build a backstop using his own money. He spent all day raking out the rocks, putting down bases, and overseeing any help he could get from the kids. He was already a fan favorite, because he was one of those guys who could speak a little Spanish and fake a lot, and he was personable. He really enjoyed being there. I don't know where Mongo is today or what he's doing, but he was a guy who really gave something back. Who knows if ten years later that little stadium is still kept up, or if the new generation of kids knows how it got there. But it doesn't matter, because I'm sure all the guys on the team remember him for that. I can't tell you what he did on the field or how many wins and losses he had. I just saw a guy who cared enough to reach out to kids in a country that he'd never call home.

At times the level of poverty we witnessed was over-whelming. Who were we to come to a new place and judge people? But it seemed to me that half the people appearing to be down on their luck could have worked if they had wanted to.

One day on our way to breakfast, we ran into a ten-year-old kid trying to sell us stuff. In his box he had sparklers and outdated Chicklets gum, neither of which we wanted. We all knew the kid should have been in school but there was no way we'd be able to make him understand that, so we motioned for him to come with us to eat. The look on his face was priceless when his food came. In the short time it took him to finish, and with the help of others, we conveyed to him that we were proud of him for trying to make money by working hard, and that certain rewards would come to him because of that. It didn't matter that what he had to sell was worthless, but that he was working. He wasn't stupid either — from that day on we had a breakfast partner every morning.

At one point during the season, our team was picked to play a game in a town five hours away. The town was contemplating entering the league with their own team next season so it was like a goodwill trip. I got nervous anytime we had to travel, but a ten-hour trip to play one game was ridiculous, and in our minds dangerous. About three hours into the trip we stopped at some sort of checkpoint for another search of the bus. Presumably everything was okay, but when we were leaving, our bus was bombarded with rocks, tin cans, and anything else handy to throw. Nobody on the bus was hurt, but as it turned out we were in an area of the country where they were not Magallanes fans. Less than five minutes later, there was a huge explosion in the front of the bus, and the front windshield shattered into a million pieces. At the time, I was lying in the aisle between the seats trying to sleep when I was showered with pebbles of glass. We all thought we'd been shot at by somebody. I was so scared I couldn't move. Guys were screaming and diving for cover. The bus slowly pulled to the side of the road and stopped. When everything began to calm down, one of the Latin players explained to us that we were safe and nobody was shooting at us. It turned out that sometimes when the heat reached a certain point and the conditions were just right, the windshield of a bus could explode if it hit a bump a certain way.

Our bus driver was the only one hurt. His face was cut and bleeding in a few places. But this guy was like Clint Eastwood in a movie. He just pulled over, stepped out of the bus, grabbed a handkerchief, and wiped off his face. Then he jumped back on the bus and said "vamos," (let's go).

I often think back to those days of winter ball (and about my career in baseball) and realize that South America isn't a place I'd love to go back to visit. I feel extremely fortunate to be an American. But those experiences helped shape my life, continue to influence my thoughts and opinions, and I'm glad I had the opportunity to live them. Through these writings, I think I'll make it clear what baseball means to me. I can't help but think that without it, I would have been born in Washington, raised in Oregon, and never gone anywhere else. Because of baseball, I've been in nearly every state in our country, South America, and Canada. And at the ages of 17 and 10, so have my children — an experience they will appreciate more in time.

U.P.S.

It amazes me when I hear people talk about what an easy life a professional athlete has — the money, fame, and glory of it all. After my second full season of minor league ball in New Britain, Connecticut (1983), I decided to stay there for the winter and not return to Oregon, where I called home. The biggest factor in that decision was money. We couldn't afford to go cross country only to return for spring training 4 1/2 months later. Married, with one daughter at the time, my $1,400 per month salary didn't take us far, especially when my salary ended when the season did.

Other players seemed to have something going in the off season. It amazed me how most of the guys could work for their father's business or their uncle's store or work construction with their brother. It was never like that for me. My dad worked for someone else selling insurance, and I didn't have relatives that could give me work in the off-season.

I knocked on doors to find off-season work, but I came with a stigma — I needed a job, but could only work for four months because spring training started in March. Not too many employers want to hire someone who's not going to hang around for a while. So I found a lot of work through a temporary agency. That's right, I was a "Kelly Girl." That winter I did a little of everything: drove a forklift for the *Hartford Courant* receiving department, designed packaging for the Stanley Tool Factory, worked for Hadfield's Sporting Goods in Berlin, CT, and was a waiter at the Holiday Inn in downtown New Britain. But by far, the toughest job I ever had was driving a truck for U.P.S. It's pretty well known that U.P.S. hires part-time drivers to get them through their Christmas rush period, and since they started hiring in October at $11.40 an hour, it gave me an opportunity to make good money for a couple of months.

I should have known from my initial interview that things wouldn't work out. I failed the driver's test by running a red light. For some reason I was really nervous and didn't even see the light. When the supervisor told me to pull over and turn off the truck, I thought he was joking. If you pass that initial driver's test and interview, U.P.S. puts you through a four-day workshop to teach you the basics of their system, driver's safety, and so forth. I was sent home shortly after my driving test, with apparently no hope of getting a job. But ten days later, they called me back and put me directly on a route with a supervisor delivering packages. They must have been shorthanded, because I had flunked the driving test, had no training period, no four-day workshop — just "go get 'em."

Halfway through that first day, the supervisor got an emergency call to help another driver. So he gave me the keys and said "good luck." I was new to the Hartford area and had no idea where I was. I had no training on how to set up and follow a route, so the packages could be delivered in an orderly, organized way. Plus, I had no idea how to distinguish the difference between packages I was supposed to deliver from those that I had picked up!

While delivering my first package to some business, a guy walked in the door and said it looked like my truck was inching its way down the driveway where I had parked. I rushed outside and saw the truck halfway into the street, slowly sliding down the road. The parking brake was shot and couldn't handle the weight of the truck, but luckily, nothing happened — But I made sure I always left the truck in gear when I stopped. The next day at work, I was given my own route. I thought I had been hired to be a runner — the guy who helps the driver during those busy periods by actually jumping out of the truck 150 times a day delivering the brown bags. But now, second day on the job, I had my own route in a rural area covering five communities in "Nowheresville." The only thing that made it better was they gave me a temporary vehicle to drive, a "Ryder Rents Trucks" truck. It wasn't as huge as some of those U.P.S. trucks and looked easier to handle and drive. Or so I thought.

For the next four days I worked 12-hour days from 8 a.m. until 8 p.m., in an area I didn't know, using a system I hadn't learned, in a rented truck with a bad transmission. After limping in every evening with a truck never emptied, I look back on the next day's events as a blessing. I quickly realized that swinging a bat for a living was much more precious than I realized, even on those days when I didn't do it well. Working for U.P.S., I found myself doing nothing but working, eating dinner, and going to bed so I could start all over again the next day. So on that sixth day of work, I was determined to make my own system, learn my route and recognize "cast-offs" (packages that veteran drivers throw onto your truck that they don't want to deliver. Rookie drivers spend a lot of time delivering other drivers' packages). I knew if I could do that, I'd cut my time down significantly and be home at a decent hour.

My biggest problem was my route. It was mostly residential and finding people home to accept a package was impossible. I'd spend sometimes 15 minutes going to five different homes before finding someone to take their neighbor's mail. Once again, that training period would have come in handy — you know, the one I never had. During the holidays, the U.P.S. drivers adopt a policy called "Driver's Release" which means drivers can sign for your package even if you're not home, and leave it on your doorstep. Nobody ever told me.

Even so, I was getting the hang of it, getting a workout, and feeling good about working hard. At about 1 p.m. I was right on schedule: half my packages were gone, and I actually knew where I was. My only challenge was keeping the truck in the right gear. It was an automatic, but it kept slipping into neutral, and it just wouldn't stay in gear like it was supposed to. That afternoon, I stopped along the side of the road to make a delivery at a fire station. As the secretary signed the log — I'm not sure what possessed me to do it, but I turned around to look outside and what I saw was my "Ryder Rents Trucks" truck going down the street without me! I sprinted out of the firehouse in a deep panic. I had never, before or since, run faster than I did chasing that truck down the street. It was maybe 50 yards ahead of me, just cruising along, obeying all the posted speed laws in the area. Another car even filed in behind it. Finally, it began drifting into the oncoming lane of traffic. Luckily, there were no cars coming in the other direction.

As I was running, I could only imagine the fate of this runaway truck, scoping out its path, and hoping for the best. The street was lined with beautiful oak trees all shedding their leaves of red and gold. I could see that if I was lucky, my truck would cross both lanes of traffic, jump the curb, and skip right over the sidewalk. Then it could slip right between two giant oaks and come to rest in a 6-foot high hedge bordering someone's front yard. That hedge was looking like a gigantic pillow to me, and I had my plan all worked out. I'd just jump in the truck, back out of the hedge, into the street, and act as though nothing happened. But my luck ran out a lot quicker than I was able to run down the street. The front end of the truck narrowly missed the first big tree, but it was at an angle in which the truck sort of sideswiped the tree, crushing the outside rear view mirror, and smashing the upper portion of the cargo compartment. I was gaining fast now, trailing the crash by only seconds — out of breath, embarrassed, and relieved that no one was hurt, all at the same time. Worst of all, I was locked out of my truck! The tree lodged itself against the driver's side door, so that it couldn't be opened and the passenger's side door was locked. A lot of things were going through my head at this point, but the biggest was, how would I explain having an accident without actually being in the truck?

The only thing that saved me was the little door inside the cab of the truck that leads to the cargo area. The impact of the crash knocked that door off its hinges, so I was able to open the back end, crawl into the cab, and start the truck.

My next concern was making this accident look like an accident. I knew the truck's faulty transmission was the real reason for my mishap, but since I could have used the parking break every time I stopped, I knew my argument wouldn't hold water with the brass at U.P.S. (when you get in and out of a truck 120 times a day, using the foot-applied parking break every time is out of the question).

I called to let them know that I skidded in the wet autumn leaves trying to avoid a puppy dog in the street and damaged their truck. Their biggest concern was whether or not the truck was drivable and could I finish my route? When I told them I could, they said they would take care of everything when I got back to the station. Upon returning at nearly 7 p.m. with only one rear view mirror on the passenger side and a bad transmission, I was told the supervisor wanted to see me.

I don't remember the first thing he said to me, but the second was "you're fired." I was a little stunned and puzzled when he explained that if a driver has any type of accident within the first three months of work it's an automatic dismissal. (A company policy mainly to cover their butts for legal reasons.)

As I was half listening to this guy and signing my release papers, I began to get mad at how my situation was handled. They didn't really care about how bad the truck was damaged — they could fix that. They didn't care at all if I was damaged. Somewhere in my earlier conversation I remember somebody asking me if I could continue working after the accident. The only thing they cared about were the U.P.S. brown bags. They wanted to be sure I was able to reach all my appointed rounds, get the next-day air packages delivered on time, and bust my tail for the rest of the day, when they knew I would be fired at the end of the day. I felt like telling them I was used, that they should have fired me on the spot, that their lack of concern for their employees was appalling, that this particular supervisor had the people skills of a recluse, and that I was really pissed off about getting fired for the first time in my life. But I said nothing, took my pink slip, and headed home with my tail between my legs.

Hey, Psycho, got anything to eat?

I think it's funny how nicknames come about. Most guys have at least one, some have two or three — usually names unrepeatable in mixed company. Still others have nicknames that even they don't know about, but everybody else does. Of course, the master of nicknames is ESPN's Chris Berman. Although his names for players aren't generally the most popular among his teammates, they are creative and funny. My two personal favorites were Bert "Be-home-Blyleven" and Jamie "Men-at-Quirk." Mine was easy for Berman, but he would always add some flair to it. He'd wait until I made a diving play in the field and then say "And here's Steve Lyons, and tigers, and bears, oh my!" And he timed it perfectly, with the catch and the "oh my!" happening simultaneously.

But my teammates, opposing players, fans, and media knew me as "Psycho." It's a nickname I would never have chosen for myself, but nonetheless, it's the name I had my entire career.

I always thought my nickname would be something a little more sane, something with an ironic ring to it. Considering my last name, I thought I'd be called "Tiger" in my younger years, but I wasn't. I always loved Laker forward Jammal Wilkes' nickname, "Silk." No explanation necessary. But I didn't do anything that smoothly, so I knew I'd never earn any nickname like that. At the same time, it wasn't something worth worrying about, because nobody ever nicknames themselves, somebody else does.

Most nicknames are simply the shortening of one's last name and adding a "Y." If the guy's last name is Anderson, he becomes Andy. If it's Marzano, it becomes Marzy. If the guy isn't that exciting anyway, adding a "Y" gets the process over with. You can always tell when the person you're talking to doesn't know who you are. If they're from the south they'll call you "Big un," and if they're from anywhere else they'll say, "What's up big guy?" Generally, a nickname is a term of endearment. So if people just call you Bob because that's your name, it's time to start working on your personality.

Marc Sullivan gets credit for tagging me "Psycho." Marc, the son of former Red Sox owner Haywood Sullivan, never could out-live that stigma. Sully (there's that nickname thing) could probably still be a back-up catcher in the big leagues. He never quite hit well enough to play every day, but was a gifted defensive player — a rarity today, as far as catchers are concerned.

The pressure he endured from the media and fans about being the owner's son forced him to ask for a trade. He was soon sent to the Texas Rangers, where subpar seasons due to arm problems ended his career. To this day, the Red Sox have not had a back-up catcher to match Sully's ability. He was a big part of the Rangers' turnaround as a scout for Texas, until they made some front office changes. He's now looking to hook up with another team.

We were in "AA" Bristol, Connecticut, when after striking out for the third time in the game, I threw my bat down, kicked my helmet, and sat at the end of the dugout swearing at myself. He leaned over and stared at me for a minute and said, "Man, this guy is psycho."

Of course, over the years, the name has stayed alive, and I suppose I did a few things both on and off the field to fuel the fire. I always thought that a lot of the people calling me "Psycho" were usually weirder than I was, and that I was normal and everybody else was a little off.

Some of the things I did on the field that drew attention would have been done by many people in the same situation. For instance, while playing right field in Texas, I was being pelted with all kinds of stuff from the stands, mostly peanuts and crumpled-up drink cups. After awhile, it gets annoying, and once something like that starts, it can get dangerous and might not stop until somebody gets hurt. And more than likely, that somebody would be me. Most fans just want to be acknowledged by the players or be noticed in some way. In fact, most of the fans that start out bad-mouthing you, yelling obscenities, and trying to degrade you, will change their tune if you say or do something clever or just be friendly.

That night in right field, I knew I had to do something. I reached down and picked up a peanut and in between pitches, I turned to the fans so they could see, and I ate it. They loved it, and of course, I had plenty more peanuts to eat the rest of the game. But I was safe. I wasn't going to get hit with a bottle or battery or anything like that. More importantly, those people became fans of mine even if it was for just one night.

But the story gets better. As the game moved along, the fans began yelling questions out to me and asking for baseballs. I'd answer when I could, and look back and smile if I couldn't. Finally, I told somebody that I couldn't give balls away during the game. "I'll hit you one," I said. "Yeah, right," they said, disappointed. I knew I'd take some heat for saying that. Obviously somebody checked the stat sheet because a couple of minutes later I heard, "Hey Lyons, you only have two home runs all year, you can't hit one this far."

Everybody laughed, and I was the butt of yet another joke. I had already batted once, and grounded out to first base. It took two innings after my Joe Namath-like "guarantee," until my next at-bat. Jose Guzman was still pitching for Texas, and his first pitch missed outside for a ball. Since Guzman has such a good change-up, I wanted to hit early in the count. I looked for something hard and inside and when I got it, I didn't miss. The ball landed about six rows higher and ten seats to the right of where I said I'd hit it. I kept a serious face as I rounded the bases, but was laughing inside — and couldn't wait to get back to right field.

As I jogged back out to my position, my three friends were giving me the "we're not worthy" bow of approval. I held my hands out to my sides as if to say, "Hey, I told ya."

But the belief I had just won over the entire crowd with my Ruthian call was quickly interrupted. Right before the first pitch of that inning, somebody drilled me with another peanut.

After I was traded from Boston to the White Sox, I was really excited to come back to Fenway as a visiting player. As I came to the on-deck circle, I was greeted by a few people I recognized, some other well-wishers, and still others just saying stuff like, "Hey, Psycho's back. Good to see you again." I'd usually answer everybody the same way—"It's good to be seen." But it doesn't matter who you are, you're always going to hear someone in the crowd that doesn't like you.

I suppose in some dark corner of Minnesota you can find someone who thinks Kirby Puckett could do more for the Twins! And I certainly have my share of people who didn't appreciate my ability to play baseball. "You're a bum, Lyons" I could hear somebody saying. And they weren't far away either, only about eight rows back. It's always so much nicer when the fans who don't like you sit far away from the field.

"You were a bum when you played here, and you're still a bum!" Turning in the direction of the comment, not knowing exactly who said it, I responded, "You're right. I am a bum. But I'm still fooling somebody, because I'm still wearing one of these uniforms."

My well-wishers enjoyed the comeback, and I knew most of them were on my side. As I refocused on getting ready to bat, I felt something hit my left shoulder, followed by heavy laughter. Looking down, I spotted a huge pretzel, the kind that are sold at the concession stands, complete with extra salt and mustard. By now there were at least 200 fans that noticed what happened, and they were laughing.

I knew where the pretzel had come from, and I quickly assessed my options. I could turn around and lash back with an obscenity, but that was never my style, especially when kids were there to hear my stupidity. I could have acted like nothing happened, but everybody saw it, and that, too, is not my style. So I did the only thing I could — I reached down, picked up the pretzel, and took a bite! The guy spent $3.50 on it, and went out of his way to personally deliver it, so it was the least I could do. The fans went crazy with cheering and laughter. They knew once again that I had gotten the better of my heckler.

My concentration was again shifted to my at-bat. I was usually good at putting those distractions out of my mind when it was time to perform, but after two quick strikes, "You're a bum" kept ringing in my head. I had to step out of the box and regroup. I couldn't let those guys ruin my concentration. I had to let it go and be focused on hitting—because if I didn't I might as well be just what that guy was calling me. The next pitch I sharply lined up the middle for a base hit. As I retreated back to first base, I quickly pointed to the heckler's section, tipped my helmet, and smiled.

For those four minutes, the 200 fans that saw everything happen had already gotten their money's worth. I was a major league player who got a hit in Fenway Park. I was anything but a bum.

Later in the series, I was playing second base when a pop foul went sailing down the right field line. Right fielder Ivan Calderon, first baseman Greg Walker, and I all gave chase. I knew I was the only one with a shot to catch it, but it kept drifting and ended up two rows deep into the crowd. Some fan made a great one-handed catch, and without thinking, I leaped onto the wall and gave the fan a "high five." My momentum carried me towards the wall and since he had made such a great play, it was just a natural reaction to congratulate him. He would have done the same for me, but once again, everyone thought I was weird for doing it. "Nobody else would do something like that," they said. The sad part is, they were right. I always thought it would be a nice rule change to make the players pause for just a second, take their gloves off, and applaud a fan after a great catch on a foul ball. It takes a lot of courage to try to barehand some of the screaming line drives hit into the stands. But, if a fan misses an easy pop up, the players have the right to rag on them. "You're brutal! How did you get into this game? You stink! My grandmother can watch a game better than you!"

Well, it's just a thought.

Don't believe everything you read

Like I said before, usually when people thought I was funny or doing something off the wall, I thought I was being normal. My humor generally wasn't something I planned ahead of time. It was almost always spontaneous. I was still willing to join in a practical joke, but most of the time I wasn't the sole instigator. Rick Cerone was a good instigator. He played for so many teams, he's probably seen every possible practical joke.

In 1992 when Tom Runnells got fired as manager of the Montreal Expos, he left notes in a few lockers, knowing he wouldn't see the players again. It was a way to show his appreciation for their efforts and wish them well. I had only been with the club for about ten days, but here's what my note said:

I didn't really want you here anyway. It was a front office decision. Thanks for going 2 for 10 in the at-bats I gave you. It helped get me fired. — Tom Runnells

Cerone had come in early and secretly wrote his own notes to everyone on the team. They were all similar to mine, but he added some personal touches that corresponded to the personalities of each player. Most of the guys on the club were young, so it took the veteran players a while to convince them that Runnells didn't actually write the notes.

Autographs and close encounters

I don't remember the first time I was asked for my auto-graph, but I do remember what my mother told me about signing my name. "Always write it so you can read what it says," she told me, "So if you ever become famous, some mother won't look at the signature and say, 'He makes all that money and you can't even read his name.'"

So my signature, even to this day, is legible, even at times when signing an autograph isn't at the top of my list of things to do. One year in Minneapolis, a couple of guys told me that my signature and Jim Gantner's were the best autographs in base-ball, "Cause you can read them," they said.

Through the years I've definitely signed my share of auto-graphs. Most of the time I enjoyed doing it, and I always had a positive outlook about it. I figured if someone wanted my signa-ture bad enough to ask me for it, I should take the time to sign it for them. I understood that at some point people would stop asking for it — and that's when I'll want to sign one.

In all the ballparks I've played in, autographs are always the main concern of the fans during batting practice and before the game. Some of the kids really want to add your name to their collection, and others want it for profit — to sell or trade in the future.

It's hard to tell the difference between the two, because they both know how to play the autograph game — they have profes-sional-looking notebooks where all their cards are arranged in alphabetical order or by team, for easy access. They all have a marker ready if their request is answered, and they know which card is worth the most if signed.

We see these same kids year after year in the same cities. They wait many hours to get one guy that hasn't signed yet. They're waiting as our team bus arrives in the next city at 3 a.m., they wait to catch that one player's autograph that they don't have on his way to lunch before the game, and they're back at the hotel after the game. Even though they become an annoyance, I admire their determination. Some of the more in-demand play-ers take advantage of the situation — knowing that their auto-graph is the one everybody is waiting for. They sign one or two and shun the 50 others waiting. "Later," they say—knowing that later means maybe next year, or possibly not at all.

Other kids at games don't even know why they're asking for the autograph. Their mom or dad is pushing them to get closer to the "baseball experience." Let me tell you, they make the player feel real good by saying, "Who are you?" while you're signing, or asking their parents, "Who is that?" after you signed.

I have put my name on a napkin with mustard on it and even a piece of a popcorn box and felt that by day's end, my signature either ended up in a gutter somewhere or in the wastebasket in some kid's room. Autographs for a lot of fans are just something to get caught up in for the moment, "Hey, we're at a game, we should get autographs." It's almost like going to Disneyland and buying those Mickey Mouse ears or that Donald Duck hat — lots of kids have them. It's Disneyland for God's sake! But when they get home, when will they ever wear that hat again? After awhile it finds its way into the yearly garage sale or into that same wastebasket.

Believe it or not, there are other categories of fans seeking autographs. Some have nothing else to do, some kids just have to have everything—never mind the price of their ticket, the hot dogs, the pennant and the two buddies they got to bring with them, they have to get an autograph, and it still isn't good enough. "Steve, get me a ball. Can I have your bat? How 'bout your hat?" I was always nice, even though I didn't always want to be. "What am I going to use if I give you everything I have?" I'd say. But I wanted to say, "Go sit down and watch the game you little brat. Do you know how many kids would just be happy to get a chance to come to a game but never get to?" Sometimes it's nice to be able to say one thing and think another!

Some ballparks make it hard for fans to get near the players for autographs, and some fans get creative in their attempts to get closer to the players. The most creative fans I ever saw were in Pawtucket, Rhode Island. At the Red Sox "AAA" stadium, the dugouts are under the stands, and the front row is 12 feet above the field. But that didn't stop those kids. They take plastic gallon milk containers cut in half and place the items they wanted signed inside. Then they'd lower it down on a string with a pen inside for autographing. They also used two-liter plastic soda bottles, wicker baskets, and anything else they could think of. I even saw a plastic gallon vodka bottle used to house a ball and a few cards to be signed.

But they didn't stop there. Some kids drew elaborate color pictures and taped them inside the jugs—pictures of sunny days at a ball game with a kid saying, "Please sign my ball." Others had candy and Tootsie rolls along with the ball they wanted signed—the note says, "If you sign, take two pieces of candy." How could we pass it up? After we signed, they'd reel it up as if they just snagged a rainbow trout. They'd read the name and yell out, "Thank-you!" and then drop the line down again for the next guy. The kids won either way, they got a few autographs from future major league stars, or they got to munch on Tootsie rolls throughout the game.

Legibility vs. eligibility

While signing a ball for a guy over the dugout in Dodger Stadium, an extremely nice-looking blonde (about 33) commented on how nice I was, and would I sign her ball too? (I knew that her boyfriend, sitting four rows back, had sent her down to see how much attention she would draw and how many balls she could collect.) I said I'd sign and asked her if she would be able to read it once I signed my name." "If it's eligible," she said. "Eligible," I replied, "is what half this team is wondering if you are. Legible is how I'll sign my name."

She was embarrassed, but laughed it off and proceeded to say how much she liked the charm on my necklace. "It's a gold baseball glove with a diamond where the ball would go," I told her. "Where did you get that?" she asked. "Puerto Rico," I responded. Then she said, "Does it have any significance?"

I just looked at her funny and passed the ball back to her.

Don't eat that

In Chicago, there's a fun place to eat in the near north Lincoln Park area called "Bigsby's." Good food, lots of TVs for sports fans, and a laid-back atmosphere. Before Michael Jordan opened his own restaurant, "Jordan's," he used to hang out at Bigsbys quite often. In fact, they even created a private room for him to eat in when he came there so he wouldn't be bothered.

If you go there, you'll see lots of photos of Jordan, all the Cubs, and most of the White Sox players. Sports is the general theme of this place. And if you're like me, after a nice meal and a few drinks, you may have to visit the facilities. As you make your way to the men's room, you'll notice many more pictures— from parties or events held at Bigsby's, from those picture booths, and of course, more sports pictures.

Now that you've positioned yourself in front of the urinal to take care of your business, turn around. Well, wait til you're finished! But then, that's where you'll see my picture—in the bathroom. Why does that seem appropriate?

Centerfield fans

Coming up through the Red Sox system, I always heard how tough the centerfield bleacher fans in Fenway could be if they didn't like you. Most of the seats are long-time season tickets, held by fans that are loyal, frustrated, and knowledge-able. I decided early on that I wanted them on my side, because as one of them shouted to me in my first appearance — "Hey Steve, one thing you have to remember is we're always behind you!" And he didn't mean that they would always support me.

I made an effort to let them know that I knew they were a part of the game. I answered them as best I could when someone asked a question. I acknowledged them when they cheered for me, and I got to know about 20 of them by sight and by name. On my birthday one year, they threw me a ball with all their signa-tures on it. After I got traded to Chicago, I brought back 20 t-shirts that said "Chicago White Sox" and threw them up over the wall to be passed out to the regulars.

Later in the season, the White Sox sent me down to Hawaii, their triple-A team, but when I got called back up, one of our first road trips was back to Boston. My centerfield buddies had a huge sign on the back wall that read "Aloha Psycho" and everybody wore Hawaiian shirts in my honor. The next night they brought "props" with them, so that they could reenact the shower scene from the movie "Psycho" complete with back lighting, a shower curtain, and 15 extras wielding fake knives. Dee, a shapely blonde, was the unanimous selection to be the shower victim, maybe because her real name is Dee, but her nickname is "Double D." One guy showed up every night but was known only as "Wolfie" because he talked like Wolfman Jack. Every night he'd let me know he was there by yelling, "Psycho, you're a maniac!" Nobody knew much about Wolfie and I heard one year he just stopped going to the games. He hasn't been heard from since 1989.

Paul is an M.I.T. professor in Robotics and Aeronautics, and I actually visited him on Harvard's campus for lunch one day. He'd been a centerfield season ticketholder for 18 seasons and wore the same shirt to every game. I suppose he'd actually bought more than one shirt like it, but for every season, every home game, Paul wore a blue and red striped polo shirt. Most Fenway fans know Paul from his yelling, "Wade" for about 90 seconds when Boggs comes to the plate.

So many people out there really make you think about how important the season is to them, and how they live and die with Red Sox baseball. It makes me wonder how long the cold winters are in Boston for those fans.

I knew I had sealed my fate with the bleacher fans on the day I was awarded the tenth player award. The award is given to the player who plays better than what is expected of him. It was sponsored by Toyota and the Red Sox organization, so the trophy was a Toyota truck, but most important to me was that it was voted on by the fans.

So when the game started, I trotted out to center, where I knew those people had a lot to do with me winning the award, and in about the second inning somebody yelled out, "Hey, Steve, how do you spell Toyota?" So in between pitches, and at the risk of my manager seeing me, I spelled out Toyota with my body, letter by letter as the crowd yelled each letter out. When I got to the last letter, "A," I wasn't sure how to do it so I bent over and mooned the crowd while crossing my arm from knee to knee to make an "A." They went nuts and nobody else knew what was going on.

It was people like them: Paul, Wolfie, Muzzy, Dee, and the rest who inspired me when I played. They made me get into the game and made it more fun for me to play.

Friends or fans?

The last day of every season was always an emotional day for me. I always felt like I was happiest while playing baseball and in the off-season, even though I welcomed the time off, I felt out of place. I was never good at good-byes, so I'd always pack my stuff up before that day's game and quietly skate out afterward.

But no matter what I did, I couldn't sneak past the die-hard fans that the season also had ended for. I sometimes have trouble understanding just how important the baseball season is to them. They come to every home game, and even plan their vacation time around our road trips. They have all the team logo t-shirts, and sometimes even an authentic uniform top, with their favorite player's name on the back. They come rain or shine, night or day. They keep score, they cheer with all their hearts, and they know more about my career than I do. What happens to these people in early October? Where do they go, and what do they do?

Every player knows them, whether they care to acknowledge them or not. The true fans never "boo" their team and they feel a definite connection with the team. It's a part of their lives, not just a game to go see. Look up the word "fanatic" and it says "a person filled with excessive enthusiasm or zeal for something." That's a fan.

There were so many fans that I knew well enough to say hello to over my playing days and sometimes I did wonder why they were so gung-ho over my team and how they spent their winters with no baseball or how they survived the strike of 1994.

I overstepped the boundaries of fan or friend more than a few times. Fans don't always understand that sometimes you're being nice just to be nice. It usually doesn't mean you want to form a lasting friendship. Although I've done that too. I've written countless letters to people who started off being fans and somehow after numerous conversations and times together I felt closer to them. But with very little free time and kids of my own to consider, I'd eventually lose contact, and usually end up feeling guilty about it.

In my 13 years in baseball I've seen more than a few kids go from 10-year-old fans to college graduates—people I never would have known if not for baseball. In some cases I even feel proud to think that in some way I helped inspire somebody to excel in their interests—all because they had an interest in me.

In other cases, I was the one whose life was enriched. During a visit to a hospital one time, I met a kid named Michael Dragon who had cancer. After leaving the hospital, I couldn't get him out of my mind. He was young and scared and really had no idea what was happening to him, and yet he was cheerful and optimistic, not wanting his family to worry.

I tried to stay in touch with him as best I could, but as his condition worsened he was moved to the Dana Farber Cancer Center in Boston. On our last visit, he choked back the nausea for the entire time I was there—making it hard for him to speak and even harder to hide his pain.

The cancer took Michael before he was able to graduate high school, but for all the time he was sick, he never complained or wanted any pity. He was strong for his brothers and sister as if he knew the only way he could ease their pain was to show them that he wasn't afraid. I think of him often and wish I could be more like him. He handled his dying in a way we all wish we could handle our lives—with courage, strength, and dignity.

I wasn't there the day they buried Michael Dragon. His parents told me that my Red Sox jersey that I gave him went with him. I guess he looked up to me. I hope he knows how much I looked up to him.

The popcorn bag

It's funny, as I reflect on my life and talk to others about theirs, how important my younger years have become. I think some people look at me and must think how easily everything came for me. That I must have lived the American Dream. And I don't disagree, really. I had somewhat of an "All-American boy" reputation through high school and college, and then went on to a career in major league baseball — every kid's dream. But those same people didn't see that I became a father at 17, worked my tail off through the minor leagues, and struggled to make nearly every major league team I played for. Nobody's life is ever as glorious as other people think. Yes, I did live a part of the "American Dream." But the dream has become less and less about where baseball took me, and more about how my parents got me there.

I didn't grow up around money. My father is an insurance agent, and my mother is a homemaker who sometimes worked seasonal jobs for extra money. But my three brothers and I never needed anything we didn't have. My parents were great at many things, but most of all, they loved us. They were great at teaching us the value of a dollar and disguising the things we needed as Christmas and birthday presents. I had my first job picking beans and strawberries when I was eight, and was told that by the time I reached the seventh grade, if I wanted stylish clothes like "bell-bottoms" and "loud" shirts, I'd have to buy them myself. I'd be provided with the basics only. One of my father's favorite lines, "I'll buy you your first bicycle. After that you're on your own."

So as a family, we were rich — and like most children, I'm not sure I appreciated or understood how special that was while I was growing up. There were times when I was 15 or 16 when I thought my dad was the dumbest guy around — because he wouldn't let me do something or tried to give me advice. When I got to be 22 or 23, I realized I was the dumb one, and everything he had told me was true. I just didn't want to listen.

Even my childhood nightmares and setbacks seem mild in comparison to most people's, and it seems most of those disappointments revolved around sports. When I was eight or nine, my dad would take me to see the Eugene Emeralds play. They were the "AAA" affiliate of the Philadelphia Phillies, and we saw players like Larry Bowa, Denny Doyle, Mike Schmidt, and Greg Luzinski.

We had two traditions at those games. First, we always brought a big grocery bag full of home-popped popcorn and a couple of cans of soda with us. It was primarily so we didn't have to pay the concession stand prices. Second, we were famous for leaving those 6-1, 8-2 games early. "To beat the crowd," my dad would say — only to listen to the inevitable comeback victory in the ninth inning by the other team on the car radio.

One night, while sitting in the third base stands, a foul ball ripped through the crowd, ricocheted off a seat or two above me, and came careening back towards me. With a proud leap and yell, and my hands held high above my head, I announced to all 6,500 or so fans that I had caught it! Bare-handed, no less. My smile would have been big enough to catch that ball with my teeth. I was getting hugs from my dad and low fives from everyone! (The "high fives" hadn't been invented yet.) It was an incredible moment — out of all the people in that stadium, I caught that foul ball, by myself. My dad didn't catch it and then give it to me while I ducked out of the way. I made that catch!

My elation turned to concern as I quickly remembered what would soon happen. You see, in those days, money was tight for "AAA" baseball clubs. They had to cut corners and save money wherever they could. So the Emeralds employed a "buy back the ball" policy. It was fine if you wanted to keep the ball for yourself, but they would give you the option of trading back the ball for two tickets to a future game. I had seen this process before. Shortly after a lucky fan snagged a foul ball, an usher, wearing a red uniform and hat, would come up, whisper something to the guy and then either take the ball or leave.

I was nervous as I began looking for the usher to come over to our seats. I was scared that he'd want the ball and our ticket stubs to prove those were our seats. My dad and I always bought the cheapest tickets and then snuck down to better seats.

I knew I wanted to keep the ball. It was my prize, it was my moment of fame, my proof of the great play I had made just seconds before. It was a baseball! Fouled off the bat of a future major leaguer, and now it was mine! Two tickets to Disneyland wouldn't get that ball back into the hands of that usher, and yet, that moment had come. The usher was at my side. The guy that takes your tickets at the gate, the guy that knows every seat in the house like the back of his hand; he tells you where you can sit and even more scary, where you can't. He's the guy who keeps the peace, gives the orders, and answers your questions. He is the baseball police! He is the guy, who in the most intimidating voice says, "Hey kid, trade you that ball for a couple of tickets?"

Now if there's one thing my parents taught me, it was to respect my elders and authority figures. To do what's right and to do what they said. So in some way, I felt as if I would be defying the usher's authority by refusing to trade back the ball. Like I was saying "no" to the man in charge. Like I was doing something wrong.

But I knew I had earned that ball and was willing to risk everything to keep it. So without giving it any more thought I blurted out, "No way. I want the ball." And with that answer, everybody in my section cheered for me again and one guy said, "That's right kid, keep the ball." Then I looked up at my dad and said, "Is that all right, dad?" "You bet your life," he said, and somehow I felt like I had, and won!

I sat there for the rest of that game trying to decide where the safest place to keep my ball might be. Clenched tightly between my hands, as it was most of the time, or tucked away in my jacket pocket out of sight of some ballpark bully that might be lurking. As the game wore on, so did the excitement and after dropping my ball a couple of times my dad warned me, "You better put that ball in a safe place before you lose it." So I did.

After the popcorn and soda began to take its toll, and the 7-5 thriller of a game ended, my dad and I filed out of the stadium. While the ushers directed traffic, I thought about my earlier dilemma with standing up to authority, and knew by my dad's reaction that I had done nothing wrong. So as we rode along, finally I said, "Hey dad, let me see my ball." I just wanted to feel the stitches again and smell it. And look at the infield dirt rubbed into the leather. " I don't have it," he said, "I thought you did." In a panic I searched my jacket pockets and found nothing. I dove into the back seat where I may have dropped it but came up empty. Then in absolute horror I screamed, "The popcorn bag! It's in the popcorn bag!"

We never took the popcorn bag home. It never even lasts into the seventh-inning stretch. A few "old maid" kernels of corn and two or three empty cans of soda — that's all that's ever left in the popcorn bag. We always figured one of the ushers would come by and sweep it away after the game. At the time, it seemed like the safest place for the ball when my father told me to put it away.

Sure, we scrambled back to the stadium, but we were too late. The gates were locked and nobody was in sight to help us out — not even an usher. I started to cry, even though I knew my dad wouldn't like it. I felt crushed, like I lost my dog or my best friend, and it hurt. I guess my dad understood, too, because he never told me to stop crying. He just said, "Keep your chin up, pal. There'll be lots of balls." He knew there was no explanation, no amount of scolding, nor any lecture that could teach me more than I learned that night. I felt like I had bet my life, and lost.

Collector's items and first pitches

I was really lucky to have played baseball in the era that I did. So many things happened from 1985 — 1994 in the baseball world, that it's hard to remember it all. I think of all the history that I saw and wish I could have grabbed just a piece of it. Some memento, photograph, or program of those days just to refresh my memory as I get older.

I had the opportunity. Think of some of the best players of my time: Reggie Jackson — I played against him in his last game ever. Tom Seaver — I was traded straight up for him in 1986. George Foster — The White Sox sent me down to "AAA" so they could sign him. I was directly involved with some of the big names of my baseball generation, but how about some of the hundreds of others? I played against George Brett, Nolan Ryan, Ken Griffey Jr. and Sr., Paul Molitor, Robin Yount, Andre Thornton, Jack Morris, Greg Maddux, Dave Stieb, Cal Ripken Jr., Alan Trammell, Jose Canseco, Cecil Fielder, and many others.

Stop and think how many superstar players there were in that period of time. And how about my teammates? Guys I actually played with and learned from: Dwight Evans, Steve Carlton, Frank Thomas, Dave Justice, Larry Walker, Jeff Reardon, Tom Glavine, Roger Clemens, Bobby Thigpen, Jack McDowell, Wade Boggs, and Ozzie Guillen.

A lot of these guys are going to the Hall of Fame. What do I have to remember them by? Not much! I can't believe that I was so stupid! I should have been more of a collector and asked for a few autographed balls or bats. I always thought that I didn't know what to do with it all — that I didn't have room for it. What a mistake! I was involved in four no-hitters and don't have anything to show for them. One of them was by Yankees pitcher Andy Hawkins against the White Sox in 1990. He threw a no-hitter, and lost 4-0.

As my career progressed, however, I smartened up a little. I began sending four or five baseballs to the opposing clubhouse to get autographs from the top players on every team. I have a nice little collection of items that remind me of what I used to do and who I did it with.

I tried to steal the third base bag in Toronto's Exhibition Stadium. We played the last game ever there, and I was playing third when George Bell hit a game-winning homer to end it, so I just waited until he touched third and then I pulled it up. One of the Toronto officials followed me into the locker room and took it back — but at least I was thinking. Besides, I left my mark: I'm credited with the last real stolen base ever in that stadium — during the game, that is, even if I didn't actually get the base I was trying to steal.

I had the chance at an excellent memento and at being in the record books all at the same time but blew it. The final out at ol' Comiskey Park was recorded when Harold Reynolds, then playing for Seattle, hit a grounder to second and was thrown out at first. Who was playing first? You guessed it. As I caught the last ball that would ever be used in that historic old ballpark, I was remembering all that Comiskey Park had meant to the players and fans that had come there for 81 years. It was sad that something was "dying," and across the street was its replacement, the new Comiskey Park.

I thought of all the stars and Hall of Famers that played right where I was standing, and that the future greats will no longer play on that same soil. I guess that isn't completely true, since they dug up the old infield and moved it to the new park. So the soil lives on, but that ball, the last ball ever used in the last game ever played. I don't have that ball. I suppose most people would regret giving it to someone else, but I don't.

You see, there was another record broken that day on that same grounder to second. Sox reliever Bobby Thigpen became the major league record holder for saves in a season with 57. In the excitement of the day, our resurgence as a team in 1990, and Thiggy's record, I reached out and placed the ball in his glove — as I did with every ball that represented a save for him after number 45, the previous record.

Had I thought of what that ball would mean to me today or even later in life, I might still have it. But Thigpen deserved it. His record won't be broken any time soon, and it took its toll on him. He's never been quite the same pitcher ever since that day. It was his year and his day — the rest of us were just there to share it and say good-bye to the oldest ballpark in baseball history. You're welcome, Bobby.

There is one item that will be proudly displayed in my office when I am a "suit" working 9 to 5 somewhere. There is one thing I got when I was most impressionable as a pro ballplayer and is still my most cherished item. In my first major league spring training camp with the Red Sox in 1984, we had two hitting coaches. One took a big interest in me and made me his spring training project. The other hung around the minor league complex a little more often, telling baseball stories and watching the kids in awe as he spoke. Carl Yastrzemski and Ted Williams.

It was exciting having two of the greatest players ever to put on a uniform help me with my game. But it was well known around camp that these two legends didn't hang around the same spot at the same time too often. They had differing opinions on how to hit, and there was no field big enough to hold both personalities. One day at lunch, I got up the nerve to ask if they would both pose for a picture with me: Ted on one side, Yaz on the other — by far my most prized possession. I'll never forget what Williams said while we were standing there. He leaned over to Yaz and said, "There's going to be quite a few career hits between us three before it's over." Thanks Ted. Sorry I didn't quite keep up my part of the bargain. Later I got them both to sign two copies of the photo, one for me, and of course, one for my Dad.

Along those lines, photos with movie and TV stars were easy to get while playing in Chicago. Somebody was always in town doing something, and they'd usually throw out the first pitch at a game. Being the third catcher meant that I usually had to catch it. I've caught pitches from people ranging from Brian Boitano to Elke Sommers — who almost lost her top while throwing the ball. Billy Crystal, John Travolta, Mary Hart, David Copperfield, Dwight Yokam, Kurt Russell and Goldie Hawn, Brian Denehy, The Oak Ridge Boys, and Tom Selleck were among the stars that passed through the locker room.

My biggest fear was that I'd drop the pitch or make the star look bad, but it never happened. By far the worst pitch I ever had to catch was tossed by John Tesh of "Entertainment Tonight." It bounced about halfway to the plate and about ten feet to my right. I took a couple quick steps to the right and made a desperation back hand stab and somehow it went into my glove.

I had two favorite "first pitches" over the years. The first was from George Wendt of "Cheers." He wanted to do something funny, so we set it up where he threw a wild pitch all the way up on the backstop screen. George is from the South Side of Chicago and was a huge White Sox fan, and we've become friends since that moment. In 1992, I saw him in Boston while they were taping an episode of "Cheers" at the real Cheers. Since I was playing in Boston, I brought him a Red Sox uniform to try to convert him. I'm not sure if it will ever fit him. He works out hard, but let's face it, he's a pretty big guy.

My all-time favorite first pitch was by *Sports Illustrated* swimsuit model Kathy Ireland. This lady is every bit as beautiful in person as she is in *S.I.*, and she has a great arm, among other things. I gave her a peck on the cheek when I brought the ball back to her. For some reason, after that kiss I got at least two hits in every game I played for the next week, going 16 for 31.

Ironically, that streak ended when another lady jumped out of the stands in New York to give me a kiss. She was drunk, but said somebody bet her $1,000 to do it. She made out fine, considering it cost her $250 to get out of jail. (In New York, they don't mess around with people who jump onto the field.) But I went 0 for 4. (I'm still looking for Kathy to bring back some good luck.)

For a long time in Chicago, I had a running joke with my teammates. I was making $525,000 but not playing much. After the ceremonial first pitch, I'd come running in and say, "another $3,000 dollars, guys. I did my job, now go out and do yours — only in America!"

My first at-bat

In my rookie season of 1985, I took a lot of time to make sure I stopped to smell the roses. After all, with all the baseball I had played to that point, I hadn't played in the big leagues, and it was really a whole new experience. I was now playing with some legends in Boston and some possible future Hall of Famers like Jim Rice and Dwight Evans. With Tony Armas as our regular centerfielder, I took in the atmosphere more than I took in game time. No matter what happens in a player's life there are a few things you'll never forget: your first at-bat, your first hit, and most likely, your first home run. For the pitchers it's the first hitter you faced, your first strike out, and probably the first guy who hits a home run off you! It's amazing how the home run has such a lasting effect on people.

My first at-bat came in a game in Chicago after an hour-long rain delay. Armas had stiffened up, and I got the call to fill in. My first at-bat was against Juan Agosto. He was a left-handed pitcher with a huge sweeping curve ball, a slider, and a fastball that was at best 85 M.P.H.

I lined the first pitch I saw down the right field line. I got a great jump out of the box and knew I could get a double — if only it was a fair ball. It bounced just inches foul, and I had to regroup and come back to face those nasty curve balls. Agosto tried to get me to swing at a couple of bad pitches in the dirt, but I worked the count to three balls and two strikes.

After fouling off the next two pitches, I took a slider just outside for ball four. What a rip-off I thought — all that work. All those years of practicing, striving for the first of what I hoped would be many moments in the sun, and I walked — in the rain, no less. I could never have a great first-at-bat story now to tell my grandkids or the old timers in the bar. There would be no deep drive into the gap or even a bloop single over the outstretched glove of the shortstop to talk about. Nope. I walked. Not even an official at-bat. If I had a heart attack trying to steal second base, my official line score for history's sake would be nonexistent, nowhere to be found — a bunch of zeros next to my name.

Which brings up a question I ask of a lot of guys I've played with: "If your career in the major leagues lasted only one day, would you rather go 0 for 4 or not bat at all?" You'd be surprised by the number of guys who say they don't want that 0 for 4. It's that fear of failure. I would take the 0 for 4. Give me the chance to fail rather than killing me with wondering what might have been. I did get another day and a few more at-bats after that too, but my best day ever in baseball was my first major league start.

I had been on the team since opening day, but had only made a few pinch hit and defensive appearances in the outfield. Then, on Memorial Day, Tony Armas' knee was too painful to play on, and I saw my name on the line-up card, hitting second, playing centerfield.

Before that day was over I had three hits, including my first and second major league home runs and 4 RBIs — and I didn't walk. I almost can't wait to get old so I can tell the stories of that day. Ken Schrom and Ron Davis were the Minnesota pitchers who are forever etched in my memory for throwing those home run balls. There is one thing, though. If I admit that my single greatest highlight of a nine-year career was the very first game I ever started, does that mean that the rest of my career was a steady decline? I guess the answer isn't really important, but it does bring me back to my question: Could I have ever been happy with just that day, knowing I may go my entire career and never match it — or roll the dice and play on? For me, it was an easy answer.

Dinger Days

I have this theory about my 19 major league home runs. I figure anybody who gave up a long ball to me must be out of the game. After all, how good could the guy be if I took him deep?

Turns out I'm wrong about that. There are a few guys still

hanging around, but there are some interesting twists and turns involving some of those mammoth blasts I hit. Indulge me.

The first time I ever took the field as a starter in the major leagues was May 27, 1985 against the Minnesota Twins. I hit two home runs that day. The pitchers: Ken Schrom and Ron Davis. Both are out of the game. The next time I connected was in Seattle on my mother's birthday, with her at the game to see me do it. That victim was Billy Swift, now playing for the Colorado Rockies and doing just fine. Then in August, I blasted one against the Kansas City Royals and Mike Jones. Who? He's gone. Finally, I ended my rookie season on an 0 for 19 slump—until my final at bat. I jumped the yard against Pete Ladd, also no longer playing.

In '86 I hit a dry spell—my only tater came against Jose Guzman who now pitches for the Cubs—wait, we'll hear more about him. Moving on to 1987, again, I only jacked one out of the park and that was off Chuck Crim who was pitching at the time for Milwaukee and is also now with the Cubs. (Are we starting to understand the problem with Cub pitching?)

In 1988, I got hot. I juiced John Candelaria and Tommy John on consecutive nights in New York. Steinbrenner began to inquire about the young phenom. Candelaria and John—both history. But I didn't stop there. I took Don August deep in Milwaukee, came back three days later and poked my only game-winning home run off Jerry Don Gleaton against Kansas City, and added Jose Nunez to my ever-lengthening list in Toronto. Where are all these guys now? They're just like a towering blast off of a Frank Thomas bat—gone.

In 1989, the best year of my career, I proved that you don't have to hit home runs to drive in runs. I hit eighth all year on the worst team in baseball that season (White Sox), and with only 443 at bats I drove in 50 runs—with just two homers. Tom Niedenfuer gave up one of the bombs—it landed in the first row of the cheap seats, and Frank Williams was collared with my only major league grandslam. That one, I did crush—way into the upper deck in Detroit. You may wonder if those two guys are still making a living playing ball? No.

1990 was so much fun for me. I hit .192 and came to the plate just 143 times. One day I decided to go and bitch about my playing time to Jeff Torborg, my manager. Robin Ventura was in the middle of his famed 0-41 slump, Scott Fletcher was hitting about .160, and I figured I should at least get a chance to give one of those guys a day off so they could regroup.

Torborg asked me if I checked the line-up for that day's game. I said, "No. I never check it anymore because I'm never on it. Every day I come in hoping to be in there, and every day I just get more and more disappointed. Now I just never look!" "You're on it today," he said. So I shut up and went to get ready to play. Maybe I should have waited one more day to go talk to him. Anyway, I hit my only home run of the year that day. Steve Cummings was the pitcher. Is he still pitching? No. Did I play the next day? No.

1991 was much better—right after re-signing with the Red Sox, I hit two bombs in the span of eight days. The funny thing was, both balls were helped over the fence by the outfielders trying to catch them. First, Juan Gonzalez caught the ball, hit the wall, and dropped it into the bullpen in Boston for a round tripper against Kenny Rogers. Then Chris Bosio dished one up that glanced off Robin Yount's glove before also ending up in the bully. Thanks, guys!

Of course, Rogers and Bosio are still making millions to pitch—and not so coincidentally, Bosio threw a no-hitter for Seattle and Rogers, a perfect game for Texas. I guess they shouldn't even appear on my list because both of those balls should have been caught.

Later in '91, I jumped all over pitches from Eric Plunk and Juan Guzman—Guzman being the only guy in my home run book twice.

Certainly, I wish the list was much longer. There's only one thing I know of that feels better than hitting a home run in a major league game.

I was pretty close—most of the guys who had to endure the pain of watching me use my home run trot are now doing something else for a living. And for those pitchers still hanging in there, I know they rest much easier knowing they don't have to face my potent bat any more. Yeah, right.

It's the guys

It's not the game, it's not the money, is it? It's not the crowds, the glory, the competition, or the winning. I never thought I'd say it's not the winning, but it isn't. It's the guys. It's the interests you share outside the game. It's being around baseball that keeps us all coming back. It's the guys you hang out with and the ones you never would hang out with. They're the ones you talk about when you're with the ones you do hang out with. It's knowing you're a veteran when you can hang out in the trainers' room—when you're not hurt. It's shared loneliness.

It's a suitcase that you're not sure if it's half packed or half unpacked, but it's not totally one way or the other. It's learning about life by knowing each other — the guy from the south, another from the north, one from California, and still another from a Latin town you can't pronounce. It's living with those prejudices and having your own exposed.

That's what keeps us trying to sign just one more contract. Fighting over what kind of music is playing and learning what a collard green is. Jeff Torborg tried to call us a family in Chicago when he managed there. He was exactly right. It's being part of a family.

There's a certain pride that goes with wearing a uniform that says the same thing on it as the person standing next to you. You may not even like him off the field, but he's the guy you turn the double play with — and you do it well together. It's being around the game, because the guys are there.

The clubhouse

When 25 guys play baseball together for almost eight months a year, they get to know each other pretty well. During that period we spend more time with our teammates than we do with our own families. In fact, the team becomes a family of sorts. We eat together, play the games together, travel, dress, shower, shop, and even kill time together. Because of this, we become a lot less private about the more embarrassing aspects of life. Those things you wouldn't do or talk about in front of a stranger or a first date. But after a while, those same things become fair game in the clubhouse or on the bench.

Leave it to me to take a somewhat different approach to these events as they happen than everybody else. For instance, five guys are sitting in the same area on the bench and then one of them scatters out of the way and says, "Who ate lunch at Taco Bell, that's brutal. How can you do that here?"

Soon after, everybody smells the problem, and they all pick a new location for the conversation with everybody blaming the other guy for farting. If I was in that group, I'd never move. Instead, I'd just sit there and tell the guys that if they gave me a few seconds I could analyze what his last meal was, just from the smell. Of course I couldn't do it, but I'd always take a quick guess. In fact, if I was the guilty party of producing the foul aroma, I'd be the first to claim it. I figured if I was going to get that much attention, I might as well own up to it!

The best way to get a reaction from everybody was to "crop dust"—Pass your gas at one end of the dugout and casually stroll down to the other end and sit. That way the whole team gets to sample your work. Some guys took it too far, though. It's like they save up until they show up at the clubhouse, just so they can blow people away. I've known guys that have had to evacuate their room for half an hour with the air conditioner cranked up and the doors open, just because his roommate was at his best.

Two of the more famous members of the 1987 World Champion Minnesota Twins actually taped some of their best efforts for others to enjoy. I heard it over our clubhouse stereo system while I was playing in Chicago. They even titled the tape "Morning Thunder," saying that they were usually in rare form the morning after a night out for a few beers. I'm almost envious that I didn't think of the idea. It takes a special state of mind to actually remember to grab a tape recorder on your way to the toilet in the morning.

Some guys would really get obsessed with those taboo subjects. I remember John Marzano of the Red Sox always had a healthy sense of humor. Nothing seemed to get him down, and he was always joking around. What sticks out most in my mind was how proud he always was of his toilet masterpieces. He'd always ask if anybody would be interested in seeing one and then rate it according to texture and staying power — whether it was a double-flusher or if one flush was enough.

None of these guys would even think of doing this stuff in public, but in the clubhouse it's okay. If you ever accidentally caught somebody picking their nose, they may feel a little embarrassed. If you caught one of our guys doing it, he may ask you if you'd like to keep it as a souvenir.

One time I was sitting in front of my locker getting dressed for batting practice when I noticed what looked like a huge booger in my shoe. I thought somebody was messing with me so I did everything I could to get it out without touching it. I shook my shoe, banged it on my chair, everything. It wouldn't budge. After making sure I wasn't secretly being watched, I reached in and plucked it out. To my surprise, it was just a piece of excess rubber glue that attaches the arch support to the bottom of my shoe. I figured if it fooled me, it would be a good prank on somebody else.

I spotted our trainer, Pete Youngman, working on second baseman Cheo Garcia's leg in the training room. I placed the fake booger in my nose and went to go have a chat with Pete. When I got into the training room, I just said, "Hello," and waited for a few seconds. When I knew I had Pete's attention I told him I needed him to stretch my back when he was finished with Cheo. At the same time I casually reached in and picked out the perfectly placed booger. Looking at it for just a second, I reached over and wiped it on Pete's shirt. He was stunned at first, but then quickly flicked it off his shirt, right onto Cheo's leg. He felt it land on his leg and started screaming, "Get it off, get it off!" Pete grabbed a towel and wiped the booger off Cheo's leg and tossed the towel out of the trainer's room. I knew Pete was pissed because he wasn't saying a word, but I couldn't keep a straight face anymore and two guys that knew what was going on were already rolling on the clubhouse floor laughing. I went over to retrieve the rubber booger and let Pete in on the joke. He said he was a little perturbed because he thought even I wouldn't do anything like that!

None of that stuff ever phases me. I can handle almost anything that might be perceived as gross by other people's standards. Everything except Tim Wallach. Not Tim himself, he seemed like a great guy for the short time we played together in

Montreal. It was his sinuses I couldn't handle. He had some medical problem that made his sinuses clog up and cause a lot of pressure. So occasionally, he'd have to relieve the pressure by choking up these green, fuzzy potato-chip-sized boogers. He knew I couldn't stand it. They looked like something no human could produce, but he loved to point them out to me whenever he could.

Let's face it, there are only two topics that are off limits in the clubhouse: you don't get personal with another guy's ability, and you don't get on another guy's family. Other than that, nothing is too rude to say or too crude to do. It's the one place the guys can really let it all hang out. I think that's the real reason guys get to the park so early. It's a second home to everybody where anything can happen, and when it does, you don't want to miss it.

Coming through the Boston minor league system, I played with one guy who decided to get circumcised at age 28. He was in extreme pain after his surgery and even had to go on the 10-day disabled list because of it. None of the players could relate to his pain, and we all laughed when he made his way from the trainer's table to the showers every day. He'd be all wrapped up in gauze and trying to stay as motionless as possible to avoid pain. Everybody joked that all was not lost — that he had a wallet made out of the remains of his operation.

Every guy that ever played any pro baseball could write a book based solely on his clubhouse stories. I've told just a few, mainly because like your own home, most of what happens in the clubhouse should be left with the players. That's why it's not uncommon to read these words on the doors of many club-houses: "What you see here, what you hear here, let it stay here, when you leave here."

Ladies in the locker room

What's the big deal with female reporters? Are they any less ladies because they're sports reporters? Should they be deprived of the opportunity to do their jobs because of their sex? Should they be banned from the locker rooms? No.

I'll be the first one to admit that I may have acted differently in the clubhouse if I knew a female reporter was there. Men never act the same way around women as they do when it's just the boys—that is if they've been taught anything about respect. But then again, I feel that the clubhouse is *my* house, and if you come in, you must adjust to the rules in my house.

Of course we had players who couldn't stand the fact that women could waltz right into the clubhouse without knocking first. I don't know what it was, maybe their religion. Chauvinism more likely. Embarrassment that someone might see "Mr. Winkie" when he's not at his best, and when you think about it, that is the biggest reason. A locker room has a bunch of naked men wandering around in it, and some guys don't think that's the best place for women.

To me it's no big deal. It's the '90s, after all. I don't feel I have the right to keep someone else from doing her job. There's no way to get around it or change the rules to accommodate everyone's feelings. Let's face it— it's hard enough to get athletes to talk to the media—nobody's going to like the idea of special circumstances or separate interviewing areas for women.

I tried to take it all in stride. I was never the shyest guy in the room, but I would never purposely undress in the middle of an interview, either. If I was on the way to the showers in my birthday suit, I was in plain view of whoever might glance my way, male or female.

No team I ever played on had a major problem with the women who covered our games, but we were also lucky to have had reporters who always had a professional attitude when they did their jobs. Cheryl Raye in Chicago, Susan Waldman in New York and Jennifer Briggs in Philadelphia were always knowledgeable, fair and trustworthy. And in that way they were more like "one of the guys" than a lot of the guys.

But even that isn't enough. Female reporters have to do the same quality work that their male counterparts do—but they must also check their sexuality at the door. When a man comes in to ask, "How did it feel to hit that home run in the sixth inning?," he doesn't have to worry about who or what he's looking at. But if a female reporter gets labeled a "pecker checker" because she has wandering eyes—she loses all her credibility. Unlike baseball, for female reporters, this is a game where you truly don't want to keep your eye on the ball(s).

It's even more difficult for the women who are beginning to break the gender restrictions in professional sports. Maneau Rehume, the first woman to play professional hockey, has to dress and shower separately, and therefore misses out on some of the most unifying times a team shares together—time spent in the locker room.

If I were her or any other woman in that situation, I'd probably walk right into the locker room on the first day, strip off my uniform and say, "That's right, I'm a girl. So take a good look and get over it. Now let's play some hockey." But that's just me.

The bottom line is, women in the locker room is a sign of the times. Everything around us is constantly changing. Some changes we like, some we don't, but this one just isn't a big enough deal to worry about.

Play hard, play well

People tell you when you're a little leaguer that if you have a dream, practice and work hard, you can play ball in high school. Then the dream becomes a college scholarship—if you play well enough. From there you balance your academic schedule with the focus toward the possibility of a professional baseball career—if you play hard and play well.

Somehow, someone notices you and the spark of that dream stays alive when you get drafted and begin playing minor league baseball. When you get there, the first thing you hear is, "If you work hard enough and play well enough, in about four or five years you may become a major leaguer."

We know all about the guys who had that dream, did what they had to do, and now reap the benefits of a successful major league career. But what about the guy whose dream turns into a nightmare? The guy who envisioned it, worked at it, played well enough, but still couldn't crack the major league ranks? There have been hundreds of these guys over the years. You don't know who they are, because their careers died in towns like Syracuse, Portland, and Indianapolis. They remain nameless, because although they played hard and put up good numbers, somebody "up there" saw something missing. Maybe too much glove and not enough bat—or vice versa. Maybe he didn't have a regular position or maybe it was just a numbers game at the big-league level — too many guys, and not enough spots on the roster.

We don't really care about this guy — he never graced a major league ballpark, or if he did you don't remember him. He's 31 now, with a wife and two kids. For him, baseball never did pay the rent anyway, and now he's found a real job. In a couple of years he'll hook up with a beer league softball team and somebody will remember that he used to play pro ball. But nothing they remember is very accurate, and the recognition only brings back his personal pain of wondering what could have been—if he had just played harder or played better.

But what if he was lied to by those "in the know"? It's been done many times before. What if that speech given every year, by every manager, on the first day of spring training is a lie? "You guys have to work hard, play well—we're taking our best 25 players with us to the big leagues this year." Why would they lie about something like that? Money. We've been taught that winning is the most important thing, ever since grade school relay races or playing jacks with your sister — play hard, play well — win!

But it can be a lie, because at the major-league level, winning is not the most important thing, money is. And if the front office has to lie to you to save face or save money, they will.

I think Ken Ryan was lied to. Of course, you'll hear plenty more about him as time goes by. He'll be one of the lucky ones who lives the dream. He's got a 96 M.P.H. fastball and a frightening "hook" to go with it, and some people even have the gall to call him "Rocket" — a nickname reserved solely for Roger Clemens. But in 1993, during a great winning streak the Red Sox had in June and July, Ryan was demoted back to "AAA" Pawtucket. Ken Ryan played hard for five years as a starter and then two more as "the closer of the future." And he played well (4-0 with a 2.45 ERA while in Boston during that span). But it was a numbers game.

"The toughest roster move I ever had to make," said Red Sox Manager Butch Hobson. The Red Sox had 12 pitchers on their roster, an unusual load and somebody had to go. They should have made a pitching move two weeks earlier, but for some reason, they didn't — so they sent me down and kept 12 pitchers, hoping one of them would screw up bad enough to warrant a demotion or release. Sending me out should have been the tough decision for them to make, but it didn't seem to bother them too much. During those two weeks, Ryan pitched flawlessly, and the Boston press was calling for the release of veteran lefty Joe Hesketh. He was admittedly pitching terribly but had a guaranteed contract that was worth about $2.6 million if he was released. (The remainder of 1993 plus $1.7 million for 1994.)

The Red Sox couldn't pull the trigger, and sent Ken Ryan and his $109,000 contract down instead. Play hard, play well.

These kinds of decisions aren't unique to the Red Sox; every organization faces them, many times every year. It just seems like they make the "financial" move most of the time.

The message they sent was: We would rather pay Joe Hesketh to pitch poorly, than pay him not to pitch at all and let Ryan get the job done right. They talk about keeping the 25 best players, but what they don't say is that it's the 25 best players for what they want to do, and sometimes the most talented doesn't matter. And that makes me wonder about that dream — play hard, play well. . .

Waiting for the call

After my first successful season in 1984, I thought I'd be called up to Boston in September after our playoffs in Pawtucket. I was voted to the "AAA" all-star team, voted best defensive third baseman, and infielder with the best arm. I hit .269 with 17 home runs, and led our team to the International League championship.

After an hour of celebration in the clubhouse on championship night, I was called to the manager's office. Tony Torchia and Minor League Director of players Ed Kenny Sr. were there. They told me I would not be going to Boston. They said since our playoffs lasted so long, and there were only two weeks left in the major league season, I wouldn't play much, if at all. Wade Boggs had a chance to get 200 hits, and they wanted to see that happen. They also said I tailed off in the second half of the season, and wasn't as productive as I was in the first half.

I sat there stunned, fighting back my emotions and the tears that went with them. I had spent 3-1/2 years busting my ass and leaving my heart and soul on the field for that organization — waiting for that one call that said, "you're going to Boston." But on the same night that I became a champion, they shattered my dream of becoming a major leaguer. I thought of everything I could have said, but I said nothing and walked out.

I didn't care if I got a chance to play. Let Boggs get his 200 hits — I just wanted to be there. I wanted to sit there, on the bench in Fenway, in between Dwight Evans and Jim Rice — in the same spot Ted Williams once sat. I wanted to take batting practice in a major-league stadium. I wanted to sit in front of my locker, try on my new uniform — just fit in. I just wanted to call my mom and say, "I made it."

The difference between .250 and .300

For most of my career I was a utility player — a guy who can play many positions. To the organization, I didn't play them as well as somebody else, but I played well enough so they couldn't get rid of me. I was always the 24th or 25th guy on a 25-man team. I showed up before everyone else, put in extra work, and was usually one of the last to leave the park. But I sometimes went weeks between appearances in games and got paid a fraction of the "stars'" salaries. And what's the difference between me and a guy who hit .300? He makes $2 to $5 million per year as long as he's got a rear end, and I'll struggle every year to make a club — continuously trying to prove my worth.

But what's the real difference between hitting .250 and .300? One hit per week. If a player plays every day during the season, he'd get nearly 600 at-bats. To hit .300, he'd get at least 180 hits. A .250 hitter, an average or below player, gets 150 hits. That's a difference of 30 hits, and with roughly 30 weeks in a season, the .300 hitter gets about one hit more a week than the average hitter.

One more hit. As Kevin Costner put it in the movie *Bull Durham*, "he gets a duck snort, a dying quail, a Texas leaguer — a 99 hop seeing eye grounder up the middle." He hits that weak pop-up that nobody wanted to catch — the same one you hit and guys were waiting in line just to get you out. His tough play was ruled a hit, yours was called an error. And your last at-bat was a screaming liner right to the second baseman. You hit the same as the other guy every day, week after week, except for that one day every week when you went 1 for 4 off that tough lefty, and he went 2 for 4, and you don't even remember his two hits.

At the end of the year the brass looks at the numbers and says, "Well, he's hanging in there, so we better keep our eyes on him. As for the other guy, he hit .300 again. He is really going to be a star."

So as your careers go on, the similarities lessen. Sure enough, he's now making millions, as you endlessly negotiate minimal non-guaranteed raises, and have no promises of a future with the team.

Your locker is still next to his, but now he's got two. He needs more room to house his endless supply of shiny new spikes and cartons of batting gloves. He not only gets both for free, but he also gets paid to wear them. Every once in a while you look at some of the pamphlets that litter his auxiliary locker. There are instruction manuals on how to use his new cellular phone and portable TV/VCR/CD player. *Money Magazine* is delivered to him. The German car manufacturers actually send him literature on their latest model cars — of which he owns two or three.

Somebody else is admiring his new set of golf clubs — given to him by one of the pros he knows. It's cool sitting here because all the movie stars and other athletes want to meet him. If you play your cards right, usually you get introduced.

He's got old batting practice bats in his locker with wood grain in them that you only dream of getting to use as your "gamer." Sometimes you order your bats under his name to try to get better wood, but it never seems to work.

When you go shopping, you notice a commotion in the center of the mall. He's there, too — signing autographs for two hours. And for that, they pay him around $15,000 — more than you just put down on your new house this off-season.

When you see him out at dinner, he orders anything he wants, because he knows the owner of the place and the maitre 'd will pick up the tab. His date for the night looks like she just jumped off the cover of Cosmo. And you wonder how he does it. It's a stupid question. Your waiter stumbles over you while leaving the check, but quickly apologizes and says he's in a hurry, because he has a chance to meet "him" before he leaves.

In the off-season you worry about a lot of things: moving back home, if and where you're going to play next year, and how are you going to keep making your house payment if you don't? Meanwhile, he spends the off-season sifting through appearance offers, planning extended vacations, and being bothered by his builder — it's a lot of work building a 12,000 square foot home.

He's still your friend and not a bad guy really. It just seems like you have different interests now. When you call him, you get his business line, and it always takes a couple of days to hear back from him. "Come over anytime," he says, "you know I've got that batting cage out back and you're welcome to use it." You never go over.

It's not something that consumes your life, but you can't help but notice the differences. You can't get away from it. Last night he was on "Letterman" and next week a guest appearance on "NYPD Blue."

One extra hit a week. Maybe if I just change my stance a little. . . . .

Let's make a deal . . .

When I finished playing baseball, I took a temporary job with a publishing company that was trying to get into the sports card industry. My job was to interview every player in the major leagues for a bio on the back of the cards. My boss owned a baseball card shop and he knew the business well. Unfortunately, he didn't know about much of anything else.

He had never worked for anyone until this job, and he got upset with me when I was unwilling to work for the company's first offer. He had never negotiated anything before and was pretty unaware of how that game was played. I, on the other hand, was used to negotiating. Everything in baseball is some kind of compromise, from signing a contract every year to getting enough swings in batting practice. I'm not sure what he was being paid, but I had a much different salary in mind. So after a few cordial meetings, I ended up working for more than twice the original offer.

In baseball, the negotiations are fierce. The main reason ballplayers have agents is to utilize the professional negotiating skills they possess. Agents have a greater knowledge and understanding of the process and also have more time to devote to the business of baseball. I always used my agent, Tom Demakis, to handle my tough situations — to be the bad guy. He'd say the right things and also heard things I didn't want to hear. Tom was formerly one of the top five attorneys out of 200 in the New York District Attorney's office, and a superior litigation lawyer; I felt safe having him negotiate my deals. Here's how my contract unfolded for the 1992 season:

Nov. 1, 1991

The Red Sox faxed Tom their original offer. 1992 base salary $500,000.

Incentives:

If player appears in 65 games	$25,000
If player appears in 80 games	$25,000
If player appears in 95 games	$50,000
If player appears in 110 games	$50,000
If player appears in 125 games	$50,000
Earning Potential	$700,000

We sincerely desire to have Steve Lyons on our ball club and we feel this proposal is very fair for a player performing in a utility role

> Signed Lou Gorman
> Senior Vice Pres/General Manager
> Boston Red Sox

Nov. 2, 1991

I discussed with Tom what I would like to see in a contract: a two-year deal at $750,000 per year (I was a free agent and wanted some security).

Arguments in my favor:

- Average major league salary is more than I'm asking for
- Possibly their best defensive outfielder
- Never on the Disabled List
- I am a free agent
- Starter Ellis Burks is always hurt and has back problems
- Best utility player in baseball
- Compare my stats thru '91 with Tony Phillips' stats thru '88. Almost identical numbers through same length of service time.
- Positive relationship with team and fans

Nov. 14, 1991

Tom relayed conversations he had with Gorman citing Lou's unwillingness to agree to a two-year contract.

Nov. 25, 1991

Red Sox fax to Tom.

Dear Tom:

The Red Sox hereby propose the following one-year guaranteed contract tender for the 1992 season for player Steve Lyons.

1992 base salary	$550,000

Incentives:

If player appears in 60 games	$25,000
If player appears in 80 games	$25,000
If player appears in 100 games	$50,000
If player appears in 120 games	$50,000

Nov. 25, 1991

Tom contacted me by phone to discuss the new offer. We agreed that they just shifted money from the incentives to the base. Definitely a step in the right direction, but nowhere near the two-year, $1.5 million we were looking for. I instructed Tom to keep banging away at Gorman, something he loved doing. Unfortunately, it seemed like Lou loved it just as much.

Nov. 28 - Dec. 10, 1991

Numerous conversations between Tom and Lou with confirming conversations with me. No significant movement.

Dec. 16, 1991

A new offer came from the Red Sox:

$575,000 base salary, same incentives
Option year for 1993: $700,000
Incentives:

75 games	$25,000
100 games	$50,000
120 games	$50,000

1993 would be guaranteed if I played in 100 games in 1992.

Dec. 22, 1991

Atlanta Braves showed an interest in me. General Manager John Schuerholz made an offer to Tom:

1992: $ 550,000 guaranteed
Incentives:

75 games	$50,000
100 games	$50,000
Option for 1993:	$600,000
Incentives:	
75 games	$50,000
100 games	$50,000

1993 would be guaranteed if I played in 80 games or got 222 plate appearances.

Tom and I discussed the advantages of having two teams interested in my services and whether or not I wanted to leave Boston. I always wanted to play in the National League, and the Braves were coming off their World Series appearance of the '91 season. There wasn't a team in the National League that I would have rather played for. My concerns were whether or not the Braves were going to trade Jeff Treadway, and if they would let me compete with Mark Lemke for the second base job. They also had a hole in centerfield with Otis Nixon serving an 18-day drug suspension to open the season. I was excited about the possibilities, and I knew I had a little bit of leverage on my side.

Tom tried to get the Braves to agree to a two-year contract. They wouldn't do it because of the uncertainty with Treadway. If they didn't trade him, they didn't want to be locked in to a two-year deal with me. Obviously, Tom asked for all of the same extras as he had in the Boston negotiation: single room, award bonuses, and higher level bonuses for 1993 (in case I was traded to an expansion team or got more playing time).

Then we added a few things. First, moving expenses. I was hearing so many good things about Atlanta and how many players made it their permanent home. I wanted to be covered if I decided to move there myself. The basic agreement with the players association also calls for reasonable moving expenses to be paid by the club if the player moves there within a two-year period. Second, I asked for a signing bonus. I hadn't had one since I originally signed in1981, and they were sort of "in style." Of course, whatever signing bonus I received would be deducted from my 1992 salary. I asked for $50,000.

Schuerholz was vacationing in Hawaii and said he'd respond to Tom soon. In the meantime, Boston was still in the race. Tom made sure Boston knew there was another party interested and asked Gorman for another proposal, still pushing for a two-year guaranteed deal.

Dec. 30, 1991

Gorman upped the offer of a one-year plus an option contract calling for $700,000 in 1992 and $700,000 in 1993. But along with the offer there was this silly proposal of games played before the All-Star break and games played after the All-Star break to determine whether or not the '93 salary would be guaranteed.

We liked the range of money that was being talked about. They basically guaranteed most of the incentive money, so my contract wasn't tied to plate appearances or games played. We knew that after two months of negotiations, we had pushed as far as we could to get two years guaranteed; it wasn't going to happen.

Gorman in some sense is like a used car salesman. He loved asking, "What's it going to take to get it done?"

Tom and I got serious and put together a proposal we could be happy with and got ready to submit it. We had already done hours of preliminary checking of players stats and contracts. There was groundwork that could help us in the contracts of Jamie Quirk, Herm Winningham, Dale Sveum, Mike Pagliarulo, and Luis Salazar.

We backed off the two-year guarantee, but proposed that the second year of the deal become guaranteed if I appeared in 70 games. All the other numbers and award bonuses were the same as we had talked about in previous negotiations. After numerous phone calls between Tom and Lou, they agreed on the number of games, 84. If I played in that many during '92, I would be set for 1993.

Tom called Schuerholz and made him aware of the Red Sox's latest offer. He said he didn't want to be involved in a bidding war, but asked if we would give him the opportunity to make an offer before I signed anything. We agreed that we would.

With the Boston offer being potentially $250,000 more over the two-year period, Tom and I both knew that my best option was to stay in Boston.

That's when the whole deal got tricky.

After telling Schuerholz that we planned on signing in Boston, I gave the go ahead to Tom to agree to the terms of this contract:

1992 Base Salary	$700,000
$25,000	Gold Glove
$25,000	L.C.S / M.V.P.
$50,000	W.S. / M.V.P.
Single Room	
Option '93 Base Salary	$700,000
Bonuses same as '92	
1993 salary guaranteed if player appears in 84 games in '92.	

The 1993 salary would be automatically guaranteed if I appeared in 84 games during the 1992 championship season including post season games.

The next time I talked to Tom, I expected him to say what he always said after we signed a deal: "Congratulations, you're signed to play for the Red Sox," and then reiterate the contract in detail. Instead I was told, "You're not going to like this. We have a problem."

During the conversation with Lou, Tom casually said, "The first year of this contract is obviously guaranteed, right?" There had never been a contract written up that contained option language for a second year when the first year was not guaranteed. The very fact that you're even discussing a second year assures that the first year is a given.

Not in this contract. The Red Sox expected me to be the first person in history to sign a non-guaranteed one-year plus an option contract. In other words, I had to make the team in spring training like any rookie. I was sure of my ability to make the team, but that wasn't the point. I had played seven years in the big leagues and they wanted me to sign a deal that allowed them to make a trade, change their minds, or do whatever else they wanted, and I would be on the outside looking in. They could have released me in spring training without any obligation except some severance pay. I was willing to put my name on the contract and dedicate myself once again to the Red Sox organization, and I wanted the same consideration from them!

It got worse. They went on to say that the 84-game plateau I had to reach to guarantee my second year was no longer valid. Rather, the option year would be strictly that— a club option. If I played in 84 games or 162, the Red Sox could pick up the option or not, completely at their discretion.

Why did we have a week's worth of frustrating conversations about how many games would vest the '93 season? Why had that all changed? We were stunned and confused as to what had gone wrong. There was no mention of taking any deals off the table, no miscommunication that would have indicated that we thought they offered something that they hadn't.

I suppose I'll never know what really happened, but I do have some idea. Gorman always liked me as a ballplayer and treated me fairly. He may have overstepped his bounds with the offer he made: $700,000 and $700,000 for consecutive years was pretty good money. I think somebody above him (such as General Partner John Harrington) didn't like the deal and told him to back off. After all I hadn't actually signed anything and they could change their minds if they wanted to. It's been done before, but we all know that's not good business practice. They made me an offer and then changed it when I was ready to agree to it.

I was extremely upset, feeling very betrayed. I ordered Tom to reopen negotiations with the Braves and authorized him to agree to any deal that came close to the former Red Sox offer.

Then the Boston newspapers became involved. Pitcher Frank Viola had already signed with the Sox, so I became the headline news. The January 6 *Boston Globe*: "Sox Face Utility Shut-Off - Lyons May Exit In Deal Dispute." "Angry Lyons Set For Exit", wrote the *Boston Herald*. The Red Sox had to sign me by January 8, because of the deadline to re-sign free agent players. Time was running out, and if I passed the deadline, my only option would be to sign with Atlanta. At least until the 8th, I had a choice.

The Red Sox called an emergency meeting to discuss what they wanted to do and later that day called Tom to discuss a "new" offer. I guess they realized they made a mistake on the first year and decided to guarantee 1992. But they would not reinstate the 84 games to guarantee 1993.

Tom was now in more serious negotiations with Schuerholz. The Braves made their final offer:

1992:	$650,000	($50,000 signing bonus)
	$ 25,000	60 game appearances
	$ 35,000	80 game appearances
	$ 50,000	100 game appearances
	$ 25,000	L.C.S./M.V.P.
	$ 50,000	W.S./M.V.P.
	$ 50,000	Gold Glove
	Single Room	
	Option for 1993	Same as 1992

If player appears in 80 games or has 220 plate appearances in the 1992 championship season, club shall be deemed to have exercised the option.

I was mad at the Sox, and this was a fair offer from the Braves. With the National league style of pinch hitting and double switches, I thought I'd have a good chance to play in 80 games. Plus, the incentives gave me the opportunity to make more money. During my negotiations with the Red Sox, I got the feeling that they didn't believe me when I said there was another team interested.

Tom called Lou and told him this would be the last phone call between them if their offer didn't change. We were prepared to sign with Atlanta, and in effect we were giving them the last right of refusal. They didn't take it.

"Psycho II, Now Playing In Atlanta. Lyons Leaves Sox, Signs With Braves" read the January 9 *Boston Herald*.

It was by far the most complex negotiation I was involved in, and the problems it caused made it a time that I don't remember with a smile. As it turned out, I was back in a Red Sox uniform by the end of June anyway. I got released by Atlanta in April, signed with Montreal and was traded to Boston in June.

On the following pages is a copy of my 1992 contract. I thought it might be interesting if you've never seen one. Note on page 4 the list of activities and sports that baseball players are not allowed to participate in.

UNIFORM PLAYER'S CONTRACT

THE NATIONAL LEAGUE OF
PROFESSIONAL BASEBALL CLUBS

Parties

Between __*THE ATLANTA NATIONAL LEAGUE BASEBALL CLUB, INC.*__ herein called the Club

and __*STEPHEN J. LYONS*__

of __*SCOTTSDALE, ARIZONA*__ , herein called the Player

Recital

The Club is a member of The National League of Professional Baseball Clubs, a voluntary association of member Clubs which has subscribed to the Major League Rules with The American League of Professional Baseball Clubs and its constituent Clubs and to The Professional Baseball Rules with that League and the National Association of Baseball Leagues.

Agreement

In consideration of the facts above recited and of the promises of each to the other, the parties agree as follows:

Employment

1. The Club hereby employs the Player to render, and the Player agrees to render, skilled services as a baseball player during the year(s) 19_92_ and _1993 Option_ including the Club's training season, the Club's exhibition games, the Club's playing season, the League Championship Series and the World Series (or any other official series in which the Club may participate and in any receipts of which the Player may be entitled to share)

Payment

2. For performance of the Player's services and promises hereunder the Club will pay the Player the sum of $-------------
(SEE SPECIAL COVENANTS) -------------------------------
----

in semi-monthly installments after the commencement of the championship season(s) covered by this contract except as the schedule of payments may be modified by a special covenant. Payment shall be made on the day the amount becomes due, regardless of whether the Club is "home" or "abroad." If a monthly rate of payment is stipulated above, it shall begin with the commencement of the championship season (or such subsequent date as the Player's services may commence) and end with the termination of the championship season and shall be payable in semi-monthly installments as above provided

Nothing herein shall interfere with the right of the Club and the Player by special covenant herein to mutually agree upon a method of payment whereby part of the Player's salary for the above year can be deferred to subsequent years

If the Player is in the service of the Club for part of the championship season only, he shall receive such proportion of the sum above mentioned, as the number of days of his actual employment in the championship season bears to the number of days in the championship season.

Notwithstanding the rate of payment stipulated above, the minimum rate of payment to the Player for each day of service on a Major League Club shall be at the applicable rate set forth in Article VI(B)(1) of the Basic Agreement between the American League of Professional Baseball Clubs and the National League of Professional Baseball Clubs and the Major League Baseball Players Association, effective January 1, 1985 ("Basic Agreement"). The minimum rate of payment for National Association

service for all Players (a) signing a second Major League contract (not covering the same season as any such Player's initial Major League contract) or (b) having at least one day of Major League service, shall be at the applicable rate set forth in Article VI(B)(2) of the Basic Agreement

Payment to the Player at the rate stipulated above shall be continued throughout any period in which a Player is required to attend a regularly scheduled military encampment of the Reserve of the Armed Forces or of the National Guard during the championship season

Loyalty

3 (a) The Player agrees to perform his services hereunder diligently and faithfully, to keep himself in first-class physical condition and to obey the Club's training rules, and pledges himself to the American public and to the Club to conform to high standards of personal conduct, fair play and good sportsmanship

*ADDENDUM TO UNIFORM PLAYER'S CONTRACT
BETWEEN THE ATLANTA NATIONAL LEAGUE BASEBALL CLUB, INC.
AND STEPHEN J. LYONS*

This Addendum is attached to and made part of the 1992 and 1993 Uniform Player's Contract between The Atlanta National League Baseball Club, Inc., herein referred to as "Club", and Stephen J. Lyons, herein referred to as "Player", and shall be deemed to amend and modify any other provisions, rules, and regulations inconsistent herewith.

A: SIGNING BONUS

   The Club agrees to pay the Player a signing bonus in the amount of $50,000.00 (Fifty Thousand Dollars), payable within ten days of approval of this Contract.

B. SALARY

   1. *The Club agrees to pay the Player a salary for the 1992 Major League Championship season in the amount of $600,000.00 (Six Hundred Thousand Dollars), payable in equal semi-monthly installments on the 15th and last day of each month commencing April 1, 1992, and ending October 15, 1992.*

C. CLUB OPTION FOR 1993:

   The Club shall have an option to extend this Contract for the 1993 season provided that it exercises such option by delivering written notice thereof to Player no later than 48 hours after the completion of the last game of the 1992 World Series.

   In the event Club exercises its option to extend this Contract, it shall pay Player a 1993 salary in the amount of $650,000.00 (Six Hundred Fifty Thousand Dollars), payable in equal semi-monthly installments on the 15th and last day of each month commencing April 1, 1993, and ending October 15, 1993.   Player shall be eligible in 1993 to earn all Bonuses set forth in Paragraphs D and E below and the guarantee language of Paragraph H below shall apply to the year 1993 as of the date the option is exercised.

   If Player has appeared in a total of 80 Games or has at least 220 Total Plate Appearances during the 1992 Championship Season, Club shall be deemed to have exercised its option, and this Contract shall be extended for the year 1993, as stated above, beginning as of the date the said game or appearance requirements are met.

D. PERFORMANCE BONUSES:

The Club agrees to pay the Player the following additional amounts
(if earned) during the 1992 Championship Season, and during the
1993 Championship Season, (if earned) in the event the option for
1993 is exercised:

60 game appearances during the Championship Season....$ 25,000.00
80 game appearances during the Championship Season....$ 35,000.00
100 game appearances during the Championship Season...$ 50,000.00

E. AWARD BONUSES:

The Club agrees to pay the Player the following additional amounts
(if earned) during the 1992 season, and during the 1993 season (if
earned) in the event the option for 1993 is exercised:

League Championship Series MVP................$ 25,000.00
World Series MVP.............................. 50,000.00
Gold Glove Award............................. 50,000.00

F. MAJOR LEAGUE RULE 9(e)

The Player specifically agrees in the event of assignment of this
Contract to accept the following adjustments as satisfying the
requirements of Major League Rule 9(e):

The bonus provisions set forth above in Paragraphs D and E of
this Contract, if yet to be earned, will become the responsibility
of the assignee Club under the same terms and conditions that
defined the obligation of the assignor Club, provided that upon
assignment during the season the responsibility for the bonus
payments set forth in Paragraphs D and E , if earned, shall be
prorated between the Clubs in proportion to the number of games
appeared in during the Championship Season with each Club involved.

G. SINGLE ROOM

The Club agrees to provide the Player with a single room, at the
Club's expense, at the Club's hotels during the Major League
Championship season during the term of this Contract, including
the option year (provided the Club has exercised its option to
extend this contract for the 1993 season).

H.   *SALARY GUARANTEE*

The Club and the Player agree that the salary stipulated in Paragraph B of this Addendum is "guaranteed" in the manner and under the terms and conditions set forth below:

1.   *The Club guarantees that, if this Contract is terminated pursuant to Paragraph 7 (b)(2) of this Contract, the Player shall nevertheless continue to receive the unpaid balance of the salary stipulated in Paragraph B of this Addendum for the term of this Contract. The foregoing agreement to continue the Player's salary beyond the date of termination applies whether or not such termination is due to the Player's inability to display sufficient professional skills or competitive ability, or is due to physical incapacity or death which is incurred on or off the baseball field or which is incurred before, during or after the Championship Season.*

2.   *Notwithstanding the foregoing and, regardless of whether or not this Contract is terminated, the Club shall be relieved of all obligations to pay the Player's salary in the event that:*

a)   *this Contract is terminated pursuant to Paragraph 7 (b)(1) of this Contract.*

b)   *this Contract is terminated pursuant to Paragraph 7 (b)(3) of this contract;*

c)   *the Player does not render his services under the Contract due to:*

(1)   *Voluntary retirement as an active Player;*

(2)   *A labor dispute (including a strike, lockout or sympathy strike);*

(3)   *Placement on any of the lists set out in Major League Rule 15;*

(4)   *Suspension by the Club or by action of the League President or the Commissioner of Baseball;*

(5)   *Intentional self-injury, suicide or attempted suicide;*

(6)   *The use of any type of illegal drug, the misuse of prescription or over-the-counter drugs, or alcohol dependency;*

-3-

(7)   Injury or incapacity suffered as a result of partici-
      pation in the following activities or sports:

Organized competitive automobile racing, organized motorcycle
racing, piloting of aircraft, hot air ballooning, parachuting
(except leaving an aircraft for purposes of emergency evacuation),
hanggliding, organized horse racing, fencing, organized boxing,
organized wrestling, karate, judo, jujitsu, skiing, snow-mobiling,
bobsledding, ice hockey, field hockey, squash, spelunking, organized basketball, organized football, whitewater canoeing, jai-
lai, lacrosse, organized soccer, rodeo, organized bicycle racing,
organized motor boat racing, polo, rugby, organized volleyball,
surfing, participation in the "Superteams" or "Superstars"
activities, or other television or motion picture athletic
competitions (without the written consent of the Club), or
other sports involving a substantial risk of personal injury.

(8) Incapacity due to a criminal or felonious act (including
    civil or criminal incarceration as a form of incapacity,
    but excluding traffic violations).

(9) Incapacity caused by the HIV virus, AIDS and/or any related
    conditions; provided, however, that this exclusion No. 9
    shall be null and void in the event that Player successfully
    completes an insurance examination (including an HIV test
    if required) within 30 days of the execution of this Agree-
    ment, such that the Club will be able to obtain general
    disability insurance coverage, including coverage for HIV
    and/or AIDS related disabilities.

3. The Player and the Club mutually agree and recognize that the
    Club entered into this salary guarantee provision based upon
    the Player's representation that he was in first class physical
    condition and that, in an effort to maintain his first class
    physical condition, the Player would adhere to any training rules
    and/or conditioning programs established by the Club. In the
    event that the Club determines that the Player is no longer in
    first class physical condition due to the use of any type of
    illegal drug, the misuse of prescription or over-the-counter drugs
    or alcohol dependency, the Club may, in its discretion, convert
    this guaranteed Contract into a non-guaranteed Contract by providing
    written notice of such conversion to the Player. The Player and
    the Club agree that the Club's rights under this Paragraph are in
    addition to and distinct from the rights set forth in Paragraph 7(b)
    of this Contract and that the Club's exercise of its rights under
    this Paragraph shall not effect the enforceability of any of the
    other obligations created by this Contract.

In the event the Contract is terminated and during its term the
Player signs a player contract with another Major League Club or
Clubs, notwithstanding anything to the contrary in this Addendum,
the Club's total obligations to the Player during the term of this
Contract shall be reduced by the amounts which the Player earns
during the year from any other Club or Clubs.

In the event the Player refuses to accept a reasonable Major League
Contract offered by a Club other than the Club which released him,
the Player shall forfeit that portion of salary which would not
have been payable had he accepted such other Contract.

I. AGREEMENT TO COOPERATE IN CONNECTION WITH INSURANCE REQUIREMENTS

1. The Player recognizes the significance of the Club's under-
taking hereunder and that the Club may desire to obtain term
life insurance coverage and disability insurance coverage to
cover its liability in the event of any employment or non-
employment related injury or death. The Player agrees to
cooperate fully with the Club in this regard. Notwithstanding
any provisions herein to the contrary, if the Player fails to
submit to or refuses to submit to any appropriate physical
examination (s) customarily required by the insurance company,
or companies, selected by the Club or makes any material mis-
representation or misstatement in writing to the insurance
company (ies) that would relieve the insurance company (ies) from
liability (other than a return of premium), the Club will have no
obligation under this Contract to the Player or his beneficiary for
any payment of compensation after the date of the injury or death,
other than its obligation to pay the Player for an employment-related
injury in accordance with Regulation 2 of the Contract, with the
playing season in which the injury or death was sustained being
the maximum extent of the Club's obligation.

2. Neither the Player nor his beneficiary shall have any right to
the proceeds of any insurance policy obtained by the Club hereunder nor shall either be deemed to be the owner or beneficiary
of said policy.

‾‾‾‾‾‾‾‾‾‾‾‾‾‾‾‾‾‾‾‾‾‾‾
PLAYER

‾‾‾‾‾‾‾‾‾‾‾‾‾‾‾‾‾‾‾‾‾‾‾
DATE

‾‾‾‾‾‾‾‾‾‾‾‾‾‾‾‾‾‾‾‾‾‾‾
CLUB OFFICIAL

1-25-92
‾‾‾‾‾‾‾‾‾‾‾‾‾‾‾‾‾‾‾‾‾‾‾
DATE

Endorsements

Why do people think that all athletes make millions of dollars in endorsements? Only a select few make any money at all endorsing products. Michael Jordan, Shaquille O'Neal, Reggie Jackson—those guys are in the minority. I've been at a couple of card shows, had a few speaking engagements, even got free Nike shoes for "endorsing" them, but I never got paid to endorse any company's product. I sat around and dreamed of being a big Madison Avenue icon, having to turn away endorsement opportunities, but I knew nothing like that would ever happen to me. I even made up my own Blockbuster commercial, and pitched it to them. Here's how it went:

"Hi, I'm Steve Lyons of the Boston Red Sox. Did you know I set a record for being the only person to play for the Red Sox four different times? I also played every position for the Sox, including Designated Hitter—also a record. And with a nickname like Psycho, you'd think everybody would know who I am. But because I accidentally pulled down my pants during a game, most people recognize my backside a lot quicker than my face. Blockbuster never has that problem. With so many locations, you always know where to find one, and Blockbuster's low prices and three day rental policy are always recognizable.

"Blockbuster is where you find all the greatest hit movies, newest releases, and even the classics. But if you're ever in a Blockbuster store and can't make up your mind from all the videos in stock, why not pick out one of my all-time favorites? (Stand between two cardboard cut-outs from "Psycho" and "Psycho II" movies.) Blockbuster—it's where you find what you want."

Of course I got the run-around and never got to meet with anybody. Most major marketing departments don't entertain outside offers. If they didn't come up with the idea, they're not going to use it. So my commercial endorsement career never got off the ground.

Keep your head down

Very few people in the sports world ever get so big that just their name evokes a reaction. Only the megastars. Maybe you love guys like Reggie, Dr. J, or Magic, or maybe you hate 'em — but you do react. Sherm Feller, the long-time P.A. announcer for the Red Sox who passed away in 1993, once told me that he was going to make me so famous that he'd never have to announce my name —just my number. He was joking, of course, but he was referring to Tom Seaver when he played for the Mets. After they announced number 41, the cheering was so loud that nobody heard the guy say "Tom Seaver." And they didn't have to.

Name a hitting coach in that class? In fact, try to name ten hitting coaches period, in either league. There's only one coach who is recognized for his philosophies and ideas: Walt Hriniak. The players either love him or hate him, but they all have an opinion about him.

Ask players around the league who never played for him, and they all say the same thing. They've adopted a word to describe the over-emphasized style of swing that he preaches — "snorkeling." The hitter looks as if he's bent over face first in the water, with his bat held high over head with a follow through that resembles a snorkel. Some players laugh and joke about it or say "I could never hit like that."

There are some players who had Hriniak as a coach and couldn't adjust to his style. Cory Snyder and Steve Sax were guys who never got untracked while playing for him, and they'll say, you just can't teach everybody the same style of hitting. Every hitter has his own style. Hriniak's critics say just that — "Everybody hits the same, and everyone's power numbers decline."

How about all the players who were established big leaguers before Hriniak came on the scene? Dwight Evans, Bill Buckner, Tony Armas, Harold Baines, Jerry Remy — all of these guys became better hitters under Walter and would swear by his methods. As for me, I say check his record. See if his teams are almost always at the top of their divisions in runs scored. Boston made the 1986 World Series, won the division in 1988, and the White Sox had a total turnaround in his five years in Chicago. Ask Frank Thomas and Robin Ventura about their power numbers and ask Lance Johnson how much money he's made from being a student of Hriniak's teachings. They'll tell you he was great.

I played for Walter for six years and went through periods where I loved him and periods when I didn't. There are certain areas of controversy with Walter. First, his style of hitting. It's simple really: keep your head down on the ball, and finish your swing with a high follow-through. Keeping your head down is the entire key, and it was pounded in your mind from day one. We had shirts made up in Chicago that read, "Rule no. 1 every-day, keep your f—ing head down." Walter's vocabulary in-volves that word quite often.

Second, Walter is an unbelievably passionate man — but only about three things: his family, boxing, and hitting. Only he can tell you the order of their importance. One thing that everybody agrees on, is that he is the most dedicated, hardest-working, no-nonsense coach in the game. Nobody beats him to the ballpark, and nobody is ready to work before he is.

If you ever get the chance, watch a Hriniak-coached team take batting practice. It's completely different than any other team. You won't find a circus atmosphere — players swinging from their heels seeing how far they can hit a ball with four other players around the cage egging him on and joking around. Not with Walter. Every pitch has its purpose, every swing has intent. "No freelancing," Walter would say, "or you can peel off. You won't come out here and waste your time or mine." When Walter's team hits, line drives scatter from foul line to foul line, and guys are overemphasizing the "head-down" philosophy to the point where some of them don't even see the ball after they've hit it. "Head down, through the middle," Walt would say. Time after time, pitch after pitch. Not a swing is wasted, not a pitch is missed. The man doesn't hear, see, or smell anything else when his boys are hitting. He won't have it any other way. He doesn't have time for the bullshit, the media, or people on the field. His job is to make his student a better hitter, period.

He doesn't let up. From day one in spring training until the last day of the season, he pushed us. He had drills that began when the sun came up until long after the game was over. "Flip" drills, "soft-toss," and throwing early batting practice are his methods for improvement. Some players have taken 200 swings before regular batting practice ever started. He makes you work on your swing. He makes you get better.

Understanding Walter is the player's toughest objective. He's a man who white-knuckled his way through alcoholism. It took an auto accident that claimed the life of a teammate and badly scarred his own life to wake him up. And even though the accident wasn't his fault, it did make him realize he had a problem. Late in his playing career he was introduced to the theories of hitting coach Charlie Lau at Kansas City. Walter decided to use Lau's teachings to build a career of his own as a coach. He once told me, "I messed up my career as a player. I won't screw up this second chance as a coach."

Walter's sense of humor is hard to follow sometimes. What you think is funny, he doesn't, and what he finds humorous, you're not sure about. And it almost always involves baseball. He lives and breathes baseball. It's what he knows, and your only chance of changing the subject from baseball is to bring up the next title fight or ask how his daughter is doing.

In his deep concentration, he sometimes loses sight of the obvious. More than once he'd asked me and other players if we were going to do our "flips" for that day, — 20 minutes after we had just done them. We used to have 10-minute hitting meetings with all the players that would run 30 minutes because Walter would get excited about an at-bat that someone had the night before. He'd go on and on about the position of the guy's head and his weight shift, with fire in his eyes and chew-spit spilling down his chin. We'd end up canceling infield practice for that day because Walter went off on one of his tangents. We didn't mind; we wanted to listen.

In the six years I played on a Hriniak-coached team, I took early batting practice nearly every day. For the guys who weren't playing much or needed to work on something, it was just expected. I was there, every day on the field, taking extra batting practice at 3 p.m.

One day in Boston I began my extra session by trying to go the other way with the first 10 pitches. After about eight swings, Walter stopped throwing and said, "What the hell are you doing?" I explained myself but he didn't like it. He said, "If you don't start swinging the bat like you mean it, with your head down, you can get the f— out of here. Peel off." (He loved to say "peel off.") "If you don't want to work, don't come."

The first thing you learn about arguing with Walter is that you don't. You can't win, so you just do what he says. I figured I'd better start hacking, keep my head down, and air it out a little bit. But after about 10 more pitches, Walt threw the balls down and started heading towards the dugout, yelling at me — "You don't want to work? I come out here early and you want to waste my time. You've got no time in the big leagues and you can't work? Get the hell out of here."

I was shocked. What did I do? I felt like I was trying to do what I was supposed to. I couldn't figure it out. So I chased him through the dugout and into the tunnel. "I don't know what you're mad about," I said, "But it's not me, I'm doing all I can do out there." We argued for about two minutes over what had happened. He told me not to show up anymore, and that I wasn't working.

When he turned to leave, I grabbed him by the shoulder to turn him back around because I still had something to say. He spun back around with clenched fists and a defensive stance. I was surprised and a little scared, because I thought he was going to deck me. Walter caught himself and lowered his hands, yelling, "Don't come early anymore, you don't want to work. I don't want you here anymore," as he walked back into the clubhouse.

For the rest of the day I still couldn't really understand what had happened or why Walter was so angry, but I was also pretty sure I was going to be back on the field the next day at 3 p.m. because if I wasn't, I'd be labeled a "quitter" — the one thing that I was sure I wasn't. The next day, I was there at 3 p.m. and not a word was said. It was as if nothing had ever happened. Maybe it was just some sort of test — like I said, understanding Walter isn't always easy.

What you need to play the game

I get angry when people talk about baseball players and say that we are not as athletic as other athletes. Brian Bosworth once said he thought you had to be a much better athlete to play football than baseball. I wonder, when was the last time Bosworth hit a curve ball. Better yet, when was last time he hit a running back? Baseball has always been a game without a clear definition of what it takes to play it.

You see guys like Jose Canseco, Mark McGwire, or Ruben Sierra — all are as strong as most football players. And sometimes you see guys like Mike Gallego, Luis Polonia, or Jody Reed — none of them taller than 5'7" or bigger than 160 pounds, but they play with their hearts and brains rather than their muscles. And then there are guys like Lance Johnson, who has about six percent body fat, or bigger guys like Cecil Fielder, who carry a few extra pounds. I agree that almost anyone can play baseball, but can they rise to major league caliber? I guess that was a source of pride with me, the fact that I was one of the 700 or so best in the world at what I did.

And maybe I look at athleticism a little differently (who would have guessed). I think baseball requires a variety of skills to be performed at different times during the game — more so than in any other sport.

You have to do all of the normal athletic things — run fast, jump, stretch, have agility and quickness, durability, and so forth. Those are givens. You must also learn to catch. Catch balls in the air or on the ground, catch long hops, short hops, bad hops. My dad always told me, "Anybody can catch the good hops — catching the bad hops is what makes you good." You have to catch pop ups, hot shots, looping liners, and 100 M.P.H. peas. But all of that is not enough. You have to be able to make shoestrings, backhands, and sliding catches, and an occasional, unbelievable catch.

You must, in baseball, learn to throw. And maybe "throw" isn't quite the word. When the ball leaves your hand it must leave a trail you could hang clothes on, it must have the speed to cut down even the swiftest of runners, and the accuracy to hit a glove at 300 paces. Ah, to throw. To be able to make the ball sizzle through the air as it passes by onlookers is something that even other players envy. A pitcher can make the ball dip and dive, curve and slide, and sometimes do things *they* didn't even expect. On a good day, if he masters the ball, he dominates the hitter. But on a bad day, he can't "throw" the ball the way he'd like, and the hitter lets him know it.

I can stand 100 feet away from someone and play catch for 10 minutes and never make that person move more than a step from his original position, and I take that for granted. That's what throwing is.

There is another major skill you need if you're going to call yourself a ballplayer. A little thing called hitting. It's often been said that hitting a baseball is the single most difficult thing to do in all of sports. It's the only thing in life you can do three out of ten times right, and be considered great. Not good, but great. There aren't many .300 hitters among us. They should be revered, applauded, and most of all, studied. The Ted Williams', Tony Gwynns, and Wade Boggs are few and far between in our game, and you're lucky if you get a chance to see them play, let alone be their teammate.

But why is it so tough to hit? We briefly discussed what a pitcher could do with the ball to make you miss it altogether, but if you do make contact, there are nine guys out there whose sole responsibility is to get you out. Those same guys who can catch and throw. Remember?

And the mental side of hitting keeps so many of us from being better hitters than we are — no brains, no headaches, they say. You can think yourself into a slump. It's amazing how I could get three hits in one game and feel great, then turn around and get one hit in the next week. You start to doubt your own ability and begin to wonder, "When's that next hit going to come?"

So you still think a non-athlete can excel in baseball? I think the most well-rounded athletes play baseball.

No parking

Growing up, and now well into my adult life, I always thought I was a fairly funny guy. I'm drawn to people who display a certain sense of humor, and it just seems to make every day go by a little easier if you have something to laugh at. Even if it's yourself.

My little brother, Mike, is the head cook at the Irvine, California *Improv*, a comedy club. He always keeps me up to date on who the hottest new comedian is or what the joke of the week might be. One night he hooked me up with a comedian from Phoenix who was performing in Chicago, George Kanter. George may be the world's biggest sports fan. He doesn't miss anything. He's the only guy I know who has a six-hour slow-play tape continuously taping ESPN just in case he misses some tidbit of sports news during the day.

In 1991, George visited me in Boston on what he called his "See the American League East" stadium tour. His favorite team is the Cubs, and he usually tries to schedule his national appearances based on where they happen to be playing. He came out to Fenway early one day, and I got him on the field to take early batting practice. He got the chance to take a few swings and get a picture of himself standing out by the green monster in left field. It was an experience that very few non-professional ballplayers get to enjoy, and he had a great time.

After the game we went out for a beer, and when we came out of the bar we discovered that my car had been towed. Between me, George, and George's friend, Jon, we had about $80 so we weren't sure we had enough money to spring the car after the taxi ride out to the towing site. On the way over, George was sure we could weasel our way out of paying. "You're big here," he said. "You're playing well now, and the Sox are hot and besides, the Yankees are in town. Tell the guy you'll give him a couple of tickets to a game if he lets the car go for free."

I was skeptical. Not because I didn't think it would work, but because I wasn't very good at the name-dropping game. I was good at hanging out with people that were. People who needed no introduction or guys who didn't mind talking to the doorman about who we were to get us in places without waiting in line.

At the same time, I took full advantage of those perks available to us for being big leaguers — but I was embarrassed about doing it myself. I guess I was scared that I'd stand up there one day and announce who I was and why I should get in free or without waiting, and the bouncer would say, "Steve who?" or "Who cares?" We used to call that "dropping a Red Sox bomb" on him. Basically, telling the guy who you are and who you play for, and you're in.

But now I was ready. George had me all pumped up and I figured the towing bill was going to be at least $50. If I could save that by handing over a couple of tickets, I'd do it. We agreed that George would butter the guy up first by saying a few things about that night's game and how well we were playing, just to see if we could pique the interest of the towing yard attendant. Later, I'd swoop in with the "Red Sox bomb" and offer the tickets.

But when we got there we encountered something we didn't expect. The guy running the show at the towing yard was covered in grease, had three teeth missing, and was fighting back two hungry-looking Dobermans. I don't like big dogs, so I was scared to death. George started some small talk with the guy while he was getting the dogs back into the pen and then he said it. "Hey! How about those Red Sox tonight? Those guys are playing great lately, aren't they?" The attendant stopped dead in his tracks, spun around, and said, "The Red Sox suck, man, I'm a Bruins fan." George just looked at me, reached into his pocket and said, "Here's my thirty bucks."

Since that time, I've seen George perform on stage many times and he really is one of the funniest comedians I've seen. But he says his career has gone a lot like mine. He feels like he does a good job and the crowds like his act, but sometimes he has a tough time getting bookings no matter how hard he sells himself. He just needs that one break that will give him national exposure and get him to the top. I had told him I thought if a manager would have ever sat me down and told me he really believed in me, I would have been a better player.

What I would have given for this conversation from my manager: "Steve, you're my left fielder this year. I don't care if you hit .200, you're going out there every day: lefties, righties, everybody. Except when John Candelaria pitches (I might as well make this dream conversation as good as it can get—he knows I hate to face Candelaria). So just relax, go out there and have fun this year."

No one ever said that to me. I always had to wait for someone else to slump to get my playing time. If anyone had just believed in me the way Tony Tochia did when I played for him in the minors, I know I would have responded like an every day player. I would have been a better all-around player. I would have had that sense of belonging to something important. Like I was being counted on.

George said it's the same way in comedy. When you see a well-known comic, and you like him, you're in the right frame of mind to laugh. Everything he says will be funnier because you expect it to be.

George returned the favor for letting him hit at Fenway by calling me up on stage a few times to tell a few jokes. Of course, he set me up with the jokes, but they went over well, and it was a great feeling to make people laugh.

Hitting the Town

Sometimes the life of a ballplayer, outside the game of baseball, can really endear itself to the man. I've illustrated many times how fun it can be to be known as a major leaguer. After a game in Chicago where I was 3 for 4 with 2 RBIs and we won 6-3, I'm in a good mood. We're gong to find a place to have a good time.

In that sense, though, we're no different from you. If you have a great day at work or have a very productive week, you may be apt to show up at a local happy hour spot or out on Saturday night to relax, enjoy friends and celebrate. The only real difference between my life and yours is that for me, any night is potentially Saturday night, and when I find that hot spot to party, I'm not going to have to wait to get in.

There's nothing better than hitting the town with six or seven other guys from the team knowing that one of the million-aires is buying because he had a good day too. Checking out the scene, winding down from the game and getting the flavor of the town you happen to be in.

Most of the time it just ends up being a lot of fun—the same way you would envision a great night out. Everybody's laughing and having a good time, that one friend of yours isn't constantly saying, "Let's go to that other place," and somebody just sent over a drink compliments of the house. But it isn't always like that.

Sometimes, players are drinking because they had a bad day, and they drink too much. Or maybe some local guy doesn't like the fact that these ballplayers are infringing on his turf so he starts to make stupid comments. I don't have to make a list here— we've all been in a place when it's about to turn ugly and sometimes we fail to use the only rule that makes sense: Get your buddies and get the hell out of there.

That's too easy—at this point somebody's got a lot of that liquid courage in them, making them a bigger, tougher, and dumber man than when he walked in the place, and he's not going to leave it alone.

One night, Eric King got decked by one of the bouncers in a bar and the rest of us had no idea what was going on. By the time we got over there, they had tossed him out the back and locked the doors. We went over to the window to see King sprinting through the parking lot with two guys chasing him. It's a good thing he could run. His next start was two days later against Texas and he pitched one of his best games that year—wearing make-up on his face to hide his black eye. We all thought maybe the best thing we could do for him was beat the crap out of him before he pitched, and he might have had a great year.

Jack McDowell and I hit the streets one night in Cleveland but it didn't last long. As I was paying for us to get into a club, Jack went up the flight of stairs to get inside. Before I even got my change back in my wallet, Jack was back down the stairs, the hard way. He wasn't even sure why. I guess the girl in front of him in line said something smartass to the doorman and he thought she was with Jack. Looking back up those stairs and seeing the size of the guy that just threw Jack down, we decided to use the rule. Get your buddy and get out!

The worst part was Jack doesn't notice that he's lost his national championship watch from Stanford during his tumble down the stairs. We went back later that night to find it, but it was gone.

Those barroom fights were just one of the reasons why I was never much of a drinker. I didn't drink at all until age 30. I can't stand the taste of beer or wine and the hard stuff is just too harsh for me. I knew I never wanted to put myself in a position where I wasn't in control. And I knew I could stay out late but never be hung over. In my younger days, I knew my Dad would kill me if

I ever came home drunk. Well, maybe not literally, but I'd be in trouble.

I never understood that period in our lives when we actually liked talking about how wasted we were over the weekend. It didn't make a lot of sense to me and made fools of the people making such a big deal about it. I've sat and watched as personalities changed as the night wore on—a slow loss of control as the alcohol takes its toll. And though I've been there a time or two myself, the last thing I want to do is brag about it, and at least when I've had too many, I'm a happy guy—the last thing I want to do is fight you.

The fighting, the hangovers, and the potential long-term problems from having too good a time are all things that don't interest me. It just seems to be a lot more fun when I'd acknowledge the guy at the other end of the bar for buying me a drink and he and his three friends would start chanting, "Psycho, Psycho, Psycho."

Another record-breaking day at the ballpark

One night in Montreal I set an all-time seed-eating record in a regulation nine-inning game: five bags of David's Sunflower Seeds. My cheeks and tongue were raw, and although my wife was a good cook, it would be impossible for her to put a bad meal in front of me for the next two days because my taste buds wouldn't recover until at least then.

Chris Nabholz, now pitching for the Cubs, was my competition and a witness to the feat. He only had 1.5 bags, and faded quickly out of the competition.

My claim to fame?

As Roy Hobbs sat in his hospital bed in the movie "The Natural" he contemplated the last game he would ever play. "I could have been the best there ever was," he said. "I could have broken every record in the book." Not quite understanding the importance of it all, his girlfriend asks, "And then what?" He thinks just for a moment, and says, "Then people would see me walking down the street and say, 'There goes Roy Hobbs. He was the best there ever was.'" Nothing else mattered to Hobbs except baseball. That was how he wanted to be remembered.

We will all be remembered by the impressions we made on others. In my professional career, it became obvious I would never be remembered for a Hall of Fame induction, a late-inning World Series home run, or even a great catch.

For me it will always be that single occasion, that one slip of concentration, that one little lapse into La La Land. Simply stated, a brain cramp. In 13 years of playing professional baseball, my greatest claim to fame had nothing to do with the game itself or how I played it. And yet, it had such an impact on the sporting world that I was the subject of 32 national radio shows the next day, seven live sportscasts from the stadium the next night, and was featured in a four-page article in *Sports Illustrated*.

The incident transcended the world of sports: *Playgirl Magazine* was interested in doing a pictorial layout with me. What did I do? Could I possibly have done something that nobody else had ever done? Something that would attract the attention of millions? Me? The light-hitting, sometime-playing, off-the-wall utility man of the Chicago White Sox?

The answer is obviously yes. I did go where no one else had gone, I did something no one else had done. I set a new mark; I rose to a new level. I . . . I . . . I pulled my pants down on the field. I mooned the fans in Tiger Stadium and everyone watching on TV. Nobody had ever done that. Not once. And even though it happened in 1990, not a day goes by that somebody doesn't ask me about it: "Hey Steve, ya gonna keep your pants on today,?" Or "Steve, what were you thinking?" "Obviously, I wasn't thinking," is my reply. I should probably set this whole thing up so you don't think I'm some sort of exhibitionist or idiot, or that I did it on purpose, like some people think.

It all goes back to being remembered. I knew I would never be a great player, so I wanted to be known as somebody who played hard, hustled, and had fun. On that night in Detroit I was getting anxious; I was 0 for 2 facing Dan Petry of the Tigers, and

I needed a hit. I drag bunted down the first base side of the field. Second baseman Lou Whitaker got a good jump toward the ball, but I also got first baseman Cecil Fielder to commit to the ball. Now my only chance for a hit was to race Petry to the base and get there before he and the ball did. This is when my instincts just took over.

I had this habit of sliding into first base head first on close plays. Believe me, I've heard all the lectures about running through the base — that it's quicker than sliding. But the closer I'd get to that base, something would just click in my head that said "go for it." I probably slid into first base 50 times in my career. I guess I always thought that it was a tougher call for the umpire to make if I slid, and I might get called safe on sheer effort alone. In this case I was right. Petry, the ball, and my recklessly flung body all reached first base at just about the same time. To be honest, Petry snuck his right foot on the base just before I slid into it. We simultaneously turned toward first base umpire Jim Evans. "Safe" he yelled.

Petry went nuts, knowing that his hustle enabled him to edge me out at the bag, and he and Evans got into a heated argument right there at first base. I hopped up knowing Evans wouldn't change the call, and now I was feeling good — 1 for 3 and safe at first.

As Petry and Evans went at each other face to face, I noticed an uncomfortable feeling. When I slid, a lot of dirt, dust, and little pebbles from the field went down the waistline of my pants, and when I stood up, it all rushed down my pant legs towards my feet — not an extremely comfortable feeling, but I was tuned into Petry and Evans' conversation. They definitely weren't discussing their dinner plans after the game.

With all the action around me, I literally forgot I was standing in front of 35,000 fans. Instinctively, I did what anyone else would do with dirt and pebbles in their pants. I undid the belt that held up my uniform, unsnapped the buttons, and unzipped the zipper. With the first yank of the pants, they fell to knee level, and with a couple of quick swipes, I began dusting off. With another quick tug, my pants crumpled down around my ankles.

Bent over and near naked with just my sliding shorts between me and an X rating, my senses returned, and I realized what I had done. Within a flash, my hands had those pants back around my waist where they belonged. Petry and Evans' argument came to a halt. I was standing there, now fully dressed, yet feeling more naked than I was before. The actual realization that thousands of people had seen me pull my pants down was sinking in. I don't get embarrassed easily, but my face was as red as you could possibly imagine.

Finally, I began laughing, searching for an appropriate emotional response to the situation. There was nothing else I could do — my brain cramped. I was in that place you go when you're watching T.V. and your mother calls you to set the table or do the dishes, but when you finally hear her, it's the fourth time she's called you. Your concentration was on the T.V. so everything else was just blocked out. I just zoned out, hoping to find a place that not even my own mother could find me.

As I tucked in my shirt and play resumed, I still didn't quite have it all figured out, but the next hitter hit the first pitch and forced me out at second. As I ran back to the dugout, six women were standing and waving dollar bills yelling, "Take it all off!"

That is the single moment that defines my career. It's the way people describe me: "You remember Lyons, the guy who pulled his pants down in Detroit."

Reggie Jackson once said, "even bad publicity is good publicity." In other words, as long as somebody is saying something about you, they still care. Once they stop talking, you're finished.

What amazed me about that whole incident was how important it became to others. I wasn't standing out there totally nude. I had sliding shorts on under my uniform pants. I show more going to the beach than anybody saw that night in Detroit, but believe me, the play created problems as well as humor.

Although he never personally said anything to me, I heard that my manager, Jeff Torborg, was upset with me for doing it. He thought I did it on purpose to get more "exposure" during a season in which I got very little playing time. He wasn't alone in that opinion, but it was shared mostly by people who didn't know me well. I can't think of a more ridiculous idea and am insulted by anybody who could even think I might interfere with the process of a game in that way. I had fun when I played. I played hard and played to win. I never did anything to ruin the integrity of what I was paid to do.

The next spring I was released by Torborg and the White Sox, and more than a few General Managers passed on signing me — citing the "pants" incident as one of the reasons. That one incident had nothing to do with my ability to play baseball, but it kept me from a job. I guess in the long run, pulling my pants down on the field did nothing to help my career . . . or did it? A Roy Hobbs I'll never be, but people do remember me — and when they do, they usually laugh or smile. That's good enough for me.

Tic-tac-toe

One of the most entertaining things I ever did on the field was something I can't take full credit for. I got the idea from Rusty Kuntz, who was coaching first base for Seattle at the time, and is now a coach for the Florida Marlins. He told me that when he was in the minors, he played tic-tac-toe with the opposing players. That was all I needed to hear.

In no time, I had beaten every other first baseman in the American League. It was 1989, and I was pretty much the White Sox regular first baseman. We were one of the worst teams in baseball, but that wasn't going to keep me from having fun.

Right after the National Anthem, I'd walk 15 feet past first base, and make the tic-tac-toe grid. It was usually 15 feet by 12 feet — big enough so the other first baseman couldn't miss it, but far enough down the line so that it didn't come into play often. (I didn't want to take a bad hop off one of my Xs.)

The key to enticing the other guy into playing was to never start with your X in the center square. That way he doesn't feel like you're taking an unfair advantage right at the beginning. Other than that, I had only two rules: first they had to make a move every inning, because the grounds crew re-drags the field after five innings, and the game might not be finished. Second, as soon as you know that it's going to be a "cat" game, you cheat. Make two Xs when it's your turn, draw a line through your row, and write "I cheat" in the dirt with your cleat. This way, I could stay undefeated, the other guy has to laugh, and he has no recourse.

Of course, I caught heat from some of the stuffed shirts in the league. They said I wasn't concentrating on the game enough, or that there was no place for those kinds of games during the game. Reggie Jackson was the California Angels' commentator, and at one point, jumped all over Wally Joyner for playing along. I loved the way Reggie played. He was one of the few extremely talented guys that got the most out of his ability. But in this case, I thought he was wrong.

I'm not an idiot. I understand the concentration needed to perform at a major-league level. Tic-tac-toe was always played while the pitcher was warming up before the inning started. I had the consent of both manager Jeff Torborg and owners Jerry Reinsdorf and Eddie Einhorn, who frequently laughed while watching from their skybox. Hey, we were 25 games out of first place. We were looking for any way to make Sox fans smile. Most of all, I just had a good time with it and so did the fans.

In Detroit one day, the fans in the first base upper deck helped me make my move. I'd begin putting an X in one square, and I'd hear everybody yelling, "No, No." So I kept switching squares until they were happy and cheering.

Only two players, Randy Milligan and Fred McGriff, wouldn't play. Maybe they didn't know how to play, but since they're both twice my size, I didn't want to ask.

One night while playing Minnesota, the Twins first baseman Kent Hrbek threw in a wrinkle. We had already played tic-tac-toe and when he realized he had lost, he set up his own game. When I went out to first base, I found a hangman game and four blanks. I was apprehensive about finding the answer to a four-letter word, but I went along.

It was one of those nights in April when it was so cold nobody should be playing baseball, so my first guess was a "c" thinking the word might be cold. And, if he was in a nasty mood because of the fact that Hrbek was already 0 for 2, I figured the "C" would also fit nicely in the third slot too.

When I came out the next inning, I had a head on my hangman. As the game wore on, my body began to define itself, but then I broke through. I tried a "p" and when I came back out, I saw the word filling in:

P _ _ P

I knew I had him now as I made my final move with the letter "o." The victory was short lived, however, because in the top of the eighth inning, Hrbek drove in two runs with a double to break the 3-3 tie. We lost 5-3.

The scary part of the whole thing was that winter. I participated in the White Sox caravan to promote the next year's team. There were several people that wanted to challenge my tic-tac-toe mastery. Sure, I was 11-0 on the trip, but I won eight games without cheating!

I also liked writing messages in the dirt to my opposing position mate. One night in Cleveland, Louis Aguayo was playing third base for the Indians, and I was playing third for the White Sox. Aguayo hit a big home run to put them up by two runs late in the game, so I asked Ozzie Guillen how to spell home run in Spanish. When I went back out to play defense, I left Louis a little message — "No Mas Hon Run." When he got back onto the field, it took him a few minutes but then he noticed the note. He started laughing as he searched me out in our dugout, and replied, "O.K., No Mas."

Later we played together in Pawtucket. His sense of humor was what made him one of the most well-liked guys on the team. We were involved in a hit-and-run play, with Aguayo hitting and me running. The other team saw it coming and pitched out on the play. Any time the other team pitches out on a hit-and-run, you're screwed. I was dead at second trying to steal, and Aguayo threw his bat at the ball trying anything to foul the pitch off. I was jogging back to the dugout and Louis was retrieving his bat, but was laughing the whole time, asking the home plate umpire to get some help from the first base umpire on if he swung his bat. That sense of humor has helped Aguayo land a coaching job with the Red Sox at Pawtucket (along with some knowledge of the game too).

Music and memories

Billy Ocean's "Caribbean Queen." It's one of the few things I remember about spring training of 1985. It's funny, too, because I should remember much more. It was my best spring training and it launched my major league career with the Red Sox. But the most vivid memory I have is riding around in my car with Billy Ocean's tape playing over and over, and my daughter Kori, who wasn't more than 15 days old, in the back seat.

Like for many other people, music is the most powerful trigger to my memory bank. Sometimes I'll hear a certain song that will remind me of a particular season. A season that might otherwise be lost or forgotten. One night in the clubhouse, AC/DC's "Thunder" was blasting away, and Frank Viola came in and said "Instructional League, 1982." Whether it was a good or bad memory, that song took him back to 13 years before.

It amazes me how guys like George Brett, Robin Yount, and Jim Kaat remember every season they played. Reggie Jackson says he remembers every home run he ever hit (all 563 of them). Maybe he dedicated a song to every one of them.

Like it or not, music has become a big part of sports. Huge sound systems blare out pop music between innings, at half-time, and during time-outs. Millions of dollars are spent on the musical half-time show at the Super Bowl. Music evokes more emotion from all of us than anything else. Sometimes, even more than our relationships themselves.

On any team I ever played, one of the most popular bench games was always "Name That Tune." Any time music was played, we tried to be the first one to name who sang it and what year it was done. Some guys kept a running score against each other with a bet on the outcome. The best I ever saw at this game was Jerry Reuss. The most unheard of, obscure song would be played, stumping everybody — except Jerry. He'd know the band, the year it was released, who produced it, and maybe even the record label.

It's those events of your life that are associated with a song that seem to be the most vivid and emotional. Boston's "Rock and Roll Band" was played at decibel levels unsafe to human ears before every basketball game my senior year of high school. All the guys would be hanging around in their jockstraps, air guitaring away, getting psyched up for the game. People of my era will always remember "Stairway to Heaven" as the last song of any high school dance. You could always tell who the couples were because they'd still be dancing slow even when the song picked up the pace at the end. "Song Sung Blue" was the first solo I ever did as a member of the Spring Creek Elementary school choir in sixth grade. I did it for my mom who bought me the single so I could learn the words.

Kool and the Gang's "Have Some Fun" carried us to a "AA" championship in 1983 in New Britain — the first and only for that team. Our pitching coach, Bill Denehy, had t-shirts made up for all of us with those words, "Have Some Fun," written on them. We all wore them under our uniforms for every game through the play-offs and on to the championship. That year was special for so many reasons, and it was my first taste of being a champion—But my most vivid memory of the entire season was the whole team huddled together after the final game. All of us around the boom box that was our stereo system, with tears streaming down our faces and champagne bottles being uncorked, singing "Have Some Fun."

We were never closer as a team than we were right then. For some of the guys, it would be the last professional game they would ever play— only four of us ever played in the big leagues. "Have Some Fun" doesn't get too much radio play these days, but when I do hear it, it takes me right back to that room. Everyone has their memories and the songs they associate with them.

My father's generation will tell you they can remember exactly where they were and what they were doing when they heard President Kennedy was shot in Dallas. I was only four at the time, but it was an event that would shape our future and affect our lives. I was too young to remember how I felt or what I understood. I guess that's why I prefer to remember Kool and the Gang in 1983 and Billy Ocean in 1985. They made everything easier.

A *"lucky" little boy*

One night in Detroit, I was 0 for 2 halfway through the game, and I needed a hit. I wasn't playing much that year, and an 0 for 4 wasn't going to help. I spotted a kid about nine years old sitting in the front row with his older brother. He had a Tiger hat on, a bag of popcorn, and he was laughing. He was the classic portrayal of what a kid at a ballgame should look like. As I went to the on-deck circle, I stopped and asked the kid if he had any luck in him. He was startled. I'm sure he wasn't used to players asking him questions. He had a look on his face as if he had done something wrong. "What?" he asked. So I asked again, "Are you lucky? Do you have any good luck in you?" "Sure!" he said, still wondering what I was up to. I stretched my bat out to him, and asked him to rub the barrel for good luck — "Put some hits in it," I said.

Now this is far from a Babe Ruth story, because I didn't promise anyone I'd do anything. In fact, I was banking on the kid, trying to get something from him.

But after he rubbed the bat, I roped a double to right centerfield. When I got to second base, I pointed at him, as if to say, "You did that." He was standing and cheering with his brother and parents. I knew he believed he was the reason for that hit.

On my next at-bat, we went through the same routine. But as I swung my bat to get ready, his father said, "Hey, he wants you to hit a home run." I spun around quickly in disbelief, and now there were 10 or 20 fans listening in. He was giggling and trying to hide under the bill of his cap. I said, "What? A home run? Have you taken a close look at these arms? They can't hit the ball that far. But I guess it's up to you."

Right then, Tiger pitcher Frank Williams hit the batter to load the bases. I stepped to the plate with my lucky bat and a chance to drive in some runs. The bases were loaded, so I knew Williams had to throw strikes. I hit the first pitch I saw well into the upper deck for my first and only major league grand slam. As I rounded first and headed towards second, I looked towards where the ball had landed. Normally, I could never hit the ball that far. I had the confidence and desire of a nine-year-old with me. It was a feeling of innocence. The feeling we all wish we could keep for much longer than nine years.

When I reached home plate I was greeted by "high fives" from all three base runners, and on my way back to the dugout, I made a little detour to give my good luck charm a "high five" too.

After the game, I went back to see the boy and jokingly asked his parents if I could take him with me to our next game. The kid was on cloud nine and truly believed it was his luck that got those hits. I gave him my Red Sox cap and said my good-byes. And as I walked back to the dugout, I took another look into the upper deck and wondered how could I have hit the ball that far?

The clapper

I've played every position at one time or another, but for some reason I didn't act the same way at every position. When I played third base, I was a little more nervous than when I played any other position. Because of that nervousness, I developed an unconscious habit of pounding my glove — repeatedly. Most of the time I didn't even realize I was doing it. It was just something I did to keep myself ready and stay concentrated. I would hit the pocket of my glove with the back of my fist as if to say "Let's go, I'm ready." It made a pretty loud popping sound, and it didn't take long for people to notice.

Several times in my career, the fans along the third base line picked up on it and imitated me as a group — clapping their hands at the same time I hit my glove. That was when I began to notice how often I did it. When 200 people clapped every time I hit my glove, it became obvious what was going on. That was when I started to play with them. Sometimes I'd act like I was going to hit my glove, but then scratch my elbow or cheek instead. That always faked everybody out, and they'd clap and laugh, because they knew they'd been had. I'd look over, tip my hat, and smile. There are a few memorable stadiums that played along with me. Yankee Stadium was pretty good, Seattle was okay, and Minnesota was outstanding. By far, the greatest response was in Scranton/Wilkes Barre, Pennsylvania.

I started off playing third base in a three-game series against the Barons, and by the fifth inning all the fans on the third base line were clapping along. The next night I played first base, and with the urging of the third base fans, everybody on the first base line caught on. By the end of that night, at least half of the crowd clapped at the same time I hit my glove. On the third and final game of that series, I played left field, much to the disappointment of the Scranton crowd. I really think a lot of those people came back to the game the next night to be part of more than just a game.

I decided to see how well they were paying attention. Even from left field, when I hit my glove the crowd responded, a few at first, and then more and more people. Standing in left field of the "AAA" ballpark I could control almost all of them by hitting my glove. A few of my teammates figured out what was going on, but very few others did. Everybody was wondering why the entire crowd would clap every once in a while for no reason. It was some of the most fun I ever had as a player, and it didn't bother anybody, did it?

Psycho shirts

After going back to the Red Sox for the second time, I thought it might be neat to have something commemorating the occasion. I'd seen different T-shirts like Jeff Reardon's "Terminator" shirt, a picture of him in a Boston uniform with a pair of shades on and his nickname printed under it. You see shirts with caricature drawings of star athletes all the time, but I knew there would never be a Steve Lyons t-shirt, or poster, or action figure unless I did it myself.

So with the help of Jerry Neuger, a friend in the sporting goods business, we came up with a shirt that read "Psycho II" on the front, and "He's back!" on the back. We had about 50 of them made up and I passed them out to all the guys on the team. To some of the guys, I suppose, it was just another t-shirt, but others were actually eager to wear it and enjoyed having it.

Since giving out those shirts I returned two more times to the Red Sox, and a Psycho IV shirt was designed. On the front, in the style of the Red Sox jersey, was written "Psycho." Underneath it was the number 4. The back read: "The Final Chapter...?" After being sent down to Pawtucket during my fourth Red Sox stint, the concession stands sold them — and they sold out.

One day in 1991 I was wearing the Psycho II shirt under my uniform while in the bullpen. There was a guy with his beer league softball uniform on in the bleachers, and he kept asking me to trade him uniforms. He played for a team called the "Mo Fo's." His uniform had a picture of Moe of the Three Stooges on it. We haggled awhile and finally agreed on his shirt for my "Psycho II" T-shirt.

He took his off and threw it into the bully while I took my uniform top off, went into the bathroom and changed into his uniform. I came out with his shirt under my Red Sox jersey and threw him my Psycho shirt. Everybody thought it was great, and I figure that guy has as much fun telling the story when he wears the shirt as I have. And he's the only person outside the circle of players on that team that has a "Psycho II" shirt. By now, it's probably being used to wash his truck!

I always felt a true sign of making it big in baseball was having your uniform sold in novelty shops with your name and number on it or a sports poster, doll, or action figure made of you. The closest I've ever come is being a player on one of the Nintendo video baseball games. Imagine being able to walk into any sports store and see yourself hanging on the wall, or to know that you had such an impact on baseball, that your name, face and team was used to actually market the popularity of the game.

The Nike shoe company always took care of me while I played. I grew up in Eugene, Oregon, which is the birthplace of Nike. As a teenager, I was probably among the first to ever wear their product. I gave them an idea in 1990, shortly after I played all nine positions in one game.

It was only the third time in the history of baseball it had happened and it's something I'm rather proud of (Cesar Tovar and Campy Campaneris were the other two). I suggested they use a collage of photos; a picture of me playing every position and then maybe a bigger one in the middle of me hitting. The caption under everything would read "He did it all wearing our shoes."

Because I was only known in Chicago and Boston, I wasn't a very marketable commodity, and I'm sure Nike doesn't have the warehouse space for thousands of unsold posters.

Doing it all

The first day of little league tryouts was frightening, wasn't it? You knew you were good, but you'd never even seen these other guys play, so you didn't know exactly where you'd fit in. The coach always seemed to have it all figured out, just by the way you looked. "Billy, you're tall, you play first base. Johnny, you're fat, you catch. George, er. . . you stink, you play right field."

I spent most of my younger days playing in the outfield — mainly because I was scared of the ball. I was afraid it would take a bad hop and hit me in the face. I have a big nose, but I like where it sits. I didn't want it spread out all over the place, so I knew any ball hit into the air couldn't take a bad hop.

I have to credit Jack Riley, my college coach at Oregon State, for my versatility. First, he offered me a half-scholarship to attend Oregon State. (I had planned to walk on at Portland State.) His approach was a little strange, but it worked. He said he offered me the scholarship not because I was a good ballplayer, but because I had good leadership skills, and he needed somebody like that. "We'll teach you how to play baseball when you get here," he said.

Later in my career at OSU, Riley switched me from the outfield to shortstop. Not many people change positions at the major college level, let alone from the outfield to the most demanding infield position. Especially guys who are scared of ground balls.

Just like anything else, fielding ground balls is an educational process. Riley spent hours with me every day, teaching me the right way to approach the ball, how to hold my glove, how to read the ball as it bounced, and how to position myself to make as many plays as possible. It was amazing how quickly I overcame my fear of the ball. I knew what I was doing, so I wasn't afraid to do it. Sure, I got hit in the face a few times by a bad hop, but like my dad always said, "It only stings for a minute."

I didn't know that learning to play shortstop in my junior year of college would set me up for one of my proudest professional moments. Athletically, a shortstop can usually move to the other infield spots and play effectively. A true third baseman, on the other hand, isn't always physically able to play short or second. The same is true for outfielders. Centerfielders can almost always play right or left, but not vice versa. So having my base positions of shortstop and centerfield, I found myself bouncing around and playing a lot of different positions over my career.

That experience led to the opportunity I got in 1990, while playing with the White Sox — playing all nine positions in one game. I had played every position on the field at one time or another, and later in my career, I became the only player in Red Sox history to play all nine positions and DH. But I wanted to do what only two other players in the history of baseball had done — play all nine positions in one game!

Every year the White Sox play the Cubs in the Cross-Town Classic. I talked manager Jeff Torborg into letting me do it during that game. I started off the game catching, and after a 1-2-3 inning, moved to first base, then left, center, short, second, pitcher, third, and finally right field. We won 5-3.

Of course, you'll never see my effort in any history book, because the Sox-Cubs game is an exhibition game, and technically doesn't count. But don't try to tell me it didn't mean anything. The reason only two other people had ever done it, is because there are very few people who have that ability. Cesar Tovar, Bert Campaneris, and Steve Lyons.

There's no way I could write about my experiences in professional baseball without at least describing my foray into the pitching world. Not being a pitcher, but getting the chance to do it, is something a lot of players would love to do.

I pitched 5-1/3 innings in the major leagues, and at least that many in the minors. I even recorded a win as a pitcher at "AA" New Britain in 1983.

The most exciting part about it was the feeling of getting away with something. Doing something I wasn't supposed to be doing. It was like having a substitute teacher or knowing your boss isn't going to be in the office. I got to pitch against some of the best hitters in the major leagues.

I took it seriously, even though the reason I was pitching was because we were being beaten so badly that we had no chance of winning, and our manager wanted to rest our bullpen for the next game. The scores were 14-2 or 12-1 or something ridiculous — but that didn't matter to me. Usually the scores were so bad that I was the most effective pitcher of the day for my team. I wasn't going to be one of those guys who just went in there to try to get the game over with. I wanted to get guys out. We all dream of being great pitchers, even if we really want to be a great hitter.

I had good stuff, too! A decent sinker, clocked at 88 miles per hour in Boston against the Twins, a change-up that I had no control over, and a nasty slider. But my mechanics were brutal. No wind-up to speak of, lousy extension, and I short-armed the ball.

I threw more like a catcher than a pitcher. I always came in to pitch from some other position on the field, so I usually was dirty from sliding or had eye-black under my eyes. I'd always have to change gloves and take off my batting gloves and wrist bands. I must have looked ridiculous, but I was dead serious.

I felt bad for the opposing players. You can't win if you're the hitter facing a pitcher that's really a hitter. If you get a hit, you're supposed to, and if you don't, your teammates laugh at you for getting put out by a non-pitcher.

I pitched two innings in 1989 against the Oakland A's. It was by far my worst effort on the mound. I walked four, gave up two hits, and one run. But for as badly as I pitched, if we were winning 3-1 at the time, I would have been credited with a save. Jamie Quirk thanked me for keeping him in the game for at least one more year — he got both hits.

In 1988, I pitched two innings in the Cubs-Sox classic. I ended up striking out Rafael Palmeiro, who was leading the National League in hitting at the time, and catcher Damon Berryhill. The line score: 2 innings, 1 hit (Angel Salazar), and no runs — not bad.

In 1991, I pitched a scoreless inning against the Minnesota Twins, striking out Chuck Knoblauch on a slider down and away. It wouldn't be that big a deal, except Knoblauch is one of the most difficult players to strike out in all of baseball. In 1991, he struck out only 40 times.

Roger Clemens has the most beautiful home I've ever seen, and I'm proud to say I am displayed in it. He has a workout room with everything you could possibly need. In the room is a framed picture of Roger, along with a list of the 238 players he struck out in 1986, titled "The Roger Clemens Fan Club" — I'm one of the names on the list.

My list is a little shorter: Knoblauch, Palmeiro, Berryhill, Steve Howard, and a handful of minor-league guys. But that list isn't important to me. Rather, the fact that I got a chance to stand out there, straddle the mound, challenge a big-league hitter, and shake off a sign. The fact I threw one pitch as a major leaguer will forever be noted. You can look it up: 0 Wins, 0 Losses, 3.00 ERA, 2 Games, 3 Innings Pitched, 4 Hits, 4 Walks, and 2 Strikeouts, (and this, mind you, does not include the Cubs-Sox Classic).

Sometimes real life exceeds your dreams!

Family Ties

Some of us are lucky. We grew up with two parents around who loved us. In a house with a picket fence in a neighborhood where crime and safety weren't major concerns.

Minus the picket fence, that was my life. My Dad worked his butt off to raise four sons and try to keep up with the Joneses. Pretty good considering his two oldest boys were his stepsons, and by the time I was 22 I was out-earning him.

My mother, Lillian, was divorced with two boys, Rick and Randy, when she met my father. Then they got married and had me and my younger brother, Michael. If Rick hadn't decided to live with his biological father when I was ten years old, I would never have known what a step brother is. We just always felt like brothers. And even now when it gets late after too many beers, Randy and I get philosophical, and Randy always says, "I had some tough times growing up with Dick Lyons, but he was always fair. Bottom line is, I wasn't his son, but he raised me like I was, and I'll always call him 'Dad.'"

My mother, at 4'11" and 90 pounds is mentally the strongest woman I know. My determination and will to succeed comes from her influence.

I feel lucky to be surrounded by three brothers who were always proud and supportive of my career. Rick, who's now 40 and a foreman in the construction business in Seattle, Washington, became a huge fan when I got to the major leagues—collecting all my baseball cards and giving them to all his friends. He was really the only non-athlete in the family, and I didn't even know he liked baseball.

I put these guys through hell, though, because they'd always show up to the games all decked in my team's hats and t-shirts and jackets—remember I started in Boston, then came to the White Sox. Then Boston, Atlanta, Montreal, Boston, Chicago Cubs, and Boston. They're all broke, but they have lots of Red Sox stuff!!

Randy is 39 and runs his own carpeting business in Seattle. He was my high school hero. If I couldn't be like my Dad, I was going to be like Randy: a great athlete and tough as nails. While practicing in the eighth grade, his coach was hitting fly balls and accidentally broke a window. When Randy tried to catch the ball to prevent it from breaking the window, the glass came crashing down and cut his arm between his shoulder and tricep, needing stitches to heal.

Nine months later, he bumped his arm while getting off the bus, and a piece of glass pierced through his skin just above the elbow. The hospital didn't do a good job cleaning out his arm when he was originally cut and left a 1 1/2 inch piece of glass in his arm. It burrowed its way deeper into his arm and about nine inches down toward his elbow, then popped back out looking like the blade of a knife sticking out of his arm. Recently he's been experiencing pain in his wrist and can't figure out what it's from. He thinks there may be yet another piece of glass still in there.

Michael is 31 now and is a chef at the Irvine Improv. He probably had the best God-given physique of all of us, but at 5'7", he took after my mother in the size department. He may be one of the only people in history to play on state championship football teams in two different states. In his junior year he won the Oregon State championship at Beaverton High School and then my parents moved to California and he won the California Interscholastic Federation title at Mission Viejo High.

The competition we shared, the games we played together, and the years we spent challenging each other helped make me the ballplayer I was. They never treated me like I owed them something because I was the major leaguer in the family. But more important, they never treated me any less than their brother.

Raising a baseball family

Playing baseball as a kid, I had no idea that so many opportunities would arise from the game. Growing up in Oregon doesn't lend itself to believing that some day I might see the world. I always thought that my kids have a distinct cultural and educational advantage that I didn't have in my childhood, just because they've always come along for the ride.

Aside from being born in Washington, I was 19 years old before I ever stepped foot outside the state of Oregon. My kids, however, Kristen, 17 and Kori 10, have already been in nearly every state in the country and have experienced things that I never dreamed of at their age. This is something I believe they'll appreciate much more as they get older.

Hopping on a plane is no big adventure to my girls. In fact, it usually meant that they were leaving their friends for the summer to spend three months in whatever town their Dad was playing in. Apartment complexes, rented furniture, no friends, nothing to do, moving—all things my kids have had to deal with their whole lives.

During my years as a player, they also had to put up with a lot of pressure and petty jealousies just because of who I was. After I pulled my pants down on the field, Kristen was teased about it more than I was. She's a pretty strong kid so she handled it, but it wasn't something she looked forward to.

Once, after a father-son/daughter game, Kristen was still wearing her uniform in the stands during our game. I struck out on a bad pitch and, realizing she had my name and number on her back, she scrunched down in her seat so nobody would know who she was.

Kori spent most of her younger years adoring her older sister. She had plenty of friends at home, but with so much moving around, her best friend became Kristen. Unfortunately, teenage girls don't always want their little sisters around. It made for some long, hot summers.

Tougher than anything else for a baseball family is the time spent apart. Both girls have been growing up with a part-time father. And since I wasn't always there, I found myself being the disciplinarian when I was. I was very hard on Kristen and very strict with her privileges.

Kristen was born when Lynn and I were just 17, and we were children trying to raise a child. My influence on her was based on the way I was raised. What I failed to realize is that not everybody is going to be a world-class athlete, or even wants to be, and that driving my children the way my father drove me wasn't for everybody. My dad realized that I not only had to be pushed and challenged, I wanted to be. I didn't differentiate between the way I was raised and the way I raised my own girls.

As parents, I guess we all have some things we would change if we had to do it over again, but I'm not too worried about Kristen. Lynn's patience and compassion was the perfect balance to my strict attitude and Kristen is and always has been the model child—conscientious, honest, and eager to please. Looking back, I think if I could do it over, I'd just let her be a kid.

By far the most difficult situation in our lives is my divorce from their mother. Trying to make them understand that the two people they love most don't live together anymore is overwhelming. They always say divorce is toughest on the children, and I agree. But it's also not so easy on a wife who was counting on her husband or a father who now lives without his kids.

As Kristen enters the University of Arizona in the fall of 1995, I know she'll eventually realize that sometimes relationships change—and that two people who promise to stay together don't always. She does know that I love her, have provided for her, and have raised her the best way I know how.

Kori is only 10. It will be years before she can truly comprehend how her life has changed. Right now all she knows is that when she plays softball, or has a dance recital or school play, Daddy is never there. Sometimes, the only way she can show that she loves me is through anger.

I'm working hard to make sure they know that I'll always be their father even though I'm 2,000 miles away. It is the most difficult emotional turmoil I'll ever know, but a situation that I'll never give up on.

They are lucky in perhaps the most important regard— they are loved and well cared for by their mother. Lynn is quick to find the good in every situation and gives of herself to them, first and always.

Remember when . . .

I was sorry to see Bob Boone leave the game as a player before I did. He is now the manager of the Kansas City Royals, after a great career as a catcher for 19 years. I used to get a laugh every year at a Bob Boone story. When I was a kid growing up in Eugene, Oregon I used to go watch the Eugene Emeralds play. They were the "AAA" team for the Phillies, and I saw some great players there: first base Willie Montanez, second base Denny Doyle, third base Mike Schmidt, shortstop Larry Bowa, and catcher Bob Boone.

One night I was lucky enough to get one of Boone's broken bats after a game. So every year since then, I'd go to the plate for the first time against Boone's club and exchange the normal pleasantries, "Hi, how's it going?" Then I'd always say to him, "Hey, Bob I've got one of your bats." He was always caught by surprise, thinking that I took one of his game bats earlier that day. So he'd say, "How did you get it?" And I'd tell him. "I got it when I was eight years old and you were playing in Eugene." The home-plate umpire and I would be laughing, while Boone was swearing at me from behind his mask. Nobody likes to be reminded of how old they're getting—especially in baseball. More times than not, he would call for the first pitch to be under my chin.

You win some, you lose some

What a game of unbelievable mood changes. I remember when Doug Rader was a coach for us with the White Sox in 1988 how personally upset he'd be when we lost and how happy he was when we won. People who really know me know that I put winning above everything else — but we play 162 games every year. You're going to lose quite a few. And in our case in 1988, we weren't a very good team so we lost a lot (90 losses, compared to just 71 wins).

I really think that when you lose a game, you should reflect on it for a few minutes to learn why you lost. What mistakes did you make, what kind of at-bats did you have — and what could have been done differently so the same types of losses don't keep happening. But being scared to be the first guy in line for the postgame spread, or making sure there's no stereo or TV playing, or not being able to talk to anybody louder than a whisper is ridiculous.

Baseball is a hard game to get a substantial level of consistency at. Why do you think players always talk about trying to play .500 ball and then go from there? That's losing as many as you win. That's never been a goal of mine, that's a lot of disappointment, a lot of cold food, and a lot of whispering. And you only get to listen to the stereo for half the season.

Clemens' 20 K's

On April 29, 1986, the night Roger Clemens struck out 20 Seattle Mariners, I played centerfield. It was the most dominating pitching performance I've ever seen.

Hitters were striking out three pitches at a time and weren't even fouling off balls. If you get a chance to see the most published photo of that night, you'll notice the only really excited person in the picture is me! I've got my arms raised above my head in triumph as if I did it.

But the thing that makes that night interesting to me is everything else that was going on in Boston that made it seem like just another day. For one, we almost lost the game. It took a late-inning home run by Dwight Evans to win it for us. Mike Easler, who was playing first base, dropped a foul pop-up that enabled Roger to pick up another "K," and attendance was terrible. It was cold, the Celtics had a home playoff game, and it was also the day of the NFL draft. So the media could have cared less about one of the 162 games we were playing. There were actually more people there at the end of the game than when it started because word spread about what was happening. Still, when Roger struck out Phil Bradley for the fourth time to make history, much of Boston was doing something else.

The coaches

More and more, teams are signing people who are great athletes and teaching them how to play baseball. This is one of the biggest reasons you see so many mental mistakes on the field today. Outfielders throw to the wrong bases, cutoff men are overthrown, pitchers don't back-up or cover bases the way they should. There are too many great athletes in the big leagues that never learned or refined their baseball instincts. Of course, most of the blame has to be put on the coaches for not teaching and re-teaching during spring training and before games during the regular season, but they can't teach everything. Many situations don't come up enough to learn in spring training. Many players switch positions and make on-the-job mistakes that cost the team runs and games before the players know what they're doing.

The year I was released from the Cubs (1993) I had almost all of my spring playing time in the infield — first, second, and third. I was involved in just one double play ball and took just one throw from a catcher on an attempted steal in 30 spring games. Now I had played all those positions before and was comfortable at each, but that's not enough "game" experience for any regular player to get ready for a season — let alone someone who may be just learning the position. You can take grounders until you drop, turn double plays until your arm falls off in practice, but if you don't get the chance to play in a game you'll always make mistakes when you do.

It's just like batting practice. The 60-year-old batting practice pitcher throws 70 M.P.H. right down the middle so you can whack it. Hell, even guys like me can hit home runs in batting practice! Compare that to having Roger Clemens on the mound, throwing 94 M.P.H., with the ball moving away from you, or cutting into you, or "dropping off the table" like nothing you've ever seen. It becomes a little different than batting practice. And if Clemens gets mad, he throws so hard that your only argument against a called third strike is that you thought the ball sounded like it was a little outside — because you didn't see it! Now tell me that it's just the same as 45 minutes earlier during batting practice. Fielding is the same way — unless you perform under game pressure over and over, it will eat you alive when you get the rare game chances.

That's why I believe there's a pattern developing in baseball — and it's probably always been true — but in my era, the teams I played with that had the most prepared coaching staff, won the most games. Look how the White Sox turned things around from the late 80s to early 90s. Sure, they continued to add talented players like Robin Ventura, Jack McDowell, Bo Jackson, and Frank Thomas. But they lost a few also: Bobby Thigpen (never the same after 1990, when he set the major league record with 57 saves in a season), Harold Baines, Greg Walker, and some guy named Lyons (ha ha). The biggest difference was the turnaround in coaching. Jeff Torborg brought a feeling of togetherness to a team that was otherwise in total disarray, but he also knew to surround himself with people who knew what they were doing and were willing to work at it.

Terry Bevington is a hard-nosed guy who has excellent people skills. He knew how to get guys to work at their weaknesses, but disguised it in a way to make that player think he was helping somebody else.

For example, my first year playing second base, I had a lot of trouble picking up Ozzie Guillen's tosses on double play balls. He, like a lot of Latin shortstops, likes to field the ball on the move and quickly snap a flip throw from below his glove and waist instead of fielding the ball, and pivoting to throw. Ozzie rarely made a bad throw doing it his way, and it certainly added to his flashy style, but it made it hard on the second baseman trying to complete the double play.

So Bevington went to Ozzie and told him that I was having a lot of trouble with my pivots at second and I needed work — so could he feed me some extra throws during batting practice? We did that for three days in a row, and even though Bevington didn't tell Ozzie point blank to alter his game, he was more aware that he had to help me along and it didn't create a defensive situation. It also gave me the chance to see more throws from Ozzie, and I got a better idea of where the ball might be coming from.

Bevington also had good instincts about including the utility players on the team. He made sure we all felt like we were a big part of the team even though we weren't in the lineup every day — something Torborg was not good at. But most importantly, when he saw a weakness in somebody he did something to improve the player...he coached. That's probably why he was a front runner to take over as manager of the Toronto Blue Jays when Jimy Williams was fired. They eventually chose Cito Gaston, but Bevington will manage in the big leagues someday.

Ron Clark, the infielders coach and defensive coordinator, was big on repetition — do it until you get it right. He knew fundamentals and stressed them. I used to have to give him batting gloves all the time to prevent blisters on his hands from hitting so many ground balls.

Barry Foote and Joe Nossek were two guys who knew the game inside and out. Two great people to have as bench coaches during a game. They were both masters at stealing the other team's signals. We always knew what the other team was doing, whether they were stealing, bunting, trying a hit and run, or whatever.

Dave LaRoche was the bullpen coach, a job with very little responsibility. You have to answer the bullpen phone, tell the pitchers which guy is supposed to warm up, and make sure no one out there orders pizza during the game. But Dave also had great people skills and played a part in the record-setting season of 1990 (not only Thigpen's record of 57 saves, but the bullpen set a record for most saves during a season). These guys all legitimately pulled for one another — no back stabbing, no jealousy, and no unknowns. Everybody knew what their roles were, and they played them. LaRoche had a lot to do with that chemistry.

Walt Hriniak. Just his name brings up an opinion. Nobody I've seen or heard of works harder or is more dedicated to his job than Walter.

Add in the training staff, Herm Schneider and Mark "Pride" Anderson, who are at the top of their profession. I played for enough teams to see the best and worst in action. These guys are the best, and you can see why the White Sox have turned their team around. They went out and hired excellent coaches that made their players get better. Things have changed since 1990, but Gene Lamont and his crew of coaches have the ability and mentality. Look for the White Sox to be a perennial favorite in the American League Central.

It was exactly the same story in Atlanta with Bobby Cox, Jimy Williams, Pat Corrales, Ned Yost, Leo Mazzone, and Clarence Johnson. Not too many guys can get released from a team, and still have good things to say about the personnel. However, I was cut by the Braves, they have one of the best staffs in the league, and have done nothing but win since 1990.

The dress code

I never understood what organizations think about the way the players dress. The Red Sox were big on saying, "Remember who you are and who you represent." Whenever the team traveled, we were required to wear at least a sports jacket, a decent pair of slacks, and dress shoes. Once we got to the next city, we could usually wear casual clothes, but no T-shirts or shorts. The strange part about it is that we charter all our flights, and bus directly to and from the hotels. We're never in an airport, so isn't it ironic that nobody sees us when we're best representing who we are?

The right place at the right time

It was strange spending my whole career as a middle-of-the-road utility-type player — mainly because in other players' eyes, there is no such thing. When guys talk about other players, opinions range from one end of the scale to the other, but there are always opinions. "That guy can really play," somebody will say, "I played winter ball with him last year — he should be in the big leagues!" But there's always someone else who chirps in with, "Shit, throw him sliders in the dirt, and he'll swing at 'em all day long — he sucks."

We all love to jump on the bandwagon, too. In 1993 I played against a kid named Manny Ramirez. He played for the talent-rich Cleveland Indians organization. You may balk at hearing talent-rich and Cleveland in the same sentence, but believe me, they have plenty of guys in their system who can play — they just don't have many who can pitch!

Ramirez jumped from "AA" to "AAA" and had combined totals of over 30 home runs and 120 RBIs. And had an average of over .300. One day, he hit an opposite-field home run bullet against us, and we were pretty impressed. "Did you see how quick that ball got out of here?" someone said. "How about the numbers he's put up — unbelievable! And he doesn't get cheated up there either, he looks like Juan Gonzalez." "Yeah," another guy added, "and how about this — he's only 20 years old!" Everybody had something good to say except one guy: "Last year he sucked . . . well, he didn't suck really, but he only hit .270 or .280 — something like that."

I know the same thing happens in the front office of every team — and at your office for that matter. Those guys who make the decisions on our futures don't always have the best information. Sometimes it's the luck of the draw or being at the right place at the right time. Maybe you do a great job in your office, but your boss reviewed the one time you didn't handle something that well, or maybe when the major league General Manager comes to see you play, you don't have your best day. The sun doesn't shine on the same dog's ass every day! We all have days we wish we could forget.

There are cast-offs in every line of work — guys that can't cut it in one business, but then go on to be successful in another. Baseball players who can't get on the field for one team, but become a star for another. Guys like Dave Stewart, Dennis Eckersley, Steve Farr, and Jeff Bagwell. One team didn't want them anymore, another team made them millionaire star players.

Of course, on the other side, there are people who get raises or promoted that you can't figure out. You know you can do the job as well, if you get the chance and you know it should be *you* sitting in that corner office overlooking the city. I've seen balls I would have caught, plays I would have made, and pitches I would have hit — if only I was in the game, and not just watching from the dugout.

The point is, and I've sighted numerous examples of this, baseball is indeed an enormous business, run by people who make business decisions, much the same way any business is run. People just don't want to see it that way — it's the "Grand Game," it's baseball. How could anyone who plays baseball relate to the problems you face at your nine-to-five job?

When one finger says it all

Sunday, March 28, 1993.

That ugly day came calling upon me once again. A pink slip. Nobody ever gets used to it, nor do you want to. And who knows if you handle it right when it happens to you. I know the Cubs didn't when they gave me the news. I was accidentally told by one of the coaches, Jose Martinez. He knew I was getting released, so I guess he assumed I already knew. He just walked up and said, "Hey, good luck to you, you'll be alright." Nobody had said anything to me yet. I didn' have a good spring (I rarely do), getting six hits in 36 at-bats, including a string of 19 hitless at-bats, while trying to play with a broken finger on my throwing hand. But General Manager Larry Himes had signed me to be the third catcher, and back-up everywhere else. I was told if I could do that, the job was mine. I worked my butt off catching, reported early, got in extra work, and was happy with my progress behind the plate — the one position on the field I had the least amount of experience playing. Maybe the signs of my release were staring me in the face and I just didn't notice, because during that spring season I did everything: I played first, second, third, shortstop in a "B" game, and left and right fields. In other words, everything but catch — the job they signed me to do.

During the signing of my pink slip I knew it was too late, but I decided I'd plead my case to Himes, Manager Jim Lefebvre, and coach Chuck Cottier, who were all in the room. They told me it looked like I needed to go somewhere and get some playing time; that since I had limited at-bats in 1992 while playing in Atlanta, Montreal, and Boston, my skills needed a little "tune up."

I told them that I couldn't believe I didn't get a chance to catch, and thought I had done a good job defensively at the other positions I played (I was charged with only one spring training error).

I asked why I got most of my at-bats immediately after I cracked a bone on the middle finger of my throwing hand, and could barely hold onto a bat, let alone swing it. I received dumbfounded stares from all three. Finally, I pointed out that I had been a utility player my entire career, was used to not playing (sometimes for weeks at a time), and then performed well when I got the chance. They wanted me to go somewhere and play? For what? To come back to the big leagues and sit?

Everybody knows that the main concern for a team's utility and back-up players is that they catch the ball when they play and don't make the team look bad defensively. If you get a hit or two, that's a bonus. I'm a .253 career hitter, primarily coming off the bench. Sorry for tooting my own horn, but ask any of the players, especially guys who were once everyday guys and then found themselves in a utility role; .253 is pretty damn respectable. But they released me because I didn't look good at the plate.

They panicked. Ryne Sandberg and Shawon Dunston were both starting the season on the disabled list, and they didn't know what to do. Very few guys had a good spring. Mark Grace had a string of 24 at-bats without a hit, and finished the spring with an average under .190. But three guys who had no chance of making the team on March 1 all made the club a month later because they had good springs. Tommy Shields, a 29-year-old career minor leaguer (who wasn't a bad player); Kevin Roberson, a top prospect who was coming off back surgery and should be playing somewhere everyday (not sitting on the Cubs bench behind Candy Maldonado, Sammy Sosa, Willie Wilson, Derrick May, and Dwight Smith); and Matt Walbeck, their number-one catching prospect who played in "AA" in 1992 and should play at least half of a season in "AAA" to prove he's ready for the big leagues (he also should be playing, not sitting in the big leagues).

It was my prediction (quite honestly), that two out of those three would be back in "AAA" before May 15, and they would once again be looking for a third catcher/utility guy — the guy they released on March 28, 1993.

It doesn't happen often, but every year some managers and general managers let themselves be fooled by a spring training performance. Forty at-bats determine your career: if you get hot you may open some eyes, if you don't, you may be looking for a job. Two years in a row, Gary Scott put on an awesome exhibition in the Cubs' spring training, and two years in a row he couldn't come close to even average numbers in the big leagues. Sparky Anderson called Chris Pittaro the best player he'd seen in 40 years in the spring of 1986. He didn't last half the season in Detroit.

So as I sat there with the "braintrust" of the Chicago Cubs, I got increasingly more incensed. I was in a panic. I had been fired — again, and I didn't like it or deserve it. My earlier releases from the White Sox, Braves, and Expos flashed back to me. I could feel my face flush with embarrassment and anger, and it seemed like minutes went by before another word was uttered.

These three Bozos couldn't legitimately explain to me why I hadn't made the team, and I had nothing to lose. They weren't going to change their minds, and my most vivid memory told me to do something about it. You know the one — my U.P.S. firing, where I sat and said nothing while being abused by their system. I couldn't let that happen to me again, I had to make a point no matter how childish or futile it might be.

So I said to them, "This is it? This is your decision?" None of them really acknowledged the question, even though we all knew the answer. I faced each one of them individually and extended the swollen, bent, and broken middle finger of my right hand, the major reason of my release in the first place and said, "Fuck you, Fuck you, Fuck you," and left the room.

As a footnote to that story, you should know that within 15 days of the season starting, all three players were sent to "AAA." Shields has retired, Walbeck was traded to Minnesota, and Roberson is a member of the Cubs.

Hidden ball trick

I always thought I was good at paying attention to details about the game. Managers always talk about doing the little things, executing the fundamentals. The team that does those things well stands to win more games. Someone once said, "Just by showing up every day, you'll win 60 games and lose 60. It's what you do with the other 42 that wins championships."

I wanted to make sure that when the coaches had their meetings at the end of spring training, they couldn't put many "no's" next to my name in too many categories:

Can he hit?	*A little.*
Can he field?	*Anywhere.*
Can he run?	*Not bad for a white guy.*
Can he bunt?	*Yes.*
Can he throw?	*Yes.*
Can he hit with power?	*No.*
Does he stay healthy?	*Always.*
Does he play hard?	*Yes.*
Is he coachable?	*Yes.*

Sure, I was a marginal player. I never tried to portray myself as a great player; I didn't do any one thing great. But I was well rounded, and made it a point to try to do everything well.

Sometimes, doing the little things took on a whole different meaning to me. Running to first base on a walk, hustling on and off the field, looking to take the extra base — rounding first hard on a single, just hoping the outfielder would bobble the ball a little so I could take second. I did the same thing on a sure double, so I was always ready to go to third if something unexpected happened. How many times have you seen a player trot when he hits a gapper and knows it's a sure double with no chance for a triple? But what if the cut-off man is missed or the ball is mishandled? The player is not ready to make the next move and that's a lack of hustle. It takes no ability to hustle and anticipate.

Without super talent, I always felt like I had to take full advantage of what the game had to offer; the "little things." Pick-off plays, bunting for a hit with a runner on third. (Bunting on the whole is a forgotten art in baseball. Brett Butler is the only player in the game today who could even come close to comparing with Rod Carew's ability to bunt — any time he wanted to.) I liked any kind of play that could give my team an advantage: trick plays, squeeze plays, and the hidden ball trick.

Oh yes, the hidden ball trick, my favorite. Scoffed at by most players as chicken shit, it's a play I considered myself the master of in the last two decades. Name another player who pulled it off more than twice during that period?

It's such a magical play when it works, because it requires so much communication, setup, deception, and luck to pull it off! And it's a tough call for the umpire, too. By design, you're trying to make sure everybody in the whole ballpark thinks somebody else has the ball — except the umpire. If he doesn't know you have the ball, he won't call anybody out. Rather than explain how to pull off the hidden ball trick, let me just recap a couple of times I did it.

In 1984 I was playing in "AAA" Pawtucket. We were playing the Yankee farm team, the Columbus Clippers. In a close 2-2 game, the Clippers were threatening in the bottom of the eighth. With runners on first and second, the next hitter lined a single to left, and being the third baseman, I was the cut-off man for the throw to the plate. Kevin Romine made a perfect throw, and I cut it off when I noticed the runner held up at third.

This is the perfect time to employ the hidden ball trick. Right now my biggest worry is the umpire calling time-out. Technically he shouldn't, unless someone asks for it, but at that time there was a long lapse of time — the pitcher had backed up home on the play, so he's walking back to the mound. Sometimes the umpire takes this opportunity to dust off home plate or just calm the tempo of the game.

Your hope is that everybody will lose contact with exactly where the ball is. The next hitter is getting ready to hit, the players on the bench are mildly celebrating the base hit, and the third base coach is regrouping after making the decision to hold the runner. This is the perfect time to hang onto the ball, give some sort of body language to the pitcher so that he knows you won't be giving it back to him, and sneak back to your position.

In the next 30 seconds, you need three things to happen. First, the pitcher has to be smart enough to know the rules — which is never a given. He can be on the dirt portion of the mound, but he can't straddle or toe the rubber, and he can't use the rosin bag to appear as the ball. Second, while hiding the ball in the web of your glove you must find a way to alert the third base umpire and show him the ball without being obvious. After all, the runner on third and the third base coach are less than ten feet away. Third, and by far the most important, the runner on third must take a lead off of third base. This may not sound like that big of a deal but remember, one of the first rules we ever learned in little league about leading off was, never lead off base until the pitcher is on the rubber. Never.

What made things worse in this case, was that the runner on third base was none other than Butch Hobson, a Red Sox great. (At the time, he was in the final season of the contract he signed with the Yankees). But here I was, a "AAA" rookie about to pull the hidden ball trick on a guy who once drove in over 100 runs in the big leagues — batting ninth! He represented all the things I wanted to be in the game of baseball. He played hard, played hurt, and played to win. I began to reconsider, thinking, "Maybe I should just call this one off and throw the ball back to the pitcher." But then I thought, , "Hey, he's in the game, he's not on my team, and I want to win."

I positioned myself close to the third base bag so that I could make a quick lunge at the right time. I couldn't be too close, or it would tip off the play. But I couldn't be too far away, or I would blow my chance. Butch surprised me by saying something to me, "How's it going," or something like that. I tried to act like I didn't hear him as I turned to the shortstop and said, "Hey, nobody out." Even I would call myself an asshole if I had walked over, started a conversation with the guy, asked about his kids and then spanked him with the hidden ball trick.

Finally, the moment I'd waited for. After the perfect set-up, I just needed Hobson to step off the base, just a step. When he did, he surprised even me because he quickly bounced out to a 2-1/2 step lead. I paused for just a second and realized that this was going to be an easy play. But just as I was about to move in, Hobson looked back and saw what was about to happen. The panic in his eyes was a sight I'll never forget. His last ditch effort to stretch back to the base fell painfully short and the toughest play in baseball was completed with the umpire's call, "He's out!" Hobson pulled a groin muscle on the play and had to be helped from the field, and Mike O'Berry grounded the next pitch into a double play. We got out of that inning with no runs being scored and ended up winning the game 3-2 in the ninth.

I can't help but think that play came back to haunt me later. In 1992 I was traded back to the Red Sox from Montreal and guess who was the manager? Butch Hobson. Totally overmatched in his first season, he never gave me a chance to show him what I could do. He used me in certain defensive situations for awhile, but always asked me where I'd rather play — center or right, first or left, depending on what change he wanted to make.

So before a game one day I went into his office and told him where I was most comfortable playing and where I thought I fit on the team. I just did it so he'd know what I thought, and he wouldn't have to ask me every time he wanted to make a move. Given the healthy outfielders on the team at that time, Billy Hatcher, Herm Winningham, Bob Zupcic and Phil Plantier, I felt very comfortable telling him that I was the best defensive outfielder he had. So if he needed me out there, he could feel free — left, center, right, anytime, anywhere.

When I finished, I once again saw that look of panic that I had seen eight years earlier at third base in Columbus and knew I had struck a nerve with him. Maybe he felt I was a little arrogant, or that I was trying to tell him how to do his job. What I did know was at that point, I had nothing to lose. I went on to tell him that I could back up Jody Reed at second and play a better defensive first base than anybody he had there (Mo Vaughn). Call it sour grapes, but I can't help but feel that he never got over that hidden ball trick, and he held it against me from that point on. Two days later I was sent back to "AAA" Pawtucket.

Hobson wasn't the only guy I got on the hidden ball trick. Not by a long shot. I got Scott Fletcher when he was in Milwaukee, Rick Wilkins in a spring training game, and I even got two guys within the span of one week. What makes this even more amazing to me is that I've spent at least half of my career as an outfielder, which gives you absolutely no chance to do it.

My personal favorite hidden ball trick had a selfish motive behind it. It didn't help us win a game or even save a big run. But it did give me a feeling of revenge. In 1991 when the White Sox released me after four-and-a-half years with them, I was back in Boston for Psycho II, playing second base. Ozzie Guillen was bunted over to second, and I took the throw for the out at first. This, incidentally, is another perfect time to try this play. To make a long story short, Ozzie wasn't paying attention, stepped off the base and I nabbed him. As for the revenge factor, it stems back to my playing days with Ozzie in Chicago.

Let me start off by saying Ozzie Guillen is the best defensive shortstop in baseball. I'm sure I'll get arguments from people who say the other Ozzie (Smith) is the best or maybe even somebody else. (Ozzie Smith won 13 consecutive gold gloves at one point). I watched Guillen play every day — night in, night out, and when you see somebody play that much, it gives you a chance to see his weaknesses rather than his strengths. I saw him make every routine play possible, and many more plays I thought were impossible. His defensive skills were incredible, and it was inspiring watching him work his magic.

But Ozzie and I never got along on a personal level. I felt he didn't give anybody any respect, as if his gift on the field gave him the right to be above everyone off the field. Maybe in other ways, we were too similar to get along. His smile and showmanship will always be his trademarks, and Chicago loves him. But even though we broke into the league in the same year (1985), in 1989 he still called me and others, "rookie." He spoke before thinking many times, and spoke with total disregard for his teammates' feelings. Calling himself "the franchise" and saying things like, "Don't do anything to hurt me, or they'll release you."

I've never been one to keep my feelings to myself, and I certainly wasn't the only player on that team who felt the same way, and I made it clear to him that I wouldn't stand for his shit. We almost came to blows one night in Milwaukee. He made a sarcastic remark about an error I made the inning before. I told him that there were plenty of guys in the world that I was scared of, but he wasn't one of them, and if he ever bad mouthed me again, I'd kick his little ass. I told him that he might be a better player than me, but he sure as hell wasn't a better person. After a couple of incidents like that, we pretty much learned to just stay out of each other's way.

In 1994, I was working for a publishing company that was producing a new sports card. I was hired to interview every player in the big leagues for information for the back of the card. I got the chance to sit down and talk to Ozzie about our differences.

I told him I noticed he changed since our days together in Chicago. I could tell that he finally realized what being a leader meant, and that he had become one. He had learned that to earn that kind of respect, he had to give more to his teammates. He had to be the example to follow. The new Ozzie was a less abrasive, more sensitive player who took on a father-figure role to the other Latin players, helping them with the language and U.S. lifestyle. I think his serious knee injury in 1993 helped him understand just how fragile his star status could be. I never heard him call anyone, "rookie" while I was visiting — even if they were one. Maybe in some small way, our confrontations helped him become the star he is today with the White Sox.

Jack Clark and the Crunch Bunch

There has been a huge explosion in the popularity of licensed products in both college and pro sport merchandise. Everywhere you look there are jackets, t-shirts, and hats with the kid's favorite team on them. In 1991, the Red Sox had a t-shirt called the "crunch bunch." Most of the star hitters were represented, including Tom Brunansky, Tony Peña, Roger Clemens (isn't he a pitcher?), Jack Clark, Ellis Burks, and Wade Boggs. Mike Greenwell was not on the shirt, much to his dismay. Among other things, I found those t-shirts were great for your own drawings too. Jack Clark was my victim in the "crunch bunch" shirt. During that season, he had a tough four-game series in Kansas City where he wasn't hitting. Striking out a lot, hitting weak ground balls, and missing balls he should have hit.

Jack is usually very low key. He doesn't say much and ordinarily I wouldn't know if he was 4 for 4 or 0 for 20; he was always the same. But this time he snapped—and he took it out on the dugout restroom. The sink, the toilet, the towel dispenser—demolished. There wasn't a piece of porcelain left in that bathroom that couldn't be swept into a dust pail. I thought it was kind of funny that when I checked out the damage, the mirror was untouched — seven years' bad luck!

Pitcher Joe Hesketh and I took the shirt, grabbed a felt pen, and went to work. Clark was pictured on the outside of the group of players so drawing on him, and next to him was easy. Hesketh turned out to be a pretty good artist. He drew a perfect toilet seat next to Clark — just in case he needed to use one and commemorate his Kansas City experience. After all, they sent Clark a $1,200 bill for the damage, which he gladly paid. Next, we painted a pair of dark sunglasses. When he slicked back his hair and wore his sunglasses, he looked like Marion Cobretti in the movie "Cobra." After a couple of washes, the glasses faded just enough to look like they were an original part of the shirt.

The next year, I played with Atlanta, and after a spring training game I was working out in the weight room wearing that shirt. Jeff Treadway passed by and looked at the characters of the Red Sox and said, "How come you're not on that shirt?" I said, "I am," pointing at the toilet. It may have been a bad thing to say. I didn't play that well in Atlanta and was released on April 30.

Bucking the system

Dave Gallagher has one of the driest senses of humor I've ever seen. He's now playing in Philadelphia, but when we played together in Chicago he cracked us up all the time. He would cut his own hair, using the clubhouse mirror. It never came out right, so we all used to call it his Chemo-do. He looked like somebody being treated for cancer. He didn't care, he'd just stand there and laugh, then cut some more.

His favorite thing to do was make up words and use them in conversation. He always said nobody would ever question him on the word because they would assume they didn't know what it meant—and that nobody would use a word they didn't understand. "Recalcinate." It doesn't mean anything, but Gally made it mean anything he wanted, depending on who he was talking to.

In 1989, during spring training, everybody was interested in the NCAA basketball tournament. Georgetown was getting beat at halftime in a game they should have easily won. We didn't see the second half because of our own game, but afterward we heard Georgetown had come back to win. We were all talking about the game with some reporters when Gallagher said, "Wow, [Georgetown coach] John Thompson must have gotten those guys to recalcinate at halftime for them to come back and win that one." The reporter never even raised an eyebrow and just continued the conversation, never questioning "recalcinate."

We used to try to drop subliminal messages into conversations with people we didn't know like cashiers, flight attendants, or drunks in bars. Neither of us was very good at it. It's so hard to continue your sentence after the subliminal word, but we both spent a lot of hours laughing at some of the times we tried to pull it off.

Gally was a great guy to have on my team, but not just because he was a closet class clown. I had a lot of respect for what he did on the field. He was as good a centerfielder as there was. I usually have trouble passing out compliments to others who did the same job I did, but not to Gally. He doesn't make mistakes. He doesn't break back on balls he should be coming in on. He knows the hitter and where to position himself. He charges the ball well, hits cut-off men, and has a good arm. There's not much else you can ask of an outfielder.

Above all, he had guts and was a survivor. He was destined to be a career minor leaguer, playing for eight years in the minors for Cleveland, Seattle, and the White Sox. Nobody seemed to want to give him a chance in the big leagues. He even retired in 1987 to market his own hitting tool called the "stride tutor." While doing that, somebody convinced him to give it one more shot and he's been in the big leagues ever since.

Gally had a great first year with the White Sox, hitting over .300 and playing great defense. But the Sox had some contract policies that he couldn't agree with. The White Sox liked to tie up their young players with a series of four one-year contracts that were based on incentives from the previous year. It was a very complicated system, but it forced the player to give up his first year of arbitration, base his salary on his playing time the year before, and it was non-guaranteed! It was a system that allowed the White Sox to dictate what the player's salary would be the first four years of his career, with very little variation. No matter how good a player you might be. They successfully held down the salaries of players like Lance Johnson, Robin Ventura, Frank Thomas, and Bobby Thigpen.

Gally filed a grievance against the White Sox with the players' association, charging that the Sox didn't bargain in good faith. It was a move that would set a precedent for the other clubs to utilize the White Sox structure if he lost his case, or take the chance that the owners would blackball him from the game if he won. There were many other players in the same situation with the White Sox, but they were afraid of the consequences of taking the team to court.

Gallagher lost his case, but was traded to the Orioles during it. He bounced around after that with the Angels and Mets before landing with the Atlanta Braves. At the time, he had two kids, a third one on the way, and less than two years of big league experience. Gally took a huge risk in challenging the system. You have to admire a guy for standing on his principles and showing a great deal of courage with no support from his teammates. Things have worked out well for him because of his ability, and it couldn't have happened to a nicer guy.

How many throws?

Remember when your dad used to say to you, "How many times do I have to tell you not to do that," about something you're always doing wrong? You'd never have a good answer for him but did you ever really wonder how many times he did tell you? I think a lot of people wonder how many times they're going to have to do the same thing or say the same thing or go to the same place day after day.

Don't you think a mailman wonders how many pieces of mail he's delivered? How many times has the receptionist at IBM picked up the phone and said, "Good morning, IBM?" Or how many fares has the career cab driver collected? I've thought about those types of things, and I began wondering how many times I've thrown a baseball. I asked a few guys I've played with to really think about it and come up with a number. Someone said "I wish I had a dollar for every toss I've made," but as it turns out, a dollar may not be a very good investment.

Sitting in Rochester, NY at about 2 a.m. after a few beers, Tim Naehring, Paul Toutsis, Jeff Plympton, and I tried to figure it out. We had all the perspectives present — an outfielder, infielder, a pitcher, and me.

We decided that to accurately figure the total number of the throws we've made, we'd start at the present time and work our way backwards. We factored in playing catch to get loose, throws during pre-game warm-up, and any throw made during the game. We came up with an average of 200 throws per day. Starting pitchers throw more on some days but far less on others, so they fit pretty well into the average. Catchers, however, throw considerably more, because they throw back 95 percent of the pitches thrown to them, and unlike the pitcher, they do it every day.

Then we figured how much we threw per year—roughly 10 months. Two months in preparation, two months in spring training, and six months in season. Approximately 6,000 tosses a month, 60,000 per year, which puts my 13-year pro career at roughly 800,000 throws.

Adding in a three-year college career where I threw more, but for a shorter period of time, the average stays about the same with both fall and summer schedules. Three years. That's another 180,000 throws, which puts it near the one million throw level.

Going back to childhood, there were three years of high school ball plus American Legion ball in the summer, three years of junior high and Babe Ruth baseball and four years of little league. Keep in mind that when I grew up there was no "tee-ball" nor "coaches pitch" type of leagues for the younger players. My hey-day as a pitcher came when I was a third grader—striking out every batter I didn't walk!

Then Toutsis reminded me of the pick-up games we played as kids. "We'd play for hours," he said. In my neighborhood we never had trouble finding enough guys for a tennis ball game or football or basketball at the school. We usually turned guys away. Today you can sometimes drive for miles before you find a playground being used by kids that just loved the game the way we did. (I sound just like my father.) Today, the kids can "play" baseball on their Sega Systems, or listen to their Walkman, or get on their jet-ski or motorcycle — they don't love the game the way we did. They have other things to do. Hell, I have a picture of me swinging a bat at age three. I assume I was also throwing a ball. How many, for sure, I don't know, but they have to be included.

Partly in the interest of professional pride, we decided that we throw the ball more as pro athletes than we did as amateurs. From the time I was eight through my high school career, it was about 40,000 throws per year, which, added to the previous million, puts it at right about one and one-half million throws.

So for most people, a dollar a throw would be great, but considering I made about 2.5 million during my career, I'm glad my contract wasn't constructed that way. It would be an interesting concept however.

Gone would be the $4 million plus contracts and lazy days during batting practice. You'd never have a tough time finding someone to play catch with. Guys would trade in their Oakley sunglasses for pocket calculators and pitch counters. Talk about hustle! Every player would be dying to make the play just so they could throw the ball back.

There is a down side, I guess. Everybody would either have a sore arm or want to be a catcher. You'd have the less-intelligent players standing in the outfield with their gloves off counting on their fingers how much money they made that night. And their coaches would be yelling at them: "How many times have I told you not to do that?!"

You're only as good as your word

My career took a severe turn for the worse with my release from the Cubs in spring training 1993. After expecting a $400,000 contract, I was left with nothing but my desire to keep playing. I decided that I wanted to walk away from the game when I was ready, not have some General Manager tell me I couldn't play anymore.

After making contact with nearly every major league club, I finally signed a minor-league contract with Boston to play in "AAA" Pawtucket — for $6,000 per month. It was certainly a far cry from the $650,000 I had made for the last three years, but it kept me in the game I loved.

I took awhile to get back in playing shape. Then I battled through back spasms that kept me out for two weeks. I eventually got a break and was called back up to Boston. I was in no position to barter for a great major league contract, and considering utility man Dave Milstein and top-hitting prospect Louis Ortiz were both playing well at Pawtucket, I had to take what they offered. The Red Sox organization, and General Manager Lou Gorman in particular, had always been fair to me in our past contract delaings. I always had a realistic view of my worth compared to other players, and Lou loves to play the negotiating game.

I was offered a $200,000 contract, and without the input of my agent, signed it. He was attending his 25-year college reunion in New York, and I felt it was a now or never offer. Later, he agreed that my read of the situation was correct. Maybe the team's interest in Ortiz and Milstein wasn't quite as urgent as I felt, but there was no room for negotiating the $200,000.

I spent one month in Boston before being asked to return to "AAA." This created an interesting situation for everyone involved, especially me. Being a veteran of at least five years in the big leagues I could refuse my assignment. I was no stranger to this process. I refused to be sent down in 1992 with Atlanta and accepted my release. I also refused to go to "AAA" with Montreal, and the deal was made to send me back to Boston for the third time.

I had two options, when asked to go to "AAA." I could accept my demotion and go back to my minor league salary — upped to $7,500 per month because of my call to Boston. There was no guarantee of coming back to Boston, and I would be taking the chance that my baseball career would be over at season's end.

My second option was to say no and accept my release. In that case, I would continue to be paid the remainder of my major league salary — roughly $110,000 and benefit from the major league licensing program for the rest of the year — another $40,000. In other words, I could take the $150,000 and hang out for the rest of the summer, or go back to the minors and make $15,000 to play for two more months.

For most people, the choice would be easy, but for me it wasn't. I knew I could still help a major league team. I also knew I wanted to be involved in the sport after retiring — manage, broadcast, something. I figured my best opportunity to do any of that would be with the Red Sox, so the last thing I wanted to do was piss them off. If they perceived me as somebody who took advantage of my call-up and then screwed them for the rest of my contract, they probably wouldn't go out of their way to help me in the future. But if they saw me as an organizational guy — someone who bit the bullet when he had to and did what was asked of him, they might find a way to take care of me in the future.

So, I packed my bags and went back to Pawtucket. I did get called up again, in September, recouping some of the money I gave up.

At the time of my demotion, Red Sox manager Butch Hobson told me that he noticed how hard I was working and that he wanted me back in spring training with the Red Sox in 1994. His enthusiasm towards keeping me on the squad was the biggest reason I decided to return to Pawtucket. I knew my career might be coming to an end, and staying with the Red Sox was probably my only chance to prolong it. I didn't want to blow that chance — not for any amount of money. I just wanted to keep playing baseball.

Financially and professionally, I lost that gamble. Hobson never invited me to spring training the next year. I don't think he ever intended to. He was just making sure the organization kept their $150,000.

This was not the first "screwing" I got from Hobson. During that season, I had a clause in my contract that would pay me $20,000 if I played in 30 games. Most managers don't like to know about those kinds of things, and Hobson was no different. But he knew about mine, because we had discussed it. He knew about everybody else's incentives, and made so sure they reached them, he got into some trouble.

Such was the case with relief pitcher Jeff Russell. He needed a certain number of appearances to get a $100,000 bonus. We had only three games left, and he was on the disabled list. They were supposed to take him off the DL, but somebody forgot to call the league. So that night, he pitched in the game, even though he was on the DL. The next night, Russell pitched again and got the bonus — much to the dismay of the higher-ups in the organization. We were going nowhere as a team, and they didn't want to have to make that payout. They let Hobson know it in a closed-door meeting after that game.

Of course, they had nothing to worry about with me. After my return in September, I had played in 28 games with five to go. Hobson couldn't seem to find a way to get a guy who can play all nine positions, good defense, and run pretty well in two of the last five games. Thanks, Butch.

I guess stuff like that does catch up to you sooner or later. The Red Sox finally realized that he was clueless and had no business managing a major league team and fired him. I guess he has a standing offer to go to Alabama, his alma mater, in some capacity. I'm sure he would find a way to screw that program up, too.

As for the Red Sox, I guess I can't complain too much. They gave me four different opportunities to play for them. But after the screwing I took in 1993, I received no offer to manage in the minors, no offer to coach at any level, and no offer to come back as a player in 1994. But even if my relationship with the Sox may finally be over, I sleep well knowing I earned every cent I made in this game. I never took the money and ran at any point in my career.

A kid's game

One day in 1993 before a game in Pawtucket, I was sitting on the bench with teammate Dave Milstein. We had just finished a clinic for kids who wanted to come out and learn more about baseball, and everybody had gone home except one kid and his dad. We sat there not saying anything for the longest time, watching as the boy and his father tossed the ball back and forth to each other.

My career was rapidly coming to an end. I was 33 years old, playing in "AAA," and knew I was in a bad situation. Milstein was a "AAA" utility guy who showed flashes of ability. He was one of those guys everybody knew would never get the chance to play in the big leagues, but he kept hanging in. He also knew that as long as I was his teammate, any chance of his advancement would be blocked because I already had eight years of big-league experience, and if Boston needed help they probably would choose me. But Milstein wasn't the kind of guy to hold any of that against me as a person. I considered us to be friends.

It had already been a long day for both of us and we hadn't even started batting practice yet. As we sat there in silence, we were both contemplating the direction our baseball lives had taken us. Why do things work out the way they do? How could we have changed them? And what will we do with our professional lives now that this one will soon be over? Finally, Milstein looked over at me as he stood up to go back into the clubhouse. I could see his eyes had welled up with tears. "It's amazing," he said, "how a simple game of catch with your dad can turn into the perversion and politics that is pro baseball."

The good, the bad, and the ugly

"Hey, what's it like being a big league ball player?" I've been asked that hundreds of times. Here's what it was like. For the first two months of the season, I usually froze my butt off. Playing in weather not conducive to good statistics, I sometimes took three showers a day. My body has been broken, strained, pulled, and scarred for life. I often didn't do anything, but eat, sleep, and play baseball. I was at the park by 3 p.m., home at midnight, and slept until noon. At the end of the season, I had to reintroduce myself to my kids because I was away so long. I paid rent in spring training and the regular season, while paying the mortgage on a house all the way across the country. I moved my family three times every year, and I often didn't see them for three months at a time. I lived in my "real home" for less than four months a year.

I lived for eight months a year with 30 other guys, all from various backgrounds and with different attitudes and conflicting personalities and ideas, and with really only one thing in common — the game. We didn't all get along, but we all depended on each other at different times. Sometimes it was like a family: guys got into arguments about different things, and then usually forgot about it the next day.

During the season we got one day off every 21 days and no days off in spring training. If you think about it, your leisure time is when I work. When you got together with eight of your friends to sit in the bleachers, have a few beers, and get a tan — you were coming to see me work. I saw the 1979 All-Star Game in Seattle. It was the only major league baseball I had ever seen before I played my first game for Boston in 1985. I've never experienced the rush of the crowd that anticipates a great night at 6:45 p.m. before a 7:35 game. Someday I'd like to try it.

We got into hotel rooms at 3 a.m. after traveling from one city to the next. I woke up with the sheets stuck to the cuts on my elbows and scrapes on my knees. I sat on a bench for most of the games and stared at gross puddles of chew-spit, sunflower seeds, and empty Gatorade cups all over the floor of the dug-out. I would sweat as soon as I stepped onto the field, my uniform was continuously soaked, and the dust stuck to me as if it were make-up I was supposed to be wearing.

I worked out for hours before ever getting to the game, usually in batting cages in the bowels of the stadium, unseen by everyone else except the food vendors and sanitation workers. I took extra batting practice until my hands bled. I was paid less than everyone else, forgotten by the fans, looked down on by many who said, "He stinks."

I played once a week, maybe, and only when the regular player wanted the day off. So my starts were against Roger Clemens, Dave Stewart, and Greg Maddux. I pinch hit with two outs in the ninth against Dennis Eckersley, Tom Henke, and Rob Dibble at a time when you're trying to do more as a hitter than you should—against their best pitcher.

If I wanted an extra workout, I got there long before the starters, and then during the regular workouts, I was the last to get my swings in. I was constantly asked if I could get the autograph of some star player who was in the dugout.

I went through periods of self-doubt. I started to believe that guy in Section 106 , Row J, Seat 22: "Lyons, you're a bum!" I hadn't had a hit in awhile and I wasn't sure when I was going to play again to get another chance to get one. I became the butt of my own jokes to hide how badly it hurt to just sit on the bench. An 11-year-old kid yelled, "Hey, Psycho, you starting tonight?"

"No," I would say, "We're trying to win."

But after a while I noticed other players doing the same thing to me. It was done in a joking way, but some of them were guys I felt I should have gotten a little respect from. At that Sunday day game after a night game, they saw the line-up that listed me hitting seventh and playing centerfield. So they laughed as they turned to me and said, "Have you seen this line-up? Are we trying?" Everyone laughs, but inside it hurt because I knew every time I went out there, I busted my ass to play well. I just didn't get the opportunity to play more. So I started taking those remarks personally. It was sort of like having a little brother — *I* can pick on him all I want, but don't you touch him or you'll answer to me. I can rip myself to hide my embarrassment, but you damn sure better stay off my ass.

That's what it was like to be a professional baseball player.

Dealing with the negatives are a reality that the average person doesn't always recognize. But without a doubt, my baseball career has been my greatest experience ever. It was more than I expected, and better than my dreams allowed. Why do you think they call it every kid's dream? For me, it was my chance to play little league forever, to fend off maturity and everything that goes with it. Remember those pick-up games we used to play after school? They'd last until dark or until we got called home for dinner. I lived in a world where that game became more important than being late for dinner, and there were always lights for us to play under.

I was 19 years old before I ever stepped foot outside the state of Oregon. Now, at 35, I've been in every state in the nation and even out of the country a few times, thanks to playing baseball. My office was the freshly cut green grass of the most elaborate stadiums in the world. The pencil I pushed was a Louisville Slugger T141 that was 34-1/2 inches long and weighed 32 ounces. I showed up for work at 2:00 in the afternoon wearing a pair of shorts and a brand new pair of baseball cleats. There's a special feeling I got as those cleats bit through a major league infield. As I soaked up the sun, I surveyed the situation — watched as a co-worker ironed out a problem with his swing.

Soon thousands of fans would assemble to admire and applaud my work. I would be a part of a team that boasts the greatest players of their time.

I'm proud of what I did and have gained considerable confidence from it. I've been exposed to cultures and attitudes different from mine — and have grown because of them. Because of the high profile, I have attained a level of fame and celebrity, something I'm not ashamed to say I enjoy. Recognition can be a powerful feeling.

I play in those celebrity golf tournaments for free, I haven't paid for any athletic shoes in ten years, and rarely have trouble with dinner reservations. I get free tickets and backstage passes to all the concerts in town —and you name him, I've met him.

I made lots of money due to supply and demand. I didn't invent anything, teach anybody, or run a company — I played baseball.

My kids have had lots of "experiences of a lifetime" and they're only 17 and 10. My daughter Kori calls Charles Barkley "Chaz" because she hung out with him in the locker room after a game.

Even though it amazes me, some people want to meet me. I walk down the street and am treated as if everybody is my friend. I traded my complimentary tickets for a car during the season and other perks. I got discounts on TVs and stereos and mobile phones — just because of what I did.

The job comes with a four-month paid vacation, the best health and dental plan, and a pension I've never contributed a dime to. We always traveled first class and sometimes had our own plane. We were easy to find, just check the best hotels in town — we'd be there.

I had 24 guys to pick me up when I was down, and 50,000 others to encourage me along. I have three championship rings gracing the fingers of my dad and two of my brothers. I have that autograph that you only dream of getting, and I've worked alongside legends. I didn't even have to work when it rained.

I have taken advantage of every opportunity that baseball has presented me with, and have had more now that my playing days are over. Doors are opened, connections are made, and deals are done.

All of this is secondary. It's the best of the best, but that's really not what's important. When I walked into the clubhouse and changed into that major league uniform, freshly dry cleaned and pressed, looked at my name on the back and the team's name on the front—I never took one day for granted. That's also what it's like being a major league baseball player.

Thoughts on the strike

During my days as a major leaguer from 1985 - 93 I lived through a few tough negotiating sessions between the players and the owners. In my rookie season in '85 there was a one-day strike, and then the lock-out in spring training of 1990. I became very involved in the business side of baseball because I wanted to be better informed about how my future would be affected. So I was the player representative to the Players Association for six years, both in Chicago and in Boston. Nothing I ever experienced was as bad as this past strike—the big one of '94-'95, lasting over seven months and forcing the cancellation of the play-offs and the '94 World Series as well as delaying and shortening the 1995 season to 144 games.

Let's understand a few things before getting into this too deep. I was a member of the players' union for nine years. I benefitted tremendously, not only financially, but also in terms of my pension benefits, medical coverage and conditions under which I played, due to what the union fought for. Three years in a row I made more than $600,000 as a major league utility player, and at age 62 I'll receive $113,000 a year for my pension—the legal maximum permitted by law. If that limit increases over time, so will my benefits. The players union also set up a separate Keough Account in the amount of $7,500 per year beginning in 1990 for every major league player. While you're considering how incredible this plan is, take this into account: I've never contributed one cent to the plan—no player contributes.

My medical benefits, thanks to the union, were top notch. One hundred percent coverage in many cases–never less than 80 percent. No deductible, and this included dental, vision, and even orthodontics. So if we're going to talk strike, you may be hard pressed to find me saying anything bad about the players' union.

Having said that, both sides are at fault. The caretakers of the game should have never let the business get in the way of a World Series. And don't kid yourself—baseball is a huge business, a $2 billion industry.

Over the last 25 years, the players chipped away at the owners' policies, and through the collective bargaining process, gained free agency, arbitration, and continue to have the national TV contracts fund the players' pension plan. With each passing basic agreement, the players fought hard to preserve and better the conditions of the business end of baseball.

Revenues continued to rise, attendance records are broken every year, and the TV rights fees soared into the hundreds of millions. Players' salaries were rising at an unbelievable rate.

The owners began to see a problem. How long could this go on? Rightfully, they wanted to hang on to a bigger piece of the pie, so they began to devise artificial plans to put a drag on rising salaries. In 1985 they proposed no more than a 100% increase in an arbitration victory for players and an increase in the number of years of service it takes to become arbitration- eligible. Tales of franchises losing money and containing costs have been long-time battle cries of the owners.

The players, never believing that baseball was in dire straits, pressed on and won time and time again in the negotiating wars. Citing that if owners wanted cost containment, they had the ability to set up their own individual baseball budgets and operate within them.

Well, the owners decided to set their budgets collectively— to force big- name free agents back to their original teams for less money than they'd be worth on an open market. It was a "one hand washes the other" approach to holding salaries down. Of course, the owners were sued by the players' association for collusion, and lost in court. They were ordered to pay the players $280 million in damages.

Now in the mid '90s, the game is facing change. Do the players realize it? I think they do. Are they willing to change some things and compromise for the good of the game? Absolutely. But wouldn't you have a distrust for the owners if you knew they had lied to you, colluded against you, and tried to change everything your organization had worked for for 25 years all at once? The owners proposed a salary cap, elimination of arbitration, and restricted free agency for players in the four to six year class. Then they failed—for seven months—to negotiate on any of those issues.

Once again, they lost in court. The National Labor Relations Board approved an injunction against the owners claiming that they refused to bargain in good faith. A federal judge agreed and passed the injunction.

Which brings me to the most controversial issue of the whole mess. Replacement players.

Many times in this book I've tried to put you in my shoes to help illustrate my point or to help you understand a situation. Mainly to dispel the notion that I'm this psycho off-the-wall idiot that played major league baseball. But now with the replacement player issue, I just may piss you off.

I was totally against it—and I think the union issues I spelled out earlier should be your first clue as to why. We saw players like Junior Ortiz, Dennis "Oil Can" Boyd, Herm Winningham, and Jeff Stone, among others, who all enjoyed those same advantages I did, spit in the face of the players union and cross the line to join teams as replacement players. And with Boyd making statements that the union never did anything for him. We had former minor league players who just didn't make it, coming back from their jobs as produce managers, truck drivers, and accountants to "give it one more try." To live out their dreams of being a big leaguer.

I guess I shouldn't be the one to diminish somebody else's dream, but let's at least call a spade a spade. They all did it for the money. These guys were done as potential major leaguers and they knew it. Not one of them would be invited to make any of the 28 major league teams in spring training under normal circumstances. Hey, we all had that major league dream—but we all have to have the good sense to know when it's time to move on too. And if not, the best way for the people who are closest to you to support you is to encourage you to put it behind you and move on.

Forget the integrity issues, forget about looking in the mirror and answering the question about "Do I have the right to be here?" and forget about every one of those replacement players knowing in their hearts that they were not real major leaguers. The major league players association saw replacement player baseball as a bargaining ploy of the owners to undermine the progress of the negotiations. As long as games were being played, it weakened the players' ability to get a settlement. Do I blame the owners for trying it? Not really. I just couldn't understand the fans accepting it—knowing that the owners were blatantly putting an inferior product on the field and asking us to pay for it and treat it like major league baseball.

And now that there's an agreement to play but no real contract between the two sides, we may be looking at the exact same problems in the near future. In the eleventh hour, the replacement players were sent home the day before opening day of the regularly scheduled '95 season, costing them the $25,000 they would have earned if they opened the year playing for the major league clubs. And Dennis Boyd's comment was, "They used me." I don't know why this was any big revelation, that was the owners' intent all along. Just as Oil Can used baseball.

So real major league baseball is back, and I'm happy. But both sides had better find a way to improve the image of this game we love, or the future generations of fans will play soccer or "baseball" on their Sega systems, or ride mountain bikes all day. The perceived greediness of both the players and the owners is ruining the game for the fans, and they're taking it personally— they think the players don't love the game, they think they don't care about those of us who watch it, and they think money is all the players care about. I don't think any of those things are true, but it doesn't matter if I'm right or wrong—it's a fact that if the people who are running this game do not become more harmonious in their dealings with each other, there will be no major league baseball as it was intended.

Snubbed in Montreal

1992 had become increasingly more frustrating. I'd always been one of those guys who shows up to play — every day. I've made up for my lack of talent with a desire to work. Improve and play! But for the first time in my career, I'd found myself not caring whether we won or lost. I certainly hadn't felt like part of the team, after being released by Atlanta and now only having 11 at bats in almost two months in Montreal. And I certainly wouldn't be a fan of the Expos if I wasn't playing. This game has to be played by a guy who has a lot of little boy in him. I think that's why I survived as long as I did. I'd been a kid for a long time, practical jokes, silliness — I never wanted to grow up. But four teams in 1 1/2 years was killing the little boy. He's growing up, he's got bills to pay, responsibilities to attend to, places to be. Not as much time for his sneakers and glove — no time to play ball.

After not playing for a long period of time, I finally asked Manager Felipe Alou what was up, and if I would ever get a chance to play. Felipe is a soft-spoken gentleman, 59 years old, but he still looks like he could kick your ass. He was from the Dominican Republic and his communication skills in English were not that great. He told me that they had to make some moves, but I wouldn't be involved in them. Alou added that they had the guys that were out of options and couldn't get sent down. None of it made sense to me. I didn't want anyone to get sent down, I wanted someone to sit down, every once in awhile, so that I could play a little bit. We had a doubleheader coming up and he said I'd probably play in one of those games — but I didn't.

The next day I decided to find out what my future was with the team and spoke to General Manager Dan Duquette. (In fairness to him, he told me when I signed with the Expos that he couldn't guarantee me a lot of playing time. But I didn't perceive that to mean never.) Anyway, after a five-minute conversation with somebody else, he came over and told me he couldn't talk right now, that he was late for an interview.

This floored me — my general manager couldn't find time to talk to one of his players because he had to talk to some two-bit radio guy wanting to do another worthless interview in

Montreal where nobody would hear it anyway. So I cornered him anyway and asked him what was going to happen with me. He said he talked to my agent earlier in the week and didn't have anything to add.

I said that my agent didn't wear a shirt that said Expos on it. I did. He didn't come here to work every day, I did. I told him that I've worked too damn hard, not only before I signed there, but since I got to Montreal, and I'm too good of a player to sit here for 37 straight days without starting. He couldn't look me in the eye (which is my experience with most GM's) and he told me it was something I'd have to take up with Felipe. I told him I had and couldn't get an answer I could understand and then walked away. I had work to do.

Not so coincidentally, that night after the game (one in which a situation came up where I thought I'd be used and wasn't again), I was getting a soda from a cooler outside Alou's office. I heard someone call my name but wasn't sure where it came from. When I heard it again, I realized it was Felipe striding towards me from his office chair and calling my name. Quickly, the thought in my head was that he was going to say, "Hang in there, big guy, I know you haven't played all that much but be patient with me. I'm trying to get you in there and there are still a lot of games to be played. So just keep working like you are and keep your chin up."

Sometimes that's all a utility guy has to hear every once in awhile to keep his attitude right. The guys playing every day don't have any worries, it's the reserve guys who need to know they're not forgotten and are still important to the team.

Of course all those thoughts took place in two steps of Felipe's movement towards me. Now in the doorway of his office, he looked up at me and said, "Oh, it's okay, I'll get it" and closed the door. As it turns out, the phone rang in his office and he wanted some privacy, so he just wanted someone to close the door. I just happened to be the closest person to the door. But because of the "meeting" with Duquette, another night on the bench, and the way I had been treated, I felt very small, like I meant nothing to the team. As if I should have asked if I could shine his shoes first, and then closed the door.

Psycho III

June 29, 1992. I was finally out of Montreal for good!! They sent my contract back to Boston. Psycho III !!! It's funny how times change. In 1986, I was traded from Boston for Tom Seaver, and now I get traded back for nothing. Maybe an old bag of balls. I think Duquette begged the Sox to just take the contract. The deal was probably that Duquette would buy the next lunch when he and Sox General Manager Lou Gorman got together. (Gorman and Duquette now work together in Boston as Boston hired Duquette as the new GM.)

I was back in the American League, and more bizarre than that, I became the first player in Red Sox history to play for them three different times. I extended that record the next season when I returned to the organization for the fourth time.

The deek

On July 20, 1992 I was sent back to "AAA" Pawtucket. I hadn't been in the minor leagues for what seemed like forever. I singled in my first at-bat, and as I gave my batting gloves to the first base coach, I realized he and I used to play middle infield together, and now he was my coach! Mark Meleski and I were drafted in the same year, but he had gone on to a coaching career after the 1986 season. He said, "Yeah, that's funny, but you're about the 30th guy that's said that to me."

After our rookie minor league seasons in "A" ball in 1981, Mark and I were in instructional league together in Sarasota, Florida. There was a guy on first trying to steal, when the hitter popped the ball up to centerfield. Mark and I were playing shortstop and second base and we decoyed as if it were a ground ball to me. Mark covered second and I acted as if I were flipping the ball to him. The runner slid into second, and our centerfielder caught the pop-up and threw the runner out at first as he was scampering back.

It was our first attempt at a "deek," and we pulled it off. We were laughing at second base as we threw the ball around the horn. When we came in off the field, our manager, Tony Torchia took us both aside and bitched us out. It was a great play, he said, but don't ever stand out there and laugh at another player for any reason, even if it is funny.

A whole other world

After spending almost nine years in the big leagues, it was a rude wake-up call going back down. I never had more fun playing in the big leagues than I did in the minors, and I've talked with enough players who shared the same sentiments as I do about the minor leagues.

In the minors, you get closer to the guys, you have to do more things together. You share cab rides because no one can afford to go alone, your rooms in the hotels are all on the same floor instead of spread all over the hotel. Nobody makes any money, so guys fight over the extra 50 cents that's supposed to be left as the tip. Guys don't go so much in their own directions like in the big leagues, where everyone follows "special interests." No investment talk, race car sponsorships, or thoughts of buying the in-season home you're renting. They spend their time figuring out how they're going to live on $37 for the final three days of the road trip. They wear cleats that have been thrown into a big box from the big leaguers and sent down to them.

Undoubtedly, one of the best things about getting called up to play in the big leagues is the towels. You can use as many towels as you want. In the minors, you get one towel and one only — and it usually has some kind of hotel logo on it.

When you're in "AAA" the terminology is different than when you're in the big leagues. They talk about going to "the show," being in the "Bigs." But for now you're just in "trips" (AAA). When you're in the big leagues, you never call it "the show" or the "Bigs." It's just the big leagues, and "AAA" is "AAA"—you don't want to see it any more. It's strange how that works—you struggle your whole life to get to your ultimate goal and then realize that your greatest thrill was the struggle itself.

"Popcorn here!"

In 1992 while playing in Pawtucket, I pulled a hamstring in a game against the Richmond Braves and sat out the next eight games. It marked the first time in my career that I ever missed a game because of an injury. I was going crazy while not playing. My treatments were set up with an hour in between with very little to do. So I went up to the radio booth and did some color work along with the Pawtucket announcers. While talking about my teammates, I wondered what was said about me when I was playing.

I figured they almost always said something about my pants down incident or that my nickname is "Psycho," but there was one line I wanted to guarantee was never used: "Boy, this guy has played everywhere at one time or another! He's even pitched and caught in a game. He's done everything but sell popcorn in the stands!"

You see, in one of those boring periods between my hamstring treatments, I snuck up to the vendor area and talked them into letting me sell some popcorn. I put on the apron and hat and roamed the first base box seats yelling, "Popcorn here!" Of course it wasn't long before people recognized who I was and began asking for autographs. So I worked out a deal where I would only sign if they bought some popcorn.

Later, I went inside the pizza booth and tried my hand at selling and baking Pawtucket pizza. It was fun until Pawtucket Vice President Mike Tamburo got wind of it and stopped me. He said for insurance reasons he could not allow me to do it anymore. Reluctantly, I took off my hat and apron and retreated back to the clubhouse. I was disappointed because I was having fun, selling all that stuff at a game, and getting a chance to bake pizza

— a new experience. But I was sent back to my daily grind, that nine-to-five job. Back to being a ballplayer - too bad.

Men will be boys

My reputation preceded me everywhere I went as a guy who loved to have fun, joke around, and play pranks on people. But I still maintain that while I may have done some off-the-wall things during a game and loved to have fun, I wasn't much of a prankster until 1993, and even then it was forced upon me.

I always got a kick out of putting shaving cream on the phone receiver and then telling someone they had a phone call. Or giving hot foots (lighting guys' shoelaces on fire while they're watching the game) or putting atomic balm in a guy's jock. But those pranks are old, everybody does them, and everyone knows about them.

The Pawtucket Red Sox was a team where no one was safe; not the manager, not the TV cameramen in the dugout, not even yourself from your own roommate. These guys pulled more pranks on each other than any team I played with. Every day something happened, and we were constantly looking over our shoulders.

We had guys sneak into other players' rooms, short sheet their beds, steal all the light bulbs, turn up the heat, and fill up a wastepaper basket with water and lean it against the door.

One night before a 6 a.m. flight home after a long road trip, we switched Tim Naehring's and Jeff Plympton's clothes in their suitcase so they took the wrong stuff home with them. I came back to my room one night to find both mine and my roommate's mattresses stuffed into the bathroom. We had room service and pizzas delivered to someone else's room; plants and trees from hotel lobbies were frequently delivered to people. Alarms were set, wake-up calls were made, a human turd was even discovered in somebody's bed. Of course, these things were mostly harmless. We didn't hurt anybody, destroy anything, or cause too many complaints. It was just good, clean, fair fun. And the more immature the prank, the funnier it was.

We watched our manager, Buddy Bailey, squirm his way through a 95-degree day in Norfolk, Virginia with itching powder in his uniform. He changed his undershirt three times and told the trainer he thought he had some kind of heat rash or something. (We won the game 9-3.)

Later in the year, somebody went a little too far and put the itching powder in his street clothes before a four-hour bus ride. He wasn't happy. John Malzone came back from a game and opened his door only to find an elderly couple all bedded down for the evening. Seems someone changed his room, moved his stuff, and forget to tell him — the hotel re-rented his old room — he didn't know.

Two guys got pennied in their room for half the day. Anybody who went to college knows this trick. Take five pennies, tape them together, and put them in the door jam from outside the room. The pressure from the pennies against the door makes it impossible to open the door — nobody goes anywhere until you decide.

The ultimate prank was concocted by pitcher Matt Young. He had us get some official Red Sox stationery and typed a letter to about 15 players on the team. We told them that due to some internal handling problems during their physicals, a semen sample was needed to test for enzyme deficiencies. The letter went on to ensure each player that no HIV, AIDS virus, or other sexually transmitted disease would be tested for, and that the sample must be given to the trainer within 15 minutes of production in order to ensure accurate test results.

I wrote the letter, got official-looking sample receptacles from a drug store, and even got one of the secretaries to do the typing for me. But when the General Manager somehow got wind of it, he nixed the idea. He thought it was great, but felt too many guys would call their agents about it and then he would hear from the agents. It was really just an intelligence test. I wanted to see how many guys were actually stupid enough to do it.

We're really just grown men playing kids' games — on and off the field. None of us really wants to grow up — you ought to try it some time. As you read about our antics and games, ridicule me if you will, but wouldn't you want to be on the planning end of one of those pranks at least once?

Same city, same bar, same girls

O.K. Here it is. My chapter on groupies. Please tell me it wasn't the first thing you looked for in this book. Who are these women anyway, and why are we so intrigued by stories about them?

I've got to think that most of the girls you see hanging around the players' entrances of the ballparks and well-known bars didn't start out thinking, "Wow, wouldn't it be great to be a groupie?" Do they even know that they're groupies? Or do they see other groups of girls just like them and say, "Look, there go those sluts"? Don't you think they probably want a little more out of life than just putting another notch on their bedpost? I think these girls want to have a relationship with or even marry a potentially rich, decent-looking, (although this is not mandatory) world-class athlete. Man, are they going about it the wrong way!

First of all, wake up! I played ball for 13 seasons and never once knew a player who married a groupie. And believe me, we know who you are—you know, same city, same bar, same girls. Nobody's fooling anybody here. Spotting a groupie is easier than spotting an idiot ballplayer. If the thick gold chain worn on the outside of his shirt with a number in diamonds hanging off of it doesn't give him away, a weak pair of cowboy boots, calloused hands and a stupid grin on his face will. If you're still not sure, go up and introduce yourself. When you hear, "Oh, hey, nice to meet you. I'm Billy Franklin, I play ball for the Red Sox," bingo! There's your baseball himbo.

The baseball bimbos are just as easy to spot. I'm talking 'bout the girls who wear their bikini tops to the games. You've seen them; your section may even cheer for them as they prance by. They're all done up in full make up and high heels, and they usually have on one of those tight cotton and Lycra shirts—don't tell me these women can't find their seats. They come to the games just to parade around and get attention. And they get it all right—the wrong kind. The catcalls and the stupid comments men make can't really sound like compliments to them, can they? All I know is that if I were a woman and you saw me for the first time, I'd want to be cautiously approached with respect, not with an aggressive sexual attitude.

For the players, the whole game is easy to fall into. For our whole lives, we are taught that as men, if we want a date with a woman we have to pursue it first. We bumble our way through high school, asking out girls and praying not to get shot down. Our confidence soars with each confirmed Saturday night. As time goes by, we never really get totally comfortable with the idea, so a steady girlfriend is a much better way to go.

Then, along comes that baseball contract—you're a star, a pro ballplayer, a stud. Even in those minor league towns you're playing in, people want to know you. Now, women are coming up to you, everybody smiles when you walk by, and you have so many new best friends. All of a sudden, that cutie at the end of the bar wants to meet you. So you go over and say, "Hi, I'm Steve Lyons, I play for the Red Sox." No Way! I never did that, did I?

What changed? Did I become better looking? Did my personality get better? Sooner or later we all realize that it's the baseball. We're the hot commodity, we can be used for the benefit of others because we are good business. So the guys figure it out—but some of the girls never do. They're still out there today and will be again tomorrow, trying to hook up with a ballplayer.

You've got to hand it to them though, they're persistent. They call, send letters and packages, follow you, and accidentally find themselves at the same places you are. It's amazing.

My mail at the ballpark was always a treat. But it was always more fun laughing at my teammates' mail than my own—because there was always sort of a sick feeling knowing this stuff was sent to me. Pictures of nude women with letters and phone numbers saying "I live in Cleveland or New York or Kansas City, give me a call when you come to town." Little do they know that these pictures usually end up on a bulletin board marked "The wall of shame." I've received stuffed animals, candy, flowers, t-shirts, underwear—both male and female—and lots of bras. I'd get the nastiest letters and the pages would be sprayed with the sweetest perfume—it just didn't add up.

Once in Toronto during batting practice, a lady wanted me to throw her a ball. She kept yelling and motioning to toss it up into the seats. She was part of a corporate party in one of the luxury suites in the second level of the stadium, so I was scared to throw a ball that far for fear I'd hit her with it.

Showing off my punt, pass, and kick city championship trophy as an eight year old. A sign of the times to come . . .

Receiving the "10th Player Award" for my rookie year in Boston, 1985. The award is given to the player who performs beyond all expectations. What's not pictured is the Toyota truck they also gave me. Alongside me are my Mom, Dad, and Kristen at age 7.

With my two daughters, Kori, 10, and Kristen, 17, at a Blackhawks hockey game. They're both big sports fans.

Here I am catching. As a utility player, one of my jobs was to warm up the pitcher—but as you can see, I'm hoping Carlton Fisk will hurry up and take over.

Photo by Jack Maley

Turning two against the White Sox. Don't think I didn't know it was "The Big Hurt" coming dowing on me—I'm glad he slid!

Fans will do whatever it takes to get an autograph. I was always flattered that someone would want mine, so I was usually happy to do it.

Photo by Louriann Mardo-Zayat

I played all nine positions during my major league career—I even played all nine in one game. At that point I had done everything except sell popcorn and pizza at the game—I wanted to do that too!

Hanging out with the original psycho, Stephen King, and family. Through baseball I got to meet many interesting people.

Me with Carl Yastrzemski (left) and Ted Williams, my most-prized photo.

With Michael Jordan during his brief stint in baseball.

John Travolta was one of many celebrities who came through the clubhouse.

Long hair, a goatee, and an earring. Been there, done that. So much for trend setting.

My claim to fame? Unfortunately what some people most remember about me is the infamous "pants-down" incident.

After trying to beat out a hit by sliding into first base, I felt a lot of dirt running down the inside of my pants.

Forgetting that I was standing in front of the Tiger Stadium crowd, I proceeded to pull my pants down and brush away the dirt.

After realizing what I had done I quickly yanked my pants back up. Not even God could save me from my embarrassment now—the only thing I could do was throw up my hands and laugh—along with everyone else.

Playing again in Pawtucket in 1992, praying to get back to the big leagues.

Doing an interview after a game. My former manager Jim Fregosi once said, "The best thing he does is interviews." I didn't like it then, but now as I embark on a new career in broadcasting, I sure hope it's true!

She wouldn't give up, and finally I gave in. At the end of B.P. I tossed the laziest arching ball I possibly could into her suite and sure enough, she caught it. Everybody cheered and that was it. Two weeks later, I get a package in the mail and it's this huge bra, pink with lace and all that pretty stuff. I didn't remember the lady being that big in any area, let alone her chest. Her letter explained who she was and asked if I remembered the incident. Then she finished by saying, "Maybe next time you're in Toronto you can find out if this really fits." I hope it was a joke.

One year in Boston a girl sent me an 8 x 10 photo of herself wearing nothing but shortstop Tim Neahring's Red Sox top. She somehow had it wedged between her butt cheeks to give me a good indication of what she looked like. Her letter said, "Could you please give this picture to Tim." I thought that was weird, why not send it to Tim herself? Two months later, I got a dozen roses from the same girl and a note asking me to meet her at a local bar. What? Was I her second choice, or was she just making the rounds? Did she think I was that stupid? In her letter she mentioned being a schoolteacher. Hopefully not at my children's school.

I really think these women just have a misguided sense of what's important. Maybe they have low self-esteem or are very insecure. Some of them just seem to have no pride and act as if their sexuality is all they have to offer.

I had a brief conversation with a lady in a hotel bar in Detroit. After I went to my room, I got a phone call from her asking if she could come up to my room. When I said I didn't think it was a good idea, I got four more calls in the next 45 minutes from her pleading with me to invite her up. After that the phone stopped ringing—she must have found another guy's room number.

My fiancee was with me once on a trip to Baltimore when a girl called my room and said she noticed me at the game and would I like to come out with her that night. I said, "I'm with my fiancee, I'm not interested." Even before I could hang up, she said, "Oh, should I call later when she's gone?"

What can a woman like that be thinking about? Maybe it is just sex to them—it is for the players. There's no mutual respect shown in these situations. The girls become clubhouse stories; the players generally treat these girls like dirt.

One night in Texas a bunch of us got together to play poker after a game. Soon there was a knock at the door and two girls came in. One of them had briefly met Scott Cooper before, so we didn't think it was any big deal that they were there. Right away, the second girl started acting put out that we weren't paying any attention to them. She started asking for other players' room numbers so she could call them, asking why we weren't playing strip poker now that she was there, and talking about how nice her body was.

Finally, Phil Plantier had heard enough. "Get the hell out of my room. Nobody wants you up here so just get the hell out," he said. I was kind of embarrassed; that's how we all felt, we just wanted to play cards. But I usually avoid those nasty confrontations. These two girls still didn't get it. Phil yelled at them again, "I'm not kidding, Get out of my room!" and stood up as if he was going to physically throw them out. They finally got the point and scurried to the door. We all started laughing and resumed our card game—I won $240.

Women like these are usually dead giveaways. If you're out some night and you're not sure if the woman you're talking to is easy, look for the conversation to include: "Do you think my boobs are too big to wear a shirt like this?" or "Feel my butt, I've been working out," or "Do you think anybody can tell I'm not wearing any underwear?" Either turn and run, or dig in for the night, it's your choice.

Many of the girls who hang around the ballparks are just that—young girls. I really think these girls just don't understand the trouble that they could get into. Guys who play baseball are way past the kissy-face games you play in high school—if a girl makes herself available, he may take full advantage of the situation, and may never bother asking how old the girl is.

I once received a letter from two 15-year-old sisters that read, "wine me, dine me, sixty-nine me." The rest of the letter was too graphic to relate. They were at the park every day before I got there and were the last ones to leave every night. They just stood at the players' entrance trying to talk to every player as he came and went.

I tried to talk to one of the girls, telling her that she'd end up writing one of her letters to somebody who didn't care about her at all and she'd end up pregnant or worse. She just denied ever writing the letter and left.

I felt bad about the whole mess. My own daughter was the same age at the time. I couldn't imagine her being capable of acting like that— and if she ever did, she'd never leave the house! My warning didn't do any good at all—later that season there were about 20 pictures being passed around the clubhouse of two girls seductively posed in swimming suits and less. Guess who? Maybe I'm naive, maybe trouble was exactly what they were looking for.

Daisy Buchanan's is a well-known hang out for athletes in Boston. A friend of mine who works there told me it was amazing how he'd see the same girls on the same nights that just happened to coincide with Red Sox home games. One night, a couple of guys were asking him about the girls, and he told them that he thought they were only interested in meeting ballplayers. "Because we don't play baseball, we're not good enough for them?" they said. "Well," said my buddy, "Let's test my theory. Texas is in town tonight, so let's see what we can do."

He came out from behind the bar and asked the girls if they needed a drink. He then casually added, "Hey, I see the Rangers are in town, there's a couple of their players over there now."

Within five minutes, the two girls had made their way across the room and were now making conversation with two average Joes who had suddenly become a centerfielder and a catcher. I wonder if either of those girls asked if her boobs looked too big in the shirt she was wearing.

Every year in spring training, the F.B.I. sends a representative out to talk to all the teams about the dangers of getting involved with women you don't know. Talk to any major league player and he can tell you who Dr. Boudreau is, even though he's never met him. Dr. Boudreau had a scam in which he'd pose as the father of an attractive girl who wanted to meet a particular player. He'd show up alone, make an excuse for his daughter being late and invite the player up to his room for a drink while they waited for the girl.

Once the player was in the room, the good doctor would slip a mickey into his drink and the next thing you know, the player is knocked out cold. When he wakes up a few hours later and wonders what the hell happened, it's too late. But he figures, nobody took my watch or any of my money, so I guess I just passed out. Wrong.

Two weeks later, some more pictures arrive for him in the clubhouse, only these pictures are not of Dr. Boudreau's pretty little daughter at all, they're of him! He just happens to be in some pretty compromising homosexual positions. Dr. Boudreau doesn't want much, just a hefty chunk of your paycheck to make sure these photos don't find their way into the wrong hands.

In spring training, we all think that's a funny story, but they wouldn't have been telling us about it if it hadn't happened to a few guys already. Pretty scary.

A few years ago I started getting letters from a lady who said she wanted to meet me. The letters rambled at times and spoke of times years ago, and I couldn't figure out who this person might be. After a few more letters I got a little nervous as she wrote about my "piercing blue eyes and my radiant smile." I started to think that this was somebody who had been close enough to me at some point to write about my physical characteristics.

Finally she wrote me a 19-page letter and sent along her graduation picture. She wrote poems using the letters of my name as the beginning of each sentence—really weird stuff. I decided to call the number she left just to tell her I really wasn't interested in starting a relationship with her and that I didn't have time to be pen pals. I was playing in Chicago at the time, and the number was in Cleveland.

A receptionist answered the phone, and I didn't catch the company name she gave, so I asked to speak to the woman. She asked if I was a friend or family. I said neither and asked the receptionist where I was calling.

The lady told me that I had dialed a mental institution and that the woman who was writing to me was a patient there. She had no idea how the woman got the ballpark's address, but said, "Oh, yeah, she's a big fan of yours. She has all your baseball cards."

Considering the rest of her social schedule, this was the one case when I guess it wasn't so strange that somebody devoted that much time to letter writing.

As I said before, I really think most of these women just have misguided intentions—but does that make them bad people? I don't think so. We've all lived on the edge in our lives at some point or another, and we've all done things we look back on with regret. The fact that some groupies have an attraction for ballplayers in some cases may actually make them more selective. We all know people who go out on a Saturday night and don't care who they end up with.

These stories were sort of like the gratuitous sex scenes in a movie. Groupies aren't as big a part of a ballplayer's life as people like to think, so if you want to hear more graphic and detailed stories of smut, sex, and deception, you'll have to go buy someone else's book.

A busy "Young man"

I've often talked about my role as a utility man in the big leagues and how I think it's the toughest job in the game. As for the toughest job on the team, that's not a player or a coach. Pete Youngman was the trainer for the "AAA" Pawtucket Red Sox while I was there, and his job was the toughest. In the big leagues, every team has a traveling secretary, strength and conditioning coach, and at least one assistant trainer. In Pawtucket, Pete wore all those hats and more.

First, look at his off-the-field duties. He would begin in January checking the upcoming season's schedule, trying to get a flight schedule to match — knowing that there would be a million last-minute changes and corrections as the season rolled along.

Every trip the team made, Pete was responsible for the buses transporting the guys to and from the airport, or to the next city if it was a non-flight trip. He was expected to determine which company had the best price and service for the club and to have a back-up plan if a problem arose. Problems with buses, flights, and hotels were commonplace, even in the big leagues.

He also handled hotel arrangements. Who wanted a single room when his wife made the trip? Who wanted a different roommate because his last one snored? Or, he would find out after a 4:30 a.m. wake-up call and a 6 a.m. flight, that only half of the rooms were ready for check-in. His skin would harden when he fielded angry complaints from inconsiderate players who weren't smart enough to realize that he did his job, but someone else on the other end screwed up.

And while the players took an afternoon nap or got lunch before the game, Pete went to the park to make sure all the equipment was set up for the game. Bats, helmets, supplies, and any personal gear the players had.

Finally, as players began to stroll into the clubhouse for early workouts (which he monitored) or to get a treatment for an injury, Pete finally got to do what he was hired to do — physical therapy. His office was the trainer's room, where he was buried in rolls of tape, pre-tape, and skin lube.

In the three hours prior to the game, he was at his best. He handled dozens of requests, be it a player's sore back, the radio announcer's headache, or a player's wife with the sniffles. He'd tape ankles and wrists, apply heat packs and ice. He'd order one person into the whirlpool, another to the weight room for maintenance lifting, and stretch the starting pitcher's arm all in the same instant. When he was at his busiest, he'd be in his glory. Taking care of the athletes is what he liked to do. This was his game time.

I've also watched him during a game. Most people see balls and strikes, hits and runs. He'd notice who was walking with a limp or throwing a little bit funny, making sure the health of the players wasn't overlooked in any way — knowing he'd be the first person on the scene if something went wrong. If something went wrong off the field, his phone was the first to ring, and if something went wrong on the field, you hoped his was the first face you'd see. There's an old saying in baseball, "You can't make the club in the tub," which basically means the more you stay out of the trainer's room, the better off you'll be.

After the game, Pete started again, icing down sore arms and logging in every treatment he gave for the day. Everything had to be written down for the record. Drug disbursements, supply reordering, and workmen's compensation reports were all handled by Pete.

Ten years ago, he took his first job as a trainer — for $900 per month for a four-month season. "That was big bank," he says. "Coming from $3.35 an hour working at a hardware store, that was big bank!" He topped out, nine years later, at $24,000 a year in 1992, so you know it's not the money. A player in the big leagues today who makes the average salary pulls down that much every week! So why?

Like everyone else, Pete has a dream. It's not to be a big leaguer as a player, which was the dream of everybody around him, and to be honest, his real dream isn't even to be a big league trainer, though it would be great. "Ten years in the big leagues, that's all I want. Just to qualify for the pension to have my retirement taken care of," he said, "I really want my own clinic. Be my own boss for a while." He wants to have a staff of three or four to provide physical therapy for high school kids with sports-related injuries.

"There's nothing like that around here for the kids," he said.

It's admittedly a big dream, with those ten years of big-league tenure an immediate stumbling block, but that doesn't phase him. Already a certified trainer with a B.S. in physical education, he goes to night school trying to earn a master's in physical therapy. He's a member of both the National Strength and Conditioning Association and the National Athletic Trainers Association, and he's determined to further his training and education.

But for all that he did for the team, it was his personality that set him apart. The players liked him, trusted him, and respected him for the effort he gave. His training room was frequently visited by guys who were perfectly healthy — they just stopped by to give him a hard time about something. We all considered him a teammate rather than a part of management or the coaching staff. Maybe it's because when it came to playing baseball, I considered myself to be a "gamer" — and although I couldn't even begin to handle his job, Pete Youngman came to play — every day.

In 1993, Pete got the break he was looking for. He's now the assistant trainer of the NBA Sacramento Kings, with plans to become the head trainer for the 1996 season. A change of sport, and now it's the "big leagues," but I'm sure nothing's changed. If you're the first person in the locker room, Pete will be the first guy you'll see, and if you happen to be last guy out at night, he's the person you'll say goodnight to.

The school bus

After every game in Scranton, Pennsylvania, we rode back to the hotel in a regular school bus. Big and yellow, with those green high-back vinyl- covered seats. It brought back memories of throwing spit wads and trying to check out the girl you liked without her noticing you were doing it. I thought to myself, at 32, what a privilege to ride on one of those again. Nobody really gets that opportunity ever again, after high school. And let's face it, in high school only the nerds still rode the bus, so it dates all the way back to at least junior high. After that, you're done, never again — unless you become the bus driver, or you get suckered into being a chaperone on your kid's science field trip to a museum. The bus was just as I remembered, the same windows that you had to pinch the tabs at the corners to pull down so you could stick your head out and yell at somebody. The seats were every bit as uncomfortable and the same handwritten sign was taped to the bus above the driver's mirror, "No food or drink in the bus."

Remember hopping on the bus, being so excited that school was over for the day? You'd always try to get "your" seat way in the back and save the other side for your best friend. And you couldn't just talk anymore—it was a rule that you had to yell and scream while riding the bus. Someone always had to slap you or tease you on their way by, and that one jerk you couldn't stand had to sit right behind you. I got my very first kiss on the school bus.

Where else but "AAA" baseball would you get to relive this? Unless you were making one of those long rides to a penitentiary, but I guess then, you wouldn't really enjoy it the same way.

Can you spare a dollar?

Once I'd been to the big leagues, going back to the minors was the pits. I've already talked about how close you can get to your teammates in the minor leagues, but there were many things about the minors that weren't nearly as good as playing in the big leagues — I'm sure that comes as no big surprise. One thing that comes to mind are the in-season flights we took. In the big leagues, at the very least we flew all charter flights — nobody else was even on the plane. Just us. In Boston we even had our own plane. Chartered from the MGM Grand, the plane stayed wherever we were — even the flight attendants stayed. If we were in Kansas City for four days before going on to Cleveland for three, the plane and crew stayed right there until it was time for us to go.

This plane had state rooms for the card players, first-class seating throughout and even captains chairs for guys like Roger. There were video screens visible from anywhere on the plane, a wet bar in the middle of the craft, and food that you'd never associate with flying. Crab claws, hors d'oeuvres, any drink you wanted, and entrees of chicken, beef, or fish anytime we traveled. Believe me, it was easy to get used to.

In "AAA," on the other hand, we flew on commercial flights, which usually meant we flew the next morning after a series — early. For me, flying at night was so much better, even if it was really late, because no matter what time you got to the next city, you could go to bed and wake up whenever you wanted. Those 4:30 a.m. wake-up calls for the 7:30 flights in "AAA" loomed over me like a bad smell. No matter what time I went to bed, I had to get up to catch that flight — and I would *always* be tired. And of course, I would be playing that night after we finally got to our destination sometime that afternoon.

Then there are the airports to deal with again. Since we used regular commercial flights, we spent a lot of time waiting for flights. Being the child that I can be, I had a way of making the waiting time go by a little quicker. Namely, "the dollar bill trick."

You've all seen it, but most of you would fall for it again. I'd take my trusty mending kit (found in most major-league hotel bathrooms), and find the thread that best matched the carpeting in the airport. Then I'd tie a dollar to it and leave it harmlessly in the corridor. Then, when somebody spotted it and reached to pick it up, I'd snatch it from their grasp and we'd all laugh. Sometimes even our victim laughed, but most of the time they'd be a little embarrassed and say something like, "Oh, that's real mature," or "I bet you think that's real funny." We did, and so did the sometimes hundreds of others who eventually gathered around to watch after they saw it happen to someone else. What amazed me about this little gag was that after the person went for the dollar and it jumped away from them, they'd go for it again — as if it were something that happened to them all the time.

The fun didn't stop when we got on the plane. Since we traveled with about 40 people, we took up a good percentage of the seats. So we liked playing a little game with the flight attendants. We had all heard the pre-flight safety presentation a million times so we liked to help them out a little bit.

All of us mirrored the flight attendant by doing exactly what she did — we'd hold up the safety folder and point out everything she pointed out, snap the latch on the seat belt plenty of times to make noise, point out all the emergency exits — very professionally, I might add, with the two-finger point. We demonstrated the "loss of cabin pressure oxygen mask" with our Walkman headphones, and usually the attendant had a tough time completing her spiel without laughing. The other passengers seemed to enjoy it also, and it helped relieve the tension for those who didn't like to fly. But that was about the only "positive" of commercial flights, and remember it was early, so the only thing left to do was to try to sleep. I was never very good at that. I couldn't get comfortable on a plane and my neck is so long, I couldn't get my head to lay on the headrest the right way. I guess if you gave me the choice between all the minor league silliness or the major league charter flights, I would take the big leagues — not to mention the paycheck.

Roomies

One of the luxuries I really took for granted after playing over eight years in the big leagues was having a single room on the road — no roommate. Once you establish yourself, a single room is just a throw-in on your contract and if not, you're usually making enough money to pay the team rate the hotel offers (it ends up being about $3,000 per year).

The big attraction was simply the independence of it. You could come and go as you pleased, wake up whenever you felt like it, and if you accidentally peed on the toilet seat it was no big deal — nobody else would be using it!

In 1993 I was reintroduced to the roommate thing. I was no longer making major-league money. In fact, I was almost begging for a job when the Red Sox signed me again in May and sent me to Pawtucket. To save money, I decided not to pay for a room by myself and agreed to have a roommate. It had been nearly seven years since my last roomie, and I had forgotten what it was like.

I think if you asked all the players, there would be very few players who would choose a roomie over a single room. But, there are a select few who developed friendships over the years and actually enjoyed the security of their roommates. They'd pull harder for each other during the games, eat together everyday, and count on each other for support while on the road, away from their real families. There wasn't a night that you didn't hear, "That's my roomie," from someone after a clutch hit or a nasty pitch.

It was an experimental process finding a guy you were compatible with. Someone who went to sleep and woke up at about the same time you did. Someone who liked to eat at the same places you did, and so on. You'd be spending a lot of time with this guy, so you had to find someone you could get along with. And it was not an easy process either. Maybe you'd hang around a guy during the games and decide to become roommates, only to find out that you had two totally different views on how to live. Some guys went through three, four, and five changes or more before settling on someone. And there were always at least one or two guys nobody wanted to room with.

In the beginning, it's just the little things that are important. On that first road trip, as soon as you check into the hotel, your mind starts racing — which bed should I choose, the one by the window, or the one closest to the bathroom? You're wondering if the TV show you're watching is the one he wants to watch, or if he likes to sleep in total silence or listening to the radio. Your new roomie probably wasn't worried about any of that stuff, but who knows? He might be thinking "Why doesn't that guy ever turn the fan on in the bathroom? He stinks." Or "Why does he always sleep in so late? He makes me feel like I have to be so quiet in the morning — it's my room, too."

I found that I had to be neat again, or at least not so sloppy. No more having three days' worth of clothes thrown in various corners of the room. I had to keep my stuff on my side of the bathroom, didn't get to use every towel, and couldn't always be the one to steal the extra bar of soap. All the pay movies had to be mutually agreed upon. I was much less expressive while talking on the phone, and I spoke much softer. I missed the privacy of the phone in a single room. No more king-sized beds with mints on the pillow — not in the minor-league hotels. (All the rooms are exactly the same in those hotels. We stayed in one place that had the same pictures in every room too. Pictures of Yaks, no less. Where do you find one print of a Yak, let alone 300?)

And how do you know if your roomie would rather be sleeping while you're watching the 2 a.m. showing of SportsCenter? But he's just too polite to say, "Shut up, turn the TV off and go to sleep?" Which brings me to another extremely important question. Do real men actually say "good night" to each other before going to sleep, or does the conversation become increasingly more sporadic until you both drift off?

These are things that must be worked out if you intend to get along with your roommate — and you have no time to waste. It's enough to make you seriously consider paying the extra $25 per night for a single room.

In the dark about color

Growing up in Eugene, Oregon, I didn't exactly experience a melting pot of cultures. But I still credit my parents for not teaching me prejudice. I found that on the West Coast people are far less interested in your nationality. In fact, I wasn't sure what mine was until I started playing professional baseball on the East Coast and somebody asked.

It turns out I'm French and Irish, but it never mattered to me. I didn't grow up worrying about anyone's color, the size of their nose, or their family's customs. I care about how I am treated by them and how they treat others. That is what I base my friendships on. To this day I don't know the derogatory names given to some ethnic groups and I don't care to learn them.

With all the different kinds of people who come together to make up a baseball team, I had the opportunity to see how others react to the same situations based on their upbringings and attitudes. I played with Latin players, black players, Asian players, guys from the North, South, West — lots of different people. I played with whites who didn't like blacks, blacks who didn't like whites, and guys who didn't like anyone different from them — no matter who they were. I played with guys who tried to take prejudice in stride, knowing that ignorance is the key factor as to why it exists. And I played with some guys who created prejudice where there was none and made life harder on us all.

In 1992 and 1993, I played with a shortstop named Jim Byrd, a black man very much aware of his heritage and proud of it. He was also very sensitive to anything remotely racial directed at him or anyone else within earshot of him. Of course, not being a minority myself, I don't pretend to understand the struggles that minorities deal with in life. But at times, I felt timid around Byrd, worried I might say something offensive, even though I knew I didn't mean to. Over the course of the season, I noticed that even if Byrd and I never became good friends, I liked him and respected him both as a player and a man.

One day our team was waiting for our flight to the next series and I was playing the "dollar bill" game. A few of the guys were sitting close by and laughing at each victim of the game, including Byrd. Wayne Howsie walked by and said, "Man, you guys got a nigger-rig all set up." Howsie is also black. I don't even know what a nigger-rig is, but jokingly I said to Howsie, "Then why didn't you pick it up?" Everyone, including Howsie, knew I was joking and thought it was funny — except Jim Byrd. He shook his head and gave me a cold stare. From that point on, I knew my relationship with him would change — probably forever. It was a stupid thing for me to say, but it was said with a sense of humor and was directed at somebody else, with absolutely no malicious intent whatsoever.

The next year in 1993 I found myself playing again in Pawtucket and who was the shortstop? Jim Byrd. The Red Sox wanted to teach him how to switch hit, so they made him hit from both sides of the plate. Switch-hitting is tough enough when you try to learn as a kid — it's impossible to learn it at the "AAA" level.

Byrd of course struggled, hitting about .200 most of the season. Out of nowhere, the Red Sox called Pawtucket in need of a shortstop for a couple days. John Valentin had rolled his ankle and needed a day or two off. They only had one backup on the roster, so they called up Byrd. Who knows if he'll ever get the chance in the majors again, but now "former major leaguer" will forever follow his name.

He didn't get into a game to pinch hit or play defense. He didn't get any extra shoes or equipment out of the deal, and he was up and down so quickly, half the Red Sox probably didn't bother to learn his name. But I know they were the two most important days of his baseball life.

When he came back down to Pawtucket, we were playing in Columbus, Ohio. After the game we all piled into one of the those shuttle buses to go back to the hotel. I was one of the last guys out of the clubhouse and when I got on the bus there was only one seat left. It was dark and I kind of tripped over somebody trying to get to the seat. But when I got a few feet away I noticed Byrd was sitting there. He had shaved his head for a new look and to get out of a hitting slump, and he was wearing a dark-colored shirt. In the darkness and given that Jim is black, I didn't see him when I first looked — he just blended in, and I thought the seat was open.

I stood for the 20-minute ride back to the hotel thinking about what had just happened. My relationship with Byrd had survived the nigger-rig comment of a year ago and we were friendly again. As we all got off the bus, I stopped Jim and told him the story because I thought it was funny. He knew the reason I couldn't see him in that seat was because he was black, and when he heard the story he laughed too. A year earlier, I'm not sure he would have.

Bloody knees

The other day I looked at a scar on my knee that was almost healed up. I remembered a time during the season when my right knee was a permanent bloody scab that never totally healed. I'd slide on it again and again and tear the scar tissue off. I spent every off-season since I was 18 with purple knees from the permanent scar tissue that formed there. I have that same look on the inside of my elbows, also from sliding and diving for baseballs — a voluntary abuse of my body for something I loved to do. Hustle was always my trademark.

Before games I had the reputation of a hot dog. I'd catch balls behind my back, play games with other guys on the team and maybe had too much fun during batting practice. During the games I was serious—too afraid of making a mistake so I tried to be fundamentally sound, but after the game, I wanted to be the dirtiest guy on the field. I figured that if I wasn't bleeding, then I didn't play well.

So in 1992, when I was put in to pinch run and steal a base, I smiled when I saw the blood soak through the knees of my uniform. It was my first "strawberry" of 1992. It was a long time coming and something that didn't happen often enough.

Hidden talent

I think one of the greater challenges of our lives is to discover our own unique talents. Most artists and musicians find that they are so inclined at a very early age and then spend years refining and perfecting their expressions. Others are introduced to something enjoyable and try to turn it into a career — computers, numbers, sales, or in my case, baseball. There are, however, relatively few of us who truly get paid to do what they absolutely love. We all dream about a way to parlay those quirky hidden talents of ours into a career.

During the long hours of those 10-day road trips, there was always so much time to kill. Having spent so much time in the malls, I could rattle off the sale items and prices of every store from Crate and Barrel to The Gap. I even know those hard-to-find places like the nearest restroom or the exact location of the Radio Shack. If I ever needed a second job I'd be a natural as the guy who stands under the "Ask me, I know," sign.

But my true passion isn't the mall itself. It's just the best gathering place for what I really enjoy — people watching. I'll sit there for hours, with an under-my-breath comment to a buddy about almost everyone who walks by. Sometimes I feel bad if I start to get too critical of people (as if I'm perfect). I'll whisper, "Look at this guy. Who cuts his hair, Black and Decker?" or "How can that lady wear that dress? It's amazing what people can do with kitchen curtains these days."

But let's face it, some of the off-the-wall characters you see and the outfits they wear, just set themselves up for abuse. I would never be so mean as to comment directly to those people, so I don't think there's any harm. Over the years, the joy of people-watching has revealed my true hidden talent —comparing the looks of an average person to that of a well-known person. Every day I'll point out at least 20 people who look like someone else, and whoever I'm with always chuckles and agrees it's a good call. Everybody, at one time or another has played this game, but I'm somewhat obsessed — everybody looks like someone else to me!

Sometimes I question why I exert so much time and energy on such trivial things. Maybe I should be taking correspondence courses (I never actually graduated from college) or read more, or become better informed on national and global issues, plan for my future, stuff like that. Nah. Yesterday I saw a guy who was a dead ringer for Tom Hanks, and nobody else caught it. It was a good call and the more I think about it, I am the master of that game.

Trend setting

I don't think I have the type of personality or ego that demands credit for everything, but I must say that I was at the forefront of a few recent trends in baseball. I have a certain sense of style that I'm proud of, and even if everyone doesn't agree with it, I usually feel like I've made an impact. One of the things my Dad used to tell me when I was a kid was, "Always try to look good as a ballplayer. That way if you don't play well, you might fool somebody."

Of course he meant that as a humorous comment, but he did put a lot of emphasis on wearing a uniform the right way, so I looked like I knew how to play. I guess I always took that piece of advice a little too far.

In the late 1980s, the style on the field was to pull your stirrup socks up as far as you could, so that there were just two stripes running down your leg into your shoe. For the White Sox, Larry Himes had taken over as the general manager and was big on conformity and discipline. He didn't like the show of individualism by his players on the field, so he had a lot of petty rules to follow: No beer in the clubhouse, no wearing shorts to the ballpark, always wearing socks off the field (just to name a few).

A lot of guys were mad about it and felt they were being treated like children. Most of those rules didn't bother me. I always felt like I was paid to do what they asked me to do, so if they wanted me to wear socks, I'd wear socks.

The rule that had everyone the most upset though, was the new "stirrup sock rule." Himes expected everybody to show three inches of the blue stirrup socks in front of the leg and one inch in the back. Maybe he wanted us to look the same as a team, but he was asking us to look different from every other ballplayer. Showing that much of the stirrup just wasn't the style.

As the player representative, I caught all the complaints from the guys, and I was expected to do something about it. Since Himes wasn't the kind of guy who changed his mind about discipline, I just decided to take his rule to the extreme. If he wanted us to show blue, I'd show blue. I went to a department store and bought a pair of over-the-calf blue dress socks and started wearing them with my uniform. I wore my pants a little longer, put on my sanitary socks, and then pulled on those dress socks. I told everybody else to wear their socks any way they wanted, and if they got hit with the $50 fine, I would pay it.

We went on kind of a mini-winning streak after that, and even though he may have wanted to fine us all, he didn't. It's a funny thing how winning cures everything! Eventually I gave up my dress socks, but I had no idea how the style would catch on. In the 1992 World Series, we all saw the "low rider" style of stirrups worn by Twins pitcher Scott Erickson, and now many players don't wear stirrups at all — just a solid color pair of athletic socks.

Some recent trends, though, I don't want credit for. I didn't think I'd see anybody wearing hightops in baseball. Bill Buckner was the first for that. And the sunglasses everybody wears are more for style rather than effectiveness. But on April 12, 1992, I saw something even I couldn't believe. Two pitchers were dueling it out — the Braves' Tom Glavine and the Giants' Jeff Brantley. The weird thing was, Glavine was the first pitcher ever wearing hightops and Brantley was wearing sunglasses — and it was a night game!

Styles come and go in life and in baseball. My mom always said "If you wait long enough, the style will come back." Now, sideburns are back, and I feel like I was one of the first to bring that style to the game. Davey Martinez was the first player I ever saw wearing them, and I grew them because of my daughter. Her favorite show at the time was Beverly Hills 90210, and the fad hit its peak because of the actors in the show. Brady Anderson was the most famous sideburn-wearer because they coincided with his single, star status in Baltimore.

I also had the most influence on the resurgence of the goatee on white players. Black guys have always worn it, no big deal, but when white guys started doing it, it was a style statement. There are a lot of players now who wear goatees, like Ken Caminiti and Mark McGwire. The most famous white ballplayer with a goatee? Jack McDowell.

In 1990 we were always playing around with style and searching for a new look. I told him we should both grow goatees and see how ugly we could look. Jack said he couldn't do it because his beard didn't grow well around the corners of his mouth and it wouldn't fill in. He said he didn't mind looking ugly, he just didn't want to look stupid. Jack was 1-3 at the time and I wasn't playing much, so we made a deal — I wouldn't shave until I played, and he wouldn't until he lost another game.

I went into a game as a pinch runner seven days later, so I shaved after a week, but Jack rattled off eight straight wins. When he finally lost a game he had a full beard, and at that time,

I talked him into shaving down to the goatee. He went 14-10 in 1990 and has become one of the winningest pitchers in the 90s, including a 20-win season and a Cy Young Award. So don't look for him to shave it off anytime soon.

Later in my career I'd grow a goatee a couple of times a year and somebody would always ask why. I'd tell them I was hoping the pitchers wouldn't recognize me and throw me more fastballs to hit. It never worked.

The Oakland bash

The simple "handshake" in pro sports has taken on various forms, to say the least. Everybody seems to be trying to find a way to distinguish themselves from others by the way they congratulate each other. We've gone from the "high five" to the "low five" to some kind of choreographed hop-scotch type of ritual that takes too much time to remember. By far the best "handshake" going over the last five years, is in Oakland — the "forearm bash."

Whoever invented it created something not only uniquely his own, but also swept every little league ballpark in the nation. You don't see any other major leaguers do it if they don't play for the A's — the "bash" is theirs. It represented the high-powered, confident offense of the Hendersons (Rickey and Dave), Jose Canseco, and Mark McGwire, and those who continue to carry it on in Oakland, but in Oakland only. It's a sign of power for them, a victory sign, a way to show that at that very moment, they are the best they can be. No other "high fives" have remained so individualized yet so universal at the same time.

Sayings that stick

Do you ever wonder how certain sayings get started or why some stick and some don't? Why was a home run called a "tater," then a "dinger," and before that a "jack"? How do these phrases gain universal familiarity? Players at times don't get a hit, they get a "knock." "I need some knocks." Who invented that word? Why do teams have their own phrases? All the players on one team say a certain thing, but if you get traded to another team, nobody says it. In 1989, the big thing to say in Chicago was "Oh, really." So if somebody was getting on you about something, you never had to dignify his comments with an answer. You could simply say, "Oh, really." But it never came out quite like that. It always sounded more like, "O reeeleee." One guy starts saying it a few times and everybody catches on.

The White Sox also had a strange way of agreeing with people. Instead of saying "yes" they'd just say, "what a question." For example, "How's your leg today?" - "What a question." "Did you get all of that one?" "What a question." "Are we going out after the game?" — "Oh, what a question."

I was only with the Cubs for a short time, but there were some favorite sayings there as well. If they agreed with whatever you had to say, they never replied with, "Yeah, you're right." They'd always say "Believe it." Of course the saying found its way into too many conversations: "Hey nice play." - "Believe it!" "You gonna get something to eat?" - "Believe it." "Is it my turn to hit?" - "Believe it." Ironically, their other favorite thing to say was, "Oh No!" But it sounded more like this - "OOOOH No!" So now, they were covered if they disagreed with anything you said. It was impossible to go through the Cubs' clubhouse without hearing "Believe it," or "Oooh no," at least a couple of times every day.

Bruce Kison used a phrase I never heard before when we played together in Boston. "Long-tom him," he'd say. Just another way to say "Hey, hit a home run." I always kind of liked it, and carried it with me even after Kison retired. I tried not to use it too often, but damn if somebody wouldn't hit one out every once in awhile when I'd say it.

Kison is now the pitching coach at Kansas City, so considering who he has to spend most of his time with, he probably doesn't like to hear anybody say, "Long-tom him" when his guys are pitching.

Pat Keedy used to say "Bip!" whenever somebody got hit by a bad-hop grounder. I brought that along with me back to

Boston. Half the bench would yell it out anytime someone would get hit with a ball. Those kinds of things always got taken too far—we'd be inserting the word "Bip" even when it didn't apply just to be silly. Nobody ever knew where the word might pop up. One night Scott Cooper got drilled in the arm by a pitch and Wade Boggs just looked over at me and said, "He bipped him." It was funny at the time—maybe you had to be there.

Every year there was a new saying brought in from somewhere. Jargon has been a mainstay in sports forever, but probably more so in baseball than any other sport. The simple fastball has taken on so many names over the years: smoke, BBs, gas, hemp, bullets, cheese, and seeds, just to name a few. And how about the curve ball? Uncle Charlie, hook, downer, spinner, and hammer. I can't wait for 1995 and the new sayings and names the players will think up. Do you think there's any room for new ones? Believe it!

Shagging

Where did the word "shagging" come from? In all the years I played, I spent most of my time shagging. If you weren't into sports and you heard that word out of context, would any of us know what it meant? Kids love to shag. They'd give their right arm to get the chance to roam a major league outfield during batting practice just to shag balls.

"Shagging" is simply chasing down balls that somebody else hit and throwing them back only to be hit again. The desire to be a good shagger lessens as you get older. You start thinking, "Why the hell do I want to run way over there, pick that ball up, and toss it back? Isn't there anybody else closer?" For most older players, the last thing you want to do after taking ground balls and taking your turn at-bat, is shag everyone else's balls.

I think it was a smart coach who invented the game "500": 100 points if you catch a fly, 75 for a one bouncer, 50 for two bounces and 25 if the ball is still rolling. If you make an error, you deduct the number of points that ball was worth and if you go over 500, you start over. It was a popular game. Everybody always loved to play. Really, it was just the coaches' way to get everybody to shag.

Mother's Day at the Lyons'

Many people ask me how I made it to the major leagues, and what they can do to help their children. I never thought that there was one specific way to raise a major league baseball player, but I think there are some similar characteristics that all successful people have, for one thing, competitiveness. It's a major part of my make-up, that's for sure. Getting an "A" in my classes in high school was never enough. I had to do extra credit assignments to make sure I had the highest number of points in the class. I was the guy everybody hated because I threw the grading scale way out of whack just to make sure I was #1.

I do think, however, that my Dad really encouraged me to play baseball. I played it because that's what my dad knew. He said he spent two years camping in the Army and hated it, so we weren't a family that went fishing or camping. To this day I've never been snow skiing or ice skating, and just recently shot a gun for the first time. My dad knew football, basketball, and baseball - and that's what I learned.

I remember a typical Mother's Day for me and my three brothers while growing up. That special day for moms when they get breakfast in bed, don't have to clean the house or do the dishes all day. Instead, Mom gets a nice dinner and perhaps a movie later that night.

I can remember trying to comply with some of the rituals of Mothers' Day. I tried to be especially nice to her, but I don't quite remember it going that way at my house. My Mom spent Mothers' Day standing in centerfield. My Dad would pitch, I would hit, and it was her job to shag the balls and throw 'em back so I could hit some more. She didn't complain one bit, even though it was her day.

That's the way she was all the time. She would see three innings of my game, drive across town to see three innings of Randy's game, and then to a different park for three innings of

Michael's game. She always said she would rather watch us play then go out for a steak dinner. She saw how happy it made her sons, and that was enough for her. And every time we played, she was there to cheer us on.

The conspiracy behind
non-hitting pitchers

Did you ever wonder about the real reason why the designated hitter came to be? At what point did the pitchers in the American League become so bad at hitting that some management official came up with the concept of the designated hitter? The D.H. is the solution to a managerial dilemma: you have pitchers who are an embarrassment at the plate and some outstanding power hitters who can't field a ball to save their lives. So, in 1973, the D.H. was born, the brainchild of some frustrated manager.

It's simple to understand how some guys can hit and not field so well, but how can so many pitchers be such poor hitters? What happens to pitchers as they progress to the major leagues? From Little League through high school, the pitchers always seemed like the best all-around players, they could hit and pitch. What happened? Somebody should look into it. What about the National League pitchers? They can't hit either, but they refuse to relinquish their bats. Sometimes, it's embarrassing to watch.

It's not an issue most people waver on. You either like the D.H. or you don't, and it has become one of the most classic arguments in baseball. But the arguments don't really get to the heart of the issue: Why can't pitchers hit?

Baseball's best-hitting pitchers were Jack Stivetts and Walter Johnson. Stivetts ended his ten-year career in 1899 with a lifetime average of .297. Johnson holds the season record with a .440 average in 1925. And there are a host of others who have followed them with respectable batting averages as pitchers. Why didn't the relatively new phenomenon of pitchers being lousy hitters affect them?

There may be some sort of conspiracy. Who knows, I'm not a pitcher (I wasn't noted as much of a hitter either). Since only the

American League uses the D.H., why aren't there many good hitting pitchers in the National League? Does someone pull them aside and say, "Just work on your form and mechanics. Get that delivery fine tuned and try this new grip for your change-up. And by the way, you'll never hit much, so don't worry about it?" Is it just an assumption that because he's a pitcher he can't hit and he never will?

Would anyone ever tell a catcher to just work on being a good receiver and block balls in the dirt, but don't worry about hitting? If not, why do pitchers get away with it? The beauty of baseball is the all-around ability necessary to play well.

The best explanation for pitchers lacking ability at the plate is that they don't get to hit often enough — even when they do pitch. A starter only plays once every five days, hits ninth, and oftentimes doesn't last the whole game anyway. Relievers see even less at-bats. To me, this theory makes no sense, because it brings me back to my original argument. For one, if relievers were better hitters, they wouldn't have pinch hitters as often — they'd hit for themselves and pitch more innings. Secondly, I spent my whole career as a utility player. Sometimes the thought of playing every fifth day and batting ninth would be a dream come true. I hit .253 for my career, but there are very few modern-day pitchers who even approach those numbers.

Somewhere along the line from when this game was originally thought up to the way its played today, many changes have taken place. But when Mr. Doubleday himself threw that very first pitch, he knew he was onto something big. He knew this "game" he just invented would someday become baseball—the game to rise above all others. And as that pitch sailed through the strike zone and into the catcher's glove, he paused and thought for a moment. Then, with his heart pounding and a huge grin on his face, he ran in to grab a bat. You know why? Because he could hit!

Myers' donuts

Spring training is always the time for informational meetings and speeches. We heard from the FBI about gambling, from the local police about drinking, and of course, about the dangers of chewing tobacco. And sometimes these meetings were the setting for impeccable timing.

One day we had a closed-door meeting for 30 minutes with the team nutritionist. She was explaining to us that we all had to step up our intake of carbohydrates and reduce our fat intake at the same time. During the presentation, she was explaining all the various ways to accomplish her scale of 60 percent carbohydrates, 20 percent protein, and 20 percent fat. It's tough to have a meeting like that because nobody really cares to hear about getting fat — especially if you're an athlete. But everybody appeared to be listening and getting something out of it. Then, about 20 minutes into the meeting, there was a knock at the door. A delivery for relief pitcher Randy Myers: a dozen Dunkin Donuts and two Sausage McMuffins from McDonald's.

Living and dying by the schedule

My hat's off to whoever creates the schedule for major and minor league baseball games. Imagine, at the major league level, making sure 28 teams are all playing somewhere, but not interfering with other scheduled local events, such as the Republican National Convention (Houston '92), concerts, or tractor pulls, not to mention the football, basketball, or soccer games that are also played in the stadiums. They also must assure each team of one day off every three weeks. How they figure out who starts where and who ends where is a mystery to me. And why does Cincinnati always play the season's first game?

As much of a headache as it must be to put together the schedule, it's at least that to play it. Let's put aside the glamorous view of the game and try to put it into perspective.

Saturday afternoon, while you were picnicking with your family and friends, having a few beers at the beach, somebody mentioned they had tickets for tomorrow's game. Casually turning your attention to the radio, it's the third inning, Sox up 7-2. "Yeah, " you say. "They've been playing great lately, it might be fun." It didn't even cross your mind that while you were sunning, I was working.

After a dinner, movie, and a night out on the town, you're in bed, thinking about tomorrow's day at Fenway. I've just showered and am driving home, knowing that with a 1 p.m. start tomorrow, it's going to be a short night. By the way, I'll see that movie four months later on video–after somebody's told me all about it anyway. No time for movie going now.

On Sunday, it's another great summer day. You and your three buddies spend the day pounding down pretzels and Fenway franks and arguing about everything from the D.H. to who was better, Mantle or Mays. The Sox win 3-1 and are in the American League East pennant race. I remember it being a great day also— but it wasn't quite the same for me. I was working. It was that schedule I had to follow. Much like the one you follow, but at the opposite time. You see, that schedule guy knows that if you're working while I'm working, it's no good. I have to work when it's your leisure time.

Monday comes and your schedule re-enters your life. Everybody has one. After a 9 to 5 job, you come home, roll around with the kids, have pot roast for dinner (your favorite) and crash in that recliner in front of the tube. "What's on?" you wonder as you channel surf through your cable system. "Hey, the Red Sox!"

Right away you notice that we are now wearing our road grey uniforms instead of those crisp classic home white ones. And that's not Fenway Park—hell, you were just there not more than 24 hours ago. That's Anaheim Stadium. Checking your Red Sox schedule, you see a 14-game road trip beginning for the Sox. "Wow," you think, "I just saw those guys yesterday in Boston, now they're in California?" You're amazed, but you're catching on. It's just my schedule.

We don't really work when those schedule guys tell us. We work when the T.V. man says. I've spelled it out before and we all know what bottom line matters. The last national T.V. package put about $40 million per year in each of the owners' pockets, so when the T.V. man spits, we swim.

That's why my schedule says play on Sunday night in Minnesota instead of Sunday at 1 p.m. It's a national T.V. game. Never mind that we play the next day in Boston. Nothing like getting home when the sun comes up and going back to the park by 3 p.m. Grab a sandwich, kiss the wife, see ya—it's my schedule.

I still have friends who don't understand. "Come visit for a couple days," they say. "Call in sick, you don't really play every day, do you?" The whole thing makes me think about my high school basketball coach. He was a tough S.O.B., but he taught me a valuable lesson. He said, "There's only three reasons to miss practice—your mother dies, your father dies, or you die." I didn't know it then, but he was setting me up for the rest of my professional life—he was preparing me for my schedule.

It's not polite to steal

OK, top of the ninth, two out, two on, and you're getting beat 7-5. You have a great view of what's going on, because you're the guy on second base. Marty Barrett's on first and the guy at the plate is Wade Boggs. You're thinking, "OK Wade, if ever there was a time for you to try to hit a home run this is it."

"Ball one," says the umpire. On your way back to second you check everything—just like a good baserunner always does. You check the positioning of the outfielders to see where they are. You have to know if they can or can't catch a bloop single and determine how difficult it will be to score on a sharp liner. You check the second baseman to make sure he can't pick you off with a planned play between him and the pitcher and you point at the third base coach, reminding him to let you know where that shortstop is because you can't see him.

"Come on Boggsie, air one out!" you're thinking. "Strike one," yells the umpire.

You start the same process over again, check the fielders, think about your lead, and prepare yourself to get the best jump possible. But this time it's different. You can hear somebody but it's not clear. Then you notice it's Barrett. He's whispering to you—from 90 feet away. He's shielding his mouth with his left hand and pointing to the pitcher with his right.

"If you get a good jump, go!" He yells, under his breath. He's pointing at Milwaukee pitcher Mark Clear. You remember him because last year he played with you and Marty with the Red Sox. You remember his extremely high leg kick and slow release out of his stretch. You remember his slow roundhouse curveball, and you remember how more than 40 baserunners in a row were successful when trying to steal against him.

Marty Barrett was always regarded as one of the smartest players to ever play the game. Like having another manager on the field with you. So you pause for a split second to pat yourself on the back for getting his clues. "Yes," you think to yourself, "perfect."

With Clear's slow move to the plate and Wade Boggs being the greatest singles hitter since Pete Rose, all you and Barrett have to do is pull off a double steal and you're a hero. If Boggs hits the next pitch for a single, you and Barrett score and of course, you go on to win the game.

So now you put your plan into action. You begin to get your lead. Nobody's paying that much attention to you, so you get a little more. Clear goes into his stretch and looks you back a little but he's not too concerned with you either. Another half step— you can hear the third base coach yell, "you're all right, you're all right." Your heart starts to race a little more as you try to read Clear's first movement towards home. Another half step is all you need for a great lead, and you're now in position to pivot and explode toward third.

Clear turns back to focus on the catcher's glove and all at once lifts his left leg to the plate. Like all good basestealers, you cross your left leg over your right and you're off! DON'T DO IT!

What I know and you don't is how this story ends. It was me who got thrown out at third base. Game over. Never make the third out at third base. Never steal third with two outs. Never take the bat out of Wade Boggs' hands (he was batting .400 at the time). Never steal a base if you don't have the steal sign from the coach. Are we getting this?

I had a great jump—and it was a bang, bang play at third. Catcher Rick Cerone made a perfect throw to get me. What I didn't stop to think about was how bad the play was if it didn't work. I didn't know that Mark Clear had totally changed his motion since joining the Brewers to make himself quicker. I should have thought about Boggs being a left handed hitter—making Cerone's throw to third unobstructed.

I should have known how much trouble I'd have been in if it didn't work. Above all, I should have known that it was just a stupid play.

As I slid head first into third base, I was met with a call I hadn't taken the time to consider. "Out!" When I looked up, I was staring right into our dugout. Right at Manager John McNamara. He was staring back in disbelief. Never in my career as a ballplayer did I feel more alone. I couldn't hide, I couldn't crawl under the third base bag, and I couldn't find a friend.

I sat on the bench for 15 minutes, scared to face my teammates or the media. Finally, one of the clubhouse kids told me "Mac" wanted to see me. When I got upstairs and into the clubhouse, McNamara was waiting for me and yelled, "You better just keep walking straight into my office."

He screamed at me for awhile, told me it was the stupidest play he'd ever seen in all his years managing, and fined me $300. Then he did something I still don't understand. He benched me for the next game. I guess that's what everybody does, but does that mean he thought I'd get to be a better player and make less mistakes by not playing anymore?

I still had to face the media. I was embarrassed, tired and pissed—the last thing I wanted to do was answer their stupid questions about my stupid play. For the first and only time, I was uncooperative with the press. When the first question was asked, "What happened?," I said, "I fucked up, go write that in your papers. That's all I have to say."

I only made two more appearances in a Red Sox uniform that year before being traded a month later to the White Sox.

Physicals

"Physical Day" was one of the worst days of spring training. Waiting all day with the other guys on the team to have eye tests, blood work, and an EKG. They weigh you, poke you, and

hook you up to machines. They always want a urine sample —
I hated that. Every time I went back into the bathroom to pee in
the cup I couldn't do it! I ran the water, I tried to make myself
nervous, and even drank a lot of water before I went. It took me
forever to get the job done. But that wasn't even the worst part
of the physical. They tested your reflexes, looked into your ears,
and weighed you. Stupid things really. They were just trying to
get you to relax because we knew that eventually we'd have to go
to that room down the hall. The one with the real doctor in it. The
one where the physical gets serious. The rectal exam!

Everybody joked when it was your turn to head down the
hall, but they knew it would soon be their turn. You'd start to
sweat as soon as your name was called, and the doctor did his
best to make small talk with you as he'd slip on those rubber
gloves. Your mind starts racing, trying to come up with a good
excuse as to why you shouldn't have to do this. What the hell is
a rectal exam for, anyway? What are they checking for? And isn't
there an easier way to do it?

My trance is broken by the doctor saying "Please slip down
your pants and bend over the table." Now I'm usually panicking,
thinking back to the jokes of my teammates. Second baseman
Mark Lemke had laughed, saying he liked his doctor, because
usually they put one hand on your shoulder to steady themselves
and comfort you — but his doctor did the exam with both hands
on his shoulders. Another guy said it hurt more than he thought
it would and when he turned around and pulled up his pants he
noticed the doctor washing off his forearm. Some guys were
saying that they were asked to come back again the next day!
Then, all of the sudden it was over. "You can get dressed now,"
said the doctor. I barely even felt it! It was no big deal. Not
something I'd want to do on a daily basis, but a yearly physical,
I could handle it.

As I walked out of the office and back down the hall to my
teammates, I adopted a limp and had a painful look on my face.
I had to make everybody think it was going to be terrible. I'm a
guy — it's what we do.

Taylorisms

I don't think it's any big surprise that I'm not a Rhodes scholar. I've made mistakes and done stupid things. I've really tried hard to make sure I haven't been too hard on anybody in these pages but sometimes I just can't hold back.

Every team usually has a guy or two who keeps them loose. He may be a great team leader and outstanding player, but he knows how to have fun. He might be a team clown or a guy who's just naturally funny. Sometimes it's the team idiot, or the guy nobody likes, who can often provide some comic relief.

In Pawtucket, the two guys were Bob Geren and Scott Taylor. Geren never shut up and did a killer impersonation of Rodney Dangerfield. Taylor was a left-handed pitcher who had no idea when everyone else was ripping him. Geren was merciless with Taylor. They were like a comedy team: nonstop bantering day after day.

Taylor brought so much of the abuse on himself. He wasn't smart enough to just shut up. Every time he opened his mouth, he'd step right into another trap. Everything he said became known as a "Taylorism." Here are some of the classics: "I'd use the rosin bag but I don't know how." "I don't watch sports on TV, I hate baseball, and I don't like comedy — I don't think it's funny." "Best pizza I've ever eaten? McDonald's Pizza. I love eating it the night before I pitch, because I have to have pasta that night."

When he got called up to Boston in September of 1992 we were playing in Detroit. When second baseman Lou Whitaker came up to bat, Taylor asked "Is he the guy that was in jail?" No Scottie, that was Ron LeFlore - a long time ago. Geren couldn't leave him alone. He nicknamed Taylor "Bang-Man" because he was the only guy ever to wear a spike hair cut with his bangs combed down over his forehead. He laughed at him at the team party when we went to a nice place to eat dinner. He said, "Bang-Man, let me help you order, I'm sure you've never had a menu in your hands. You're used to ordering from that board on the wall behind the girl at the counter." In spring training of 1991, President Bush visited the Red Sox clubhouse before the game. "Who's that?" Taylor asked.

He got on a kick one year when he ate nothing but Chinese food for months. He said it was the best diet he could ever be on. He finally quit when he noticed he had gained 15 pounds.

One night the Bang-Man was getting blasted and was pissed off that one particular guy from the other team had gotten a hit off him. He came storming off the field in a rage and announced, "That's it, next time he gets it, so be ready." Of course everybody knows that when a pitcher is that mad and makes a statement like that, somebody on the other team is gonna get drilled. I wasn't sure exactly why he was so upset, so I asked him, "Are you going to hit him?" "Nah," he said. "I've been working on a knuckleball - next time up, he gets it."

It got out of control as a team when Geren learned that Taylor wasn't going to be with us for that night's game. We were fighting for a berth in the International League playoffs with just two games left in the regular season, and we had to win. Taylor asked for the night off so he could attend his wife's 10-year class reunion. We were dying! First of all nobody asks for a day off in baseball. You just don't do it — unless something very serious has happened. But sure as hell not for a class reunion — and it wasn't even his, it was his wife's! None of us were mad, we just thought it was unbelievably ridiculous. Someone put a line-up card in our locker room that was titled "Taylor's High School Reunion Softball Classic." Each guy on the team took turns listing a player in the lineup, and we hung it in his locker for the next day.

Taylor was lucky the season was about to end because he would have been buried by all of us after that. Geren is now a coach in the Red Sox organization, and Taylor was released in 1994. In hindsight, maybe Taylor was really the smart one. After all, he did get permission to go to the reunion.

Riley's Fan Section
_____

Most players agree that one of the biggest hassles about playing in the big leagues is dealing with people who want tickets to the games. People you haven't heard from in years are your team's biggest fans now that you play for them — and were just wondering if you had any extra tickets to the game.

The tickets that are left by the organization for the players can also be used to negotiate deals. Many of the players trade their tickets to a car dealer in exchange for the use of a car during the season. Others get reduced rates on rental furniture or other items.

Of course, we get the tickets from the team, so players' families can all sit in a somewhat protected area of the stadium and enjoy the game without being bothered by anybody. Each player was allowed six tickets per game—four family tickets and two guest tickets. The guest section is supposed to be for friends, and although it's usually still a good seat, they aren't with the families.

Every year without fail, there are problems that arise in the family section. Somebody leaves tickets for a friend of a friend who ends up getting drunk and obnoxious. People wander into the section without those tickets and badmouth our starting pitcher while his wife and children sit two rows in front of them.

One night I followed Rick Miller into the box seats during a game in Anaheim. He noticed someone bothering his family and off he went. Hell, I was a rookie, and wasn't sure why I was going. All I knew was that Miller's shirt said "Red Sox," so I was there to help if he needed me. When we got there, he put one guy in a headlock and told another guy to "back off." The stadium police arrived quickly and calmed the situation down. We both headed back down to the field and Miller was promptly ejected from the game. Going into the stands for any reason is cause for ejection, but I would have done the same thing. Some things are worth it. Our families want to feel safe and somewhat secluded from the rest of the fans. People can get very cruel at those games, and the "family section" has become a necessity in every ball park.

Sometimes the most difficult problem you have as a player is saying "no" to everyone who wants a ticket. In my rookie season in 1985, I left 43 tickets in Minnesota. I'm not even from Minnesota, but my aunt and uncle are, and by the time I asked them how many tickets they needed, they had invited half their town to come and see their nephew play ball. I had to borrow tickets from everybody on the team to have enough. Dwight

Evans saw me listing out every ticket I needed and said, "Hey Rook, learn how to say no."

By far the strangest thing I ever saw in the family section happened in Pawtucket in 1993. Ed Riley, a local guy from Worcester, left 32 tickets for the game since he was the starting pitcher that night. Riley is one of 16 kids, and most of his brothers and sisters were on hand to cheer him on, thoroughly dominating the family section.

In the sixth inning, "Riles" was beginning to tire. We were leading 1-0, but after one out, Riley surrendered a walk and a base hit. With runners on first and third, Manager Buddy Bailey decided to pull Riley in favor of right hander Jose Melendez. Riley had done a nice job, but it was the right move to get him out of there at that point. However, his family didn't see it that way. Several of his brothers stood up and yelled in disbelief. "What are you doing? How can you take him out, Buddy? That's bullshit! That's why you'll never manage in the big leagues, that's bullshit!"

I was playing first base that night and I was kind of enjoying the scene, thinking, "I've never seen anything like this before." But Ben Mondor, who owns the team, wasn't enjoying it. At Pawtucket, they pride themselves on an honest deal and a family atmosphere at the ballpark. Within seconds, General Manager Mike Tamburo was in the stands trying to calm the Riley family.

They couldn't be restrained. "Bullshit, that's my brother. He should still be pitching, that's bullshit!" For some reason, I began counting the "bullshits" and tallied 14 before three staff ushers and four uniformed police officers escorted the Rileys out of McCoy Stadium. Four cops! Ed Riley's family got kicked out of the family section and certain members were asked never to return!

It was a strange sight to look into the family section and suddenly see a whole group of seats now vacated, only minutes after it had been packed.

The next day I asked Ed what he thought about what had happened. He said he thought it was great. "Imagine," he said, "having so much support from your brothers that they get more upset than I do about me getting taken out of a game."

No bullshit!

The Radinsky Quiz

Scott Radinsky, "Rad," has developed into one of the more feared left-handed relievers in the American League. But he'll never be accused of being a brain surgeon. When he first made the big-league team during the shortened 1990 spring training season, he had been a veteran of three minor league seasons as a pitcher. Everybody knows that the catcher gives signs to the pitcher to tell him what pitch— one finger: fastball, two fingers: curve, three fingers: slider, etc. When an opposing runner reaches second base, there is always the fear that he may watch the catcher, see the signs, and relay them to his teammate, the hitter.

So to prevent this from happening, the catcher changes his signs to a series of numbers instead of flashing just one sign. It's been done this way since the beginning of time and there are three or four ways that are fairly popular, easy to understand and well known to any pitcher in his fourth season. One way is to determine which sign was actually the "live" sign or the pitch that the catcher actually wanted you to throw. The catcher would come out to the mound and say, we've got a guy on second, we'll put down four signs and whatever sign was second, the pitcher would throw that pitch.

As time goes by, that gets easier for the other team to figure out, so you may have to change to a different sequence. Another way to do it is called "first sign indicator," which means whatever sign he flashes first is the order in which the "live" sign is found. So if he starts with a three, the live pitch is the third sign. If he starts with a four, the fourth sign the pitcher sees is the pitch he's supposed to throw.

Let's do a little quiz.

If you are the pitcher and you know you're using "first sign indicator," what pitch do you throw when the catcher puts his fingers down in this order?

2, 1, 3, 2

How about this one: 3, 1, 3, 2

And finally: 1, 2, 2, 1

If you said fastball, slider, fastball, you're right. If you said something else, you crossed up your catcher and he hates you.

Radinsky had a slight problem with all of this. Granted it was only a spring training game, but still, it's baseball. I'm playing second base, Jerry Willard is the catcher, and we bring Radinsky in to pitch. In our little meeting on the mound, Jerry tells Rad, "You got guys on first and second and one out. Let's use first sign indicator. This guy hitting is a first-pitch fastball guy, so let's start him off with a curveball, OK?"

Rad looked at him funny and said, "No, what's 'first sign indicator' mean?'"

Now you all know what it means, because you've been reading the book, but Rad should have known because at that time he had pitched in professional baseball for four years. Jerry and I looked at each other in disbelief and Jerry started explaining to Rad (while on the mound, mind you) how to do first sign indicator.

"We don't have time for this now." I said, "Let's make it easy, go with second sign—do you know second sign, Rad?" "Yeah," he said, and Jerry responded, "OK, second sign, let's start this guy off with a curve ball." We all say "great," and go back to our positions.

Now, Rad is a nasty lefty who has about a 94 M.P.H. fastball and a good slider and had been working on his curve that spring. When he looked in for the sign, Jerry gives him exactly what he said he would.

1, 2, 1, 3—curveball.

Rad winds up and throws him a fastball as hard as he can throw it. When a catcher is expecting a curveball that travels about 80 M.P.H. and curves from his right to left, but gets a 92 M.P.H. that's straight as an arrow, it's a little tough getting a glove on it.

The ball smoked Willard right in the chest. Some balls just hit you and bounce off, and some balls hit you so hard they sort of stick to you until you feel how bad it hurts. This one stuck on Willard so long he was able to cradle it with his arm before dropping to his knees in pain.

I'm at second base laughing my ass off and Jerry's steaming, back on his way to the mound. By the time I get there, I only hear the tail end of the tongue-lashing Rad's getting, but I'm there in time to hear Willard say, "Screw it, I don't give a shit if every hitter knows what's coming. I'm giving you one sign, throw that pitch. Do you think you can handle that?"

Since then, Radinsky has learned enough about pitching to fulfill his promise of being a dominating left-handed reliever.

Out of nowhere in 1994, Radinsky was diagnosed with Hodgkin's disease. While missing the entire season with his chemotherapy and rehabilitation, he vowed to be pitching again by August 1994. Unfortunately, the strike ended his quest for a comeback. The White Sox re-signed Rad for the '95 season. Let's hope during his time off he didn't forget the signs.

Front runners

It seems to me that the game of baseball is built around defeats rather than successes. I've already discussed how, if you're a hitter you can make seven outs in ten at-bats and still be considered a great player.

As players, we find ourselves becoming front runners in a game where that type of behavior isn't tolerated. For instance, whenever a pitcher does well, he is wholeheartedly congratulated by all his teammates in the dugout when he comes out of the game. But if he doesn't do well, everybody avoids the guy at all costs, as if he's their worst enemy. No pat on the back, no "hang with 'em" — nothing. The guy grabs his jacket and heads for the showers, feeling like a failure, and what's worse, like everybody could care less.

Front runners are everywhere on baseball clubs. You can be a front-runner even if you're not an athlete, it just takes on another name, "fair-weather fan." For the players, it's the guy waiting in front of his locker when he's 3 for 4 with three RBIs looking for a reporter to talk to — but hides in the trainer's room after an 0 for 4 and an error. He's loud and happy, chirping all the time when things are going well for him, but moody and hard to find when it's not going his way. We all know one or two, but we all try hard not to be labeled as one — and most would probably deny it.

Catch me if you can

They say a good writer will never write about something he hasn't experienced first hand. That challenges his credibility. To write a detailed account from the eyes of a catcher I cannot do, but I did catch a game or two, and can adequately discuss my feelings and observations about when I did. Catching is by far the toughest and most demanding position on the field. The intense concentration and awareness a catcher needs are not easily learned. Often, major league players change positions for a variety of reasons — outfielders become first basemen, catchers go to third base, shortstops turn into second basemen, and so on. But when was the last time an outfielder, second baseman, or pitcher moved to catcher? Especially for a spring training experiment. It takes years of seasoning to become a decent receiver. To be comfortable crouched in an uncomfortable position, to throw yourself willingly at the mistake pitches (they don't call catcher's gear the "tools of ignorance" for nothing), and to learn to "call" the game with intelligence are all things that can't be learned overnight.

Think about this — better yet, try it. Squat like a catcher does, just for a minute — if you can do it that long. Now imagine, if you can, a slider coming at you about 82 miles per hour and biting hard towards the dirt. You expect it to be thrown about 62 feet, but this one max's out at about 58 feet. What's your reaction? Damn right. Turn your head and bail out. Not if you're a catcher. They drop to their knees, tuck their chin and block that ball with whatever they can to make sure it doesn't get by them. And like anything else, they practice this move in spring training over and over to make sure they remember how.

This is one of the most overlooked plays in the game today. It's a 2-2 game in the eighth, a guy on third, two outs. The catcher calls for a curveball. The pitcher bounces it and the catcher blocks the ball with his chest protector, keeps it in front of him, and casually tosses it back. Everybody else acts just as casual about it because very few of us know just how difficult and important it is that he blocks that pitch. But if he doesn't, a run scores and the team loses. But because he did, the hitter pops up the next pitch and they're out of the inning. But does anybody say anything to him? No. He's a catcher — it's his job.

Now let's back up a step and put ourselves in that same situation. You just blocked that pitch in the dirt. You've got the hitter thinking off speed, so you decide to call for a fastball up and in.

This time the guy hits the ball nine miles and you lose anyway. The crowd is booing and throwing stuff at the pitcher but who takes the heat in the dugout? You do. Why? Because when something goes wrong they always second-guess the catcher. "How can you call for a fastball right there?" the manager asks. "You had him set up for another breaking ball, you gotta use your head back there." And even your gutless pitcher throws in his two cents, "Yeah, I was thinking curve ball, but he wanted the fastball." You feel like killing the guy or saying "Hey, asshole, I just called the pitch, I wasn't the one who threw it right down Broadway with a sign hanging on it saying ,'Hit me!'" But most don't. Most bite their tongue and take it — because they're catchers.

Imagine catching on one of those beautiful Sunday day games. It's about 90 degrees, the fans are in shorts and bikinis, the beer and soda are flowing — it's definitely a picnic-type atmosphere at the game. Not for the catcher. With all that gear on, it becomes about 110 degrees, and every hitter who comes up digs in and sprays dirt and dust all over you while you sit and wait.

You've got a bruise on the inside of your thigh as big as a dinner plate and gravity has pulled the excess blood in your leg down to your knee to make a pretty rainbow of colors. Just a little reminder of that foul tip you got four days ago. Your right thumb is heavily taped because of that ball you blocked last night. You can barely throw the ball back to the pitcher, so God knows how you'll throw out a base stealer. And to top it off, you're facing Roger Clemens today — just hoping he doesn't jam you because you don't know if that thumb can handle it. But when the umpire says, "Play ball!" you squat in that familiar stance, forget about the pain and let your training and instinct take over — because you're the catcher.

So why does anybody want to catch? From the conversations I've had with catchers and from my own experience back there, it's the power of the position that keeps them coming back.

It can be the most exhilarating position on the field when things go well. Knowing what the pitcher wants to throw even before he does. And he's having the type of day where he can hit the glove any place you put it. That's what being a catcher is all about. Out-thinking the hitter by never throwing the pitch he's looking for, or at least not in the spot he's looking for it. Running the team, controlling the game, being counted on — that's catching. When a pitcher throws a no-hitter, everybody congratulates the pitcher. The people who know baseball congratulate the catcher. He's the one who put down the right fingers all day, the pitcher just had a great day of following instructions.

They'll never invent a tougher job in the game than catcher. Often overlooked or taken for granted, isn't it ironic he only gets noticed when he makes a mistake?

Defensive Replacement

Isn't it strange how whenever somebody enters the game late as a defensive replacement, the first ball of that inning always seems like it gets hit to him?

Real respect (?)

I always wondered how guys in baseball gained respect off the field from their teammates and others. The guys with outstanding baseball ability always have an advantage over those who don't. Everybody wants to get close to those guys. You see people hanging on every word they say, just because they're good players. All of a sudden, their social or political views are valued—or at least, noted, and they have friends who come out of the woodwork to hang out with them. It has been my experience that you don't have to look all that hard to find a decent, well-rounded, educated ball player—but let's face it, you don't have to look long to find a borderline idiot who plays the game, either. So if there are just as many guys on either side of the talent level—good to marginal, why do so many of the idiots get a lot of respect off the field, just because they know what they're doing on it?

What's my line?

Recognition off the field is a significant part of any pro-athlete's life. There are times when it's a flattering experience and there are many more times when you'd rather go unnoticed. Early in the career, when it's new, there's that hunger for attention. But as time goes on, they find that sometimes it's more of a hassle than it's worth. Eventually, there are rarely introductions such as, "Hi, I'm Joe Blow, I play baseball for the Red Sox." As the years passed, we used different ways to introduce ourselves to people we didn't care about, especially when a group of us might be out getting something to eat or at a bar having a drink.

We've pretended to be roadies for the circus or a local band. We've said that we were in town for a convention of dentists or even frozen seafood distributors. I remember a girl told me once that her dad was also a seafood distributor and she asked what company I worked for. "Birds-Eye" I said. Right away she knew I was lying and she said "Birds-Eye only sells frozen vegetables!"

I finally settled on one story that I liked, I would say that I sold computers for IBM, mainly because I didn't want to talk about baseball. It was easier to come up with BS answers if anyone asked me questions about my business.

I told them I could set them up with a personal computer called a P72 that would handle all their household usage's: letters, tax forms, games, and so forth. Or if they wanted to have more capabilities, they could move into a C243 that could also handle specific business needs they may have. After that, they assumed I knew what I was talking about, and was really boring them, and they felt I was trying to sell them something — so they'd leave me alone. P72 and C243 are the bat model numbers that I used during the season and have nothing to do with computers. I own a personal computer and haven't touched it in two years — I have no idea how it works.

Hit this

Mark Wohlers is a promising young closer for Atlanta, and I got to know him during my time with the Braves in 1992. He possesses a fastball in the low- to mid-90s, and at times, had a good slider and change-up. He's also a soft-spoken, kind-hearted gentleman, which is rare these days. We met again later in 1992, playing against each other; Pawtucket vs. Richmond. Since we are friends, and he is a guy who loves a challenge, I figured he wanted nothing more than to strike me out. Just to get me out wasn't enough. And I figured he'd do it with his power pitch — the fastball, even though he knew that's what I'd be looking for. When he came to the game that night, I got a chance to test my theory. His first two pitches were just what I thought they'd be—hard fastballs. But he's got a great fastball and I couldn't get good wood on either of them, fouling both off. Then, out of nowhere, he struck me out with a nasty slider.

The next night, I saw him before the game and ragged on him for throwing the slider. Jokingly, I told him he had no guts. Why doesn't a guy who throws 95 M.P.H. use his fastball? He said he wanted to, but manager Chris Chambliss had made the call from the bench. And when the manager calls a pitch, you don't shake it off. "You'll get your chance again," Wohlers said, "and next time I'll throw nothing but heat." "I'll be looking for it," I said, as I went to get ready for the game. It was another close game that night, and I knew I'd get my chance to see his fastball when they brought him in to finish the game.

With the score 2-1, Richmond, and one out with the bases empty in the ninth inning, I got my chance. The first pitch I saw was a fastball, and I laced it down the right field foul line — just foul. The next pitch was a slider that I swung at and missed. When Mark got the ball back, he knew I was glaring at him as if to say, "Hey, where's that challenge we both knew was supposed to take place." He looked at me, then looked into his dugout and shrugged his shoulders as if to say "They're calling the signs."

So I turned towards their dugout searching for Chambliss, who I admire very much as a manager, and like a lot as a person. We had spent some time together during a Braves caravan, and later worked well together in spring training. When I found him at the nearest end of their dugout, I made sure we had eye contact and stuck my tongue out at him. He kind of laughed and yelled out at me, "What's that for?" But he knew what it was for — I wanted Wohlers' fastball, and he didn't want him to throw it.

Mark Wohlers is the kind of guy where in his mind, a deal is a deal. I think he has a code of ethics that we'd all be proud to have as our own — and I knew in his mind it was time to let the challenge begin.

With the 0-2 count, I stepped back into the box and studied Wohlers as he took his signs. He shook off the first sign as if to say, "No, no sliders." Then he shook another sign off — a change-up, no doubt. Then he stepped off the rubber to let everybody know he wanted to start over, and by doing that, it was almost as if he shouted to everybody in the stadium, "I want to throw him a fastball! I throw 95 M.P.H. Here it comes. Let's see if you can hit it!" When he got back on the rubber, there was no hesitation on his face when he took the sign. I knew what was coming, Chambliss knew what was coming. Hell, the soda vendors knew what was coming.

This was the war we were both waiting for. We all knew that if he threw the slider or change-up or something out of the strike zone, I'd probably chase it and strike out. But this wasn't about getting somebody out anymore — this was about honor and courage. This was the challenge of Wohlers being a power pitcher and me a fastball hitter — his strength against mine.

I tapped my spikes a couple of times and dug in at the plate. I zeroed in on his face so much that I could see the sweat dripping off his nose. There was no longer any hesitation in his gaze towards the catcher — he was only expecting one sign. As he started his wind-up it seemed as if he was in slow motion until he released his pitch. He fired a fastball as hard as any pitch I'd ever faced at any level in my career.

Even though I had two strikes, I had no thoughts of just a "protecting the plate with a compact put-the-ball-in-play swing."

I was going to put my hardest swing against his hardest pitch and see what happened. I felt like I began to swing my bat at the same instant he released the ball, attacking a white blur as it sailed high through the strike zone. The pitch was fouled straight back and out of play. I detected the scent of burning leather, as you sometimes can after fouling off a pitch.

Wohlers got a new ball from the umpire. He took his glove off and rubbed the ball down with both hands, trying to raise the seams for a better grip. As he walked around the mound he removed his cap and wiped the sweat off his forehead with the sleeve of his glove hand and returned to the rubber. I was looking for any crack in the armor of his promise to throw fastballs. There was none, and for the second time I was a part of baseball's most classic theme: ninth inning, game on the line, pitcher against hitter.

This time, Wohlers was even more focused. He was in a confident rhythm, and I felt like I should do something to break his concentration. Just as I began to motion for time-out to regroup my own thoughts and make him start over, he began his motion to the plate. It was too late. In the next two seconds, I had to reposition myself in the batter's box, blink my eyes, and refocus on his release point. His thundering fastball shot out of his arm like an assassin's bullet. I tightly gripped the bat and made a stride toward the oncoming missile, shifting my hips and swinging my weapon with bad intent. My follow-through knocked my body off balance as I stumbled out of the box and toward first base. The ball shot off my bat high into the night sky as all eyes adjusted to its flight.

Wohlers gathered himself in reaction — his eyes stayed glued to me. He knew that I would tell him how well I hit the ball by my movements and actions on my way down the line. I knew where the ball would land, there was no doubt in my mind. The competitive frustration began to show and Wohlers knew it. His worries were over with a feeling of triumph soon to follow.

As I rounded the first base bag, the ball harmlessly landed in the centerfielder's glove. A high pop-up was what I got for my efforts. The mind games, the concentration, the posturing — it was all over, and I came up empty. Wohlers knew he had won our little war within the battle of the game itself. As I ran towards him on my way back to the dugout, he continued to stare me down — trying to pull off an act of intimidation that just isn't him. As I got closer to the mound I just chuckled a little bit and he started to laugh. Nothing was really said between us — nothing had to be. Wohlers knew he had gained my respect based on that battle. What he didn't know was that he had it long before we ever played that game.

During the 1992 World Series, I watched Wohlers make a couple of appearances against the Minnesota Twins. He had been called up by the Braves and had pitched well in relief. His fastball was consistently clocked from 97 to 100 M.P.H., and I knew what those hitters were going through. Sitting on my couch far away from the game, I'm sure I felt a lot more comfortable than those hitters did.

Umpires

Throughout my career, I always seemed to throw in my two cents with the umpires. I never really knew if it was because I didn't know when to keep my mouth shut, or if I just had to make my point.

After only two months in the National League I'd already been taught who the good and bad umpires were. What makes a good or bad umpire? To me it's the enthusiasm for their job and the game itself. American League umpire Al Clark was always one of my favorites. He might not be the best umpire, but he was pleasant, happy to be in/at the game, he hustled, and he'd take a little shit if you thought he missed a call. I used to tease him about being the only umpire in the game who wore his name on his hat.

The biggest gripes that players always have is that the umpires sometimes don't look and act like they care about their jobs, they become very defensive when they're questioned, and they rarely admit when they miss a call. My Dad gave me a great piece of advice when I was a kid telling him about a game that we would have won if it wasn't for the stupid umpires. He told me that an umpire will never, ever beat you in any game you play.

And I wholeheartedly believe it to be true. Bad calls are a part of the game, and there are actually a lot fewer bad calls than you'd think (most of the time you think they missed a call, when you see it again on the replay, they are usually right).

You as a player have many opportunities to win a game, during the game. The umpires will never dictate that much of the game to beat you. Being an umpire is also an extremely difficult job. Most of us know the rules of the game, but their job is mostly judgment: ball or strike, safe or out. That's where the arguments come in. Very rarely do you see an argument on a specific ruling.

Jerry Nudecker was one of the last American League umpires to wear the outside "pillow" chest protector. He had a unique strike call: it sounded like he was saying, "strike-a-hike."

He once called a high pitch a strike on me, and I looked back and said, "Jerry, that ball was too high to be a strike." He looked at me and said, "You don't tell me that ball was high, son, you ask me if it was high." So I said, "All right, Jerry, was that pitch a little high?" He answered, "Yeah, it was up." We both just kind of laughed for a second—until I struck out swinging on the next pitch.

My first National League run-in with an umpire was with Bruce Froemming. If you asked any National League player who they were most apt to get into it with, Bruce's name would come up more often than not.

While playing with Montreal, Froemming's crew was doing a long series of ours with Atlanta and Houston at home. We saw a lot of bad calls, and of course, they all went against us—and usually at a crucial point in the game and usually involving Froemming.

Finally, Archie Cianfrocco made a great diving play at first, flipped the ball to Jeff Fassero covering first, and Froemming blew the call. Our dugout was less than 20 feet from the foul line, and all of us went nuts. Even soft-spoken, newly appointed Manager Felipe Alou went out to argue the call. Things began to settle down a little, and I had to pipe up! Most of the time when guys mouth off in the dugout, they'll do it only if the umpire doesn't know it's them talking. You don't want to blast the ump and then have to try to hit the next night when that same guy is working the plate.

Well, I stood up and said, "It's a little tiring getting it shoved up our ass night after night." When Bruce looked into the dugout to see who was on him, I kind of snapped. I turned around and pointed at my back and said, "Yes, I said it. Number 2. Lyons. You're brutal out there."

I think Froemming was so surprised that somebody was actually admitting they said something, he didn't know what to do. He didn't throw me out of the game, he just said, "Keep your mouth shut." But by this time, second base umpire Ed Montague was on his way over to see what was going on, and I continued to yell at him. "The game is out there," pointing toward the field. "Keep your eyes out of this dugout, nobody's talking to you!" The funny thing was, I wasn't even in the game. I guess that's one indication of how frustrating it was playing in Montreal.

One thing I've wondered is why a hitter can voice a complaint with the umpire, but pitchers can't. We've all seen it before: a hitter doesn't like a particular call, and lets the umpire know it. It varies from asking, "Wasn't that pitch a little outside?" to "That blankity-blank pitch was nowhere near the blanking strike zone! How can you call that blanking pitch a strike?"

Of course, if you choose the latter you better hope you're looking towards the pitcher as you're saying those choice words. Even so, if the next pitch is anywhere close, you better be swinging, because umpires want no part of your questioning their calls. And if you're waiting for one of them to say, "Yeah, you're right, I missed that one," don't hold your breath.

But a double standard exists when it comes to pitchers arguing balls and strikes. You can't do it. I guess because at 60 feet away there is no quiet or unsuspecting way to do it, and the umpires will not stand for being questioned or embarrassed by the players. They want to make sure that the 40,000 or so fans at the game think they have the game under control—even if they don't.

Striking out anger

Like most kids who ever played baseball, I had a hard time relaxing when I wasn't getting any hits. I knew very few guys who didn't get frustrated when they weren't hitting. Everybody shows their frustration in different ways and in varying degrees. I panicked. No doubt about it, I was a basketcase when things didn't go well. I got physically and verbally upset. I worried about everything. I became unapproachable and was difficult to be around. Luckily for me, those periods didn't linger for too long. Publicly, I could bounce back from a bad game by the next day, but inside I worried a lot. I always felt like I had to get enough hits in today's game in order to be in tomorrow's line-up. I think that's a common worry among utility players, even though deep down we really know that it doesn't make any difference. If we get four hits or no hits, we were only giving the regular player a day off, and he would be back tomorrow.

The part of my career that most embarrassed me was my temper. I spent a lot of time working on controlling my helmet-throwing and complaining, but I failed badly.

My Dad once told me that if I ever got 600 at-bats in a season, the most hits I'd ever get would be about 150. Based on my career average of .253, that means I was going to make about 450 outs. Was I going to get upset about every one of them? Was I going to throw my helmet every time? It didn't make sense to him or me, but unfortunately, I didn't always respond to adversity the way I would have liked — the way I saw true professionals act. Guys like Dwight Evans, Robin Yount, or Harold Baines. Even younger players like Robin Ventura. That doesn't mean these guys never got upset or threw a helmet. They did. But they picked their spots. They waited until they were out of sight or by themselves, and they didn't do it often. Because I wasn't very good in the area of self-control, I had a great amount of respect for those who did on a day-to-day basis.

I have two conflicting theories about why my temper ran wild. The first I wish were true, the second is more likely. I get so wrapped up in the heat of the battle and so competitive that nothing else matters. My concentration is so focused on my job that only two reactions are possible — satisfaction or rage. I want things to go my way so badly, that the reality of a close play appears to be an easy call, going my way. During the game, in my mind, I'm always safe on a close play. At times, I'm sure I'm right, but not all the time.

The more likely reason for my temper is that we are all skilled people, fiercely competitive, — and extremely vulnerable. With each game, with every play and every pitch, we all face the possibility of failure and embarrassment. Those of us with less confidence, less security, and less control, mask those feelings in many different ways. I know there have been many times where a strikeout or an 0 for 4 has made me so mad that I threw something, hit something, or yelled and screamed at myself.

I've come to the conclusion that most of those actions were for the benefit of everyone else. I felt it would assure them that I could do better, and I expected myself to. Hiding behind emotional blow-ups allowed me to make sure I had more time to address the possibility of a more serious problem. Even if the problem wasn't that serious, I made it more so by worrying about it. I just wanted everybody to believe in me as a player, even when I sometimes doubted myself. It's indeed a painful revelation on my part, especially when it's laid out for all who care to read it. But I take pride in knowing that I still have time to learn about my shortcomings and change them — even if it is a lifelong process.

Terrific?

One thing I noticed through all my travels in 1993, was that when I did claw my way back to Boston in mid-June, there was at least one person who was not so proud to talk about it. My first start that year was in Yankee Stadium, where Tom Seaver is now a TV analyst for the Yankees. He was saying how I had bounced around, going from Boston to Chicago, back to Boston, Atlanta, Montreal, and Boston again! What he failed to mention was that the first time I was traded from Boston to Chicago, I was traded for Tom Terrific himself. Obviously, the trade was considered to be much more a feather in my cap than his!

T.V. time

One of my bigger off-the-field thrills was when I appeared as a guest on Roy Firestone's "Sports Look" show on ESPN (now called "Up Close"). I was even a regularly scheduled guest, honest. His show was always considered by the players as a "Who's Who" in the world of sports. Not just anyone gets on the show. Of course, my appearance was related to my pants-down episode on the field, but I got my chance to intelligently answer some questions on the most elite sports talk show.

I did, however, find the experience somewhat funny in the way Firestone himself prepared for my interview. After waltzing through the "People's Court" stage, which is in the same studio as Firestone's show, I was waiting in the make-up room. Firestone came in and introduced himself and asked a few background questions: Where are you from? What does your Dad do? How's the season going? That kind of stuff. He probably left the room wondering how the hell was he going to talk to me about dropping my drawers for seven minutes.

Once the on-air interview began, he used a technique that made him seem like he knew me much better than he really did. He seemed very prepared and well-informed. Instead of asking me the same direct questions as he had earlier, he used my answers to lead to another question. For example, instead of asking me where I was from again, he said, "Now Steve, I know you're from Oregon. How did playing most of your baseball in the rain affect your progress?"

Later, when we were talking about a nasty series we had played against Oakland, I mentioned that Dave Stewart got mad at me and said I had no business playing baseball, and should be selling insurance instead. Firestone and I both kind of laughed about it, and he added, "somebody in your family is in the insurance field, aren't they?" I had told him earlier that my father sold insurance. He then moved to the next line of questions to which he already knew most of the answers.

My learning disability

What makes one player consistently better (one hit a week) than another? I have no idea. I did this stuff for more than 13 years, and if there was something I could learn other than practice, I would have come across it. I know it has a lot to do with timing and hand-eye coordination, coupled with the ability to see the ball quickly and not be fooled by its speed and trajectory. I never figured it out, that's why my timing was always off. I could never learn to wait long enough before beginning my swing. It was no secret that I couldn't hit anything off-speed, so I got a pretty steady diet of curveballs and change-ups.

I had an interesting conversation with second baseman Jody Reed in 1991. We were talking about recognizing pitches and knowing what to swing at and what to lay off. He said, "When I see a slider early in the count, I don't swing at it unless it hangs. I'd rather hit a fastball until I've got two strikes."

I said, "Bull, how do you know it's a slider until after the catcher has it in his glove?" He said, "I read the spin." I have 20-10 vision, I can read the fine print on a contract from across the room — but I couldn't see the spin on the ball as it passed me at 90 M.P.H. I never knew what pitch I was seeing until after I swung at it. Then I said, "nice slider" — as the catcher threw the ball back to the pitcher. The only time I ever knew what pitch was coming was when I guessed right.

Jody couldn't believe it, so we asked a few other guys on the bench. They all said they do try to read the spin on the ball to tip them off to the pitch that's being thrown.

Usually, I thought I had a mediocre career with not quite enough talent to get into the elite of the game. But I left that game thinking I was pretty damn good to hit .253 and never "read" one pitch ever thrown to me— to accomplish what I did, playing with this quirky baseball learning disability. I always started my swing and then, while the pitch was on its way, decided what kind of pitch it was, how fast it was going, and figured out if it was actually a strike or "my pitch," before I swung the bat.

I started watching pitchers as they warmed up in the bullpen, trying to get a "read" on their pitches. You can see the different types of spin on the ball to help you figure out each pitch, but I could never quite incorporate that knowledge during a game. It seemed so different when I actually had to swing the bat. Everything went so much faster. Even if I did read the pitch, it was by me before I had the chance to hit it! I learned about this "reading" thing way too late in my career to make it work for me. I guess the bottom line is, you never stop learning — no matter what you do.

The greatest power of all

When friends and other players ask me who has the most power in the game, I think my answer startles them a little. I watched current Red Sox outfielder Jose Canseco hit the fifth deck in the Toronto Skydome in the 1990 American League Championship Series against Toronto. I personally witnessed Fred McGriff hit the Hard Rock Cafe window in that same stadium in 1989 — and there have been countless other "bombs." Who gets my vote? How about Wade Boggs? I played with Wade for about four years. In that time, he was always known as a hard-working player. He did what he had to do to make himself better. But he rarely showed up for extra hitting — maybe six or seven times a year (with a career average of .350 you don't need too many extra swings).

When he did, it was usually because he detected something that he felt needed work before that night's game, and he'd come early and correct it.

He seemed to be able to hit a home run in batting practice anytime he wanted. I'm not an idiot, I know the difference between batting practice and a game — I didn't sit on the bench that much! But having the power and ability to hit a baseball out of the ball park in any situation takes a tremendous amount of talent.

One day in Cleveland he showed up for early batting practice and put on a show I'll never forget. In less than ten minutes he took about 60 swings, sending 50 balls into the seats. And to showcase his bat-handling ability, he hit about 25 of them to left, 15 to center, and pulled (which he rarely does) 10 more to right. The rest of us watched in amazement. I don't care who you talk about — how far the ball went, how much power a guy has, anything — I'll never see another display like that, ever. Boggs' power numbers don't really support my claim that he has as much power as anybody. His best home run year was 24 in 1987, and he never hit more than eight in any other year.

When I asked him about that, he said he wanted to be remembered as the best hitter in baseball. If he tried to hit more home runs, naturally his average would drop. He may hit 20-30 home runs and bat .310 or .320. He said he'd rather hit five to ten home runs and hit .350.

Say what you want about Wade Boggs. Hell, even I didn't always like the way he played. But give him credit for being able to do what all of us wish we could. He knew exactly what he wanted, went out and did it — Wade Boggs will indeed be remembered as one of baseball's all-time greatest hitters.

Let's play two

The first time I ever met one of the all-time greats, Ernie Banks, Mr. Cub, the man who is attributed with one of the most-quoted statements ever made in baseball, "It's a great day for baseball, let's play two," we were playing two! And that's exactly what he said to me. The Cubs had scheduled a "B" game that day at 10:30 a.m. before the regular 1 p.m. start. I asked him to autograph a ball for me and he said, "Sure I'll do it." And then out it came — "It's a beautiful day for baseball, let's play two!"

From one "psycho" to another

Stephen King is an avid Red Sox fan and attends about 20 games a year. One game in 1991 when I knew he was there, I sent a ball up to him that said, "From one Psycho to the original." Two weeks later, he visited the dugout before a game, and he brought me a signed copy of his most recent book with the inscription, "To Steve Lyons, From your #1 fan, Annie Wilkes." He then signed his name, Stephen King. Of course, Annie Wilkes is the principle character in one of his other books, *Misery*. But the most important message I got from him was a telegram in 1992, the day I was traded back to the Red Sox for my third stint with the team. The papers read "Psycho III, Here We Go Again," or "Psycho III, The Return." King's telegram simply read, "Welcome Home." He went out of his way for me, and his words couldn't have meant more.

Gifts from the heart

In the years 1992 and 1993, I was involved in a charity golf tournament in St. Croix, Virgin Islands to benefit the Queen Louise Home. The Lutheran social services run a home for children whose parents are abusive and negligent. They house about 35 children who have had rough upbringings. Some are born HIV positive, there are a few crack babies, another with Down Syndrome. But most of them were either abused, abandoned, or simply not cared for or loved.

During the week-long event, the celebrity ballplayers played three rounds of golf. Each foursome had a sponsor that paid big bucks to play with a celebrity. The ballplayers also go to the Queen Louise Home, and spend half a day with the kids in their environment to really see what they were supporting. Each player also brought some personal items such as bats, gloves, or pictures to auction off at the celebrity dinner and auction.

I've been to my share of these functions, and have also donated plenty of items to these auctions in the past, but I've never seen the outpouring of love and money like that at the Queen Louise Home.

Not only was I thrilled to meet and spend time with Hall of Famers Brooks Robinson, Al Kaline, Billy Williams, and others, but it was great to see how they, as well as current players and coaches, got involved.

At one point near the end of the auction in 1993, an item called "A Children's Package" was auctioned off. It contained various gift certificates for Stride Rite shoes, a pizza party, and other things. It was worth maybe $200. When the bidding started at $100, Randy Johnson's hand raised and stayed in the air as the bidding continued. After the price rose to $1,000, Johnson noticed there was only one other bidder that was dueling it out with him — Jaimie Navarro. It was a hard throwing lefty against a hard throwing righty, which was amusing to everyone watching. As the bidding climbed to $3,500, Navarro began imitating Johnson, refusing to lower his arm from high over his head. At $4,500, Johnson (who is 6'10" standing on the ground), stood up on his chair and raised his hand.

The crowd, which by now was cheering wildly in admiration and enjoyment, was sensing defeat for Navarro. When Johnson signaled his "go ahead" for $5,000, the crowd rose to its feet and gave him a standing ovation. The auctioneer called him up to the stage to be acknowledged. But just as the crowd quieted a little, there was a familiar voice from the back of the room.

"What?" the voice said, "We're all done?" It was Navarro answering the bell for another round, after it seemed the knock-out punch had been thrown. "$5,100," he said. And back at it they went. With a haymaker of his own, Navarro jumped from $5,200 to $6,000 by holding up all five fingers on one hand and an index finger on the other. Johnson fell back into his seat and heard "going once, going twice. . ." "$6,100," Johnson yelled, surrendering to his competitiveness and his knowledge that his pockets must be deeper than Navarro's.

"No way," thought Navarro, could Johnson have come back from that $6,000 bid, and yet he had. Now it was just a matter of time before Johnson would have victory. At $6,300, Navarro could go no further and physically bowed to Johnson and another standing ovation.

It's easy to say, "Well, they're both millionaires, they can afford to do it." That may be true, but there are many more of us out there who can afford to do something but choose not to — and when you understand that neither Johnson nor Navarro even had children of their own (Jaimie and his wife Tammy now have a son, Jaimie Jr.) it makes it even more special. They bid over $6,000 for a $200 item, just so they could donate it back to the kids at the Queen Louise Home. Navarro had already spent nearly $5,000 bidding on a refrigerator, which he donated back to the Home. Between the two of them, they spent nearly $30,000 at the auction. And it wasn't so much because they could, it was because they cared.

I hope they're listening

Even though I never became a household name as a ballplayer, I was still able to use my profession as a means to speak out. I got plenty of opportunities to speak at little league banquets, rotary clubs, high schools, and junior highs. For two straight winters, I made tours of nearly every junior high and high school in central Connecticut. I talked about things that were important to me, using three basic points: do your best, be yourself, and have fun. Plus I told stories about my dad or experiences I had in high school.

Many times, my speaking engagements coincided with drug awareness week at school and, as you might expect, I had a unique way to handle the subject. I made sure I had their attention and then told them that I would not stand in front of them and tell them not to use drugs and alcohol. I backed that statement up by saying that I didn't think it was a good idea for them to do it and that I had never used any drugs. They had their parents telling them not to use drugs, their teachers telling them to "say no to drugs" — everybody telling them not to use drugs. I didn't feel it was my job to beat a dead horse. I challenged the students to make the right choice for themselves — based on what they knew was right and stressed that the consequences of these choices would affect the rest of their lives.

The approach made me feel like I was talking to the kids, not preaching at them. I felt they could walk away from it knowing that if they were put in a situation where they had to make a tough choice, they might remember something I said. I didn't want them to feel like I was just another adult telling them what to do.

I made sure that they knew how important I felt individualism was. Going along with the crowd isn't always the thing to do, and showing somebody you can stand on your own, and standing on your own, or even alone, is a big step toward gaining self-confidence.

Kids that age were starting to find out that there were going to be a lot of things in their life they were going to have to do that they didn't necessarily want to do; you'll always have a boss or an authority figure in your life. I wanted them to understand that they would forever be judged by their effort. I wanted them to think about always doing their best in life, not just in the things that they loved.

I had a built-in way of not sounding too much like a saint. Though I didn't drink or use drugs or get in trouble with the law I openly talked with the students about living with my own decisions as a teenager. The tough realities of being a father before I graduated from high school opened some eyes in those talks. And as hard as that was for me, it was nothing compared to what Lynn sacrificed to become a mother at 17—tossing aside her own childhood to become an instant adult.

Finally, I tried to make them see the lighter side of situations, to have fun and see things in a positive, optimistic view. Life will be hard at times, but it will be ever tougher if we always see the bad in our personal situations. Being miserable never helped anybody, and it's a lot more difficult to hang around someone who is never happy.

An MVP work ethic

As you sit and watch superstar Frank Thomas, think about what he's already accomplished in his career as a two-time American League MVP.

He has become one of the most feared hitters in the league, and his rise to the top has been a quick one. For all his potential greatness and thrills yet to be seen, kids could learn a great lesson from Thomas because of something he couldn't do–throw. Can you imagine a major league ball player who never learned to throw a baseball correctly?

In 1989, when the "Big Hurt" first came up to the White Sox, he had a serious throwing problem. Due to some shoulder injuries from his football days and lack of good coaching and practice, this 6'5" 240-pound man could barely throw the ball from first to second. The coaching staff for the Sox had Thomas show up early every day to play catch. Isn't it amazing? The first thing you learn to do is throw a ball! We work on it from that very first time we fire that rattle across the room when we're babies.

So, day by day, using a new grip on the ball and learning to throw a little more over the top for better control, Thomas got better. To his credit, he worked at it early every day, when you know he would have rather been launching balls into the seats in extra batting practice. He worked on something he wasn't good at. He worked on his weaknesses as well as his strengths, and five years later as an all-star and MVP, nobody would ever guess that at one point, he couldn't throw.

My kind of owner

Ben Mondor owns the Pawtucket Red Sox. He is by far the classiest owner ever. He goes the extra mile for both the players and the fans. In 1992, the highest ticket price in the whole stadium was $5, there was free parking, and not a bad seat in the house. As a result, the attendance record was broken in 1992 for the seventh straight year.

He treats his players as if they were his own sons, and never says a bad word about his team, regardless of how well they're playing. During the playoffs one year, he invited all the wives to travel and stay with the team, and personally invited the entire organization to be his guest at every meal - fully paid for.

Our kangaroo court had raised $900 for a team party at season's end, and Ben attended the final court session. After being fined $5 for being late for court, he added $2,000 to the total so that we could have a "real" team party.

In the penny-pinching business side of baseball, Ben Mondor stands alone as a guy who anticipates problems before they happen, fixes them if they do happen, and smiles every time you see him. I was on the only championship team he ever had in 1984. Of the three championship rings I own (1983 New Britain and 1986 American League Championship in Boston) I'm most proud of the ring we won in Pawtucket.

Ballpark sounds

In almost every ballpark, the P.A. announcer has a few announcements when the home team takes the field. He usually tells the fans to be alert, because of the danger of thrown bats and balls. He mentions the alcohol policies: that it will not be sold after the seventh inning. And then my favorite part: "And as always, obscene language, running, rowdyism, throwing objects in the stands, and general misbehavior will not be tolerated, and is cause for immediate ejection from the ballpark." Isn't it ironic that the fans can't participate in the very same things they'll see during the game?

It amazes me the way a crowd sounds when it really gets into the game. When a game-winning home run is hit or a great play is made, and close to 50,000 people stand, cheer, and scream, the sound is indescribable. And it's a different sound when you're part of the crowd making the noise than when you're the subject of the cheering.

First, you can hear clapping, then other noises join in that are only partially recognizable — screaming, yelling, stomping, until very quickly the sound escalates to the point of a high-pitched shrill with a constant ringing in your ears. And it's fun. But imagine trying to explain that experience to someone who had never been part of a crowd before? It would be frightening. None of it sounds like a pleasurable experience, and yet that's how we show our appreciation for excellence.

What are they talking about out there?

People have asked me if any of the opposing players ever talked to me during the "action" of the game. It only happened a couple of times that I can remember. In my rookie year, 1985, we were playing in Toronto. I was at bat, protecting the plate on a 1-2 count, trying not to strike out. But, as the pitcher wound up and delivered, I was startled by Ernie Whitt, the catcher. As the ball was about halfway to the plate, he yelled out "Shit" just as I swung and hit the ball over the right field wall for a home run. It definitely wasn't the pitch Whitt wanted to see, and he reacted as if he knew I was going to hit it out of the park even before I did (which for a guy with 19 career home runs, that's something). I'm not sure if he scared me into hitting the ball out, or if I didn't notice him until after I swung the bat.

Later in my career, I spent all spring learning how to play second base. When the season began, I was sure I was prepared for every possible situation that might come up. I knew my relay responsibilities, how to protect myself with the bag on double-play balls, and how the guys on the other team came in hard to break them up. But I wasn't prepared for Dave Parker. One night in a game against Oakland, Parker singled to right. The next hitter grounded to short for a fairly routine double play to end the inning. As I made the pivot to throw to first, Parker let out a scream that scared the hell out of me. I'd never before heard a player scream at a guy while he was turning a double play (or making any other play for that matter). I made the play, but both of us shared a laugh before he stood up and I ran off the field.

All in all, most of the talking takes place in the dugout between innings. You can always say "hello" to the catcher or to the infielders as you make your way around the bases, but not much more than that. There's no time—and remember, every-body has to be so serious out there. It's baseball. It's a war; you're supposed to hate your opponents. I never quite understood that attitude. Why can't I get a base hit and come back to first base with a big smile? Mark Grace is there and I say, "Isn't this great? Sunny day, lots of people watching—I'm making lots of money, aren't you? Yahoo!"

It never happens. Some guys have more of a sense of humor than others. It's just your job to know who they are. Dave Lapoint was always a good guy to have around to keep guys loose, and he expected his teammates to do the same for him.

One day he began to struggle to throw strikes in the ninth inning of a game against Milwaukee. We were winning 6-1, but with two outs he walked two batters in a row. I walked in from my third base position and said, "Look, what the hell am I going to tell you about pitching but throw strikes—you want the complete game don't you?" He said, "Yeah, I'm O.K." As I started to head back to third base, I stopped and came back to say, "By the way, did you see the blonde sitting two rows behind our dugout?" He started to laugh and said, "I saw her. Why do you think I walk so slow off the field at the end of the inning?"

The next hitter hit the first pitch right to me and the game was over.

Try to have that same conversation with a player with a tight ass, and the game is over all right—you lose.

Hitting into a slump

Every hitter goes through periods when things are going so well he feels he can hit any pitch — and sometimes does. The ball seems to find a hole every time, whether he knows what pitch it was or not —he's just in a zone. Every close pitch is a ball, and he guesses right every time. Even when he makes an out, it's a bullet, right at an opposing player. The pitched ball looks like a beach ball in slow motion just waiting to be crushed.

I think you have to concentrate even more during those periods to make them last. When you get two and three hits a game for about a week, your confidence is sky high. It doesn't matter who's pitching tomorrow, because you're gonna get two knocks. But, if you fall into that trap and really do begin to think you can hit anything, it can backfire. You become a little less selective and a little too aggressive at the plate. You pay less attention to the mechanics of your swing that got you those hits in the first place, and you start to think more in terms of higher power numbers. "I'm going so good right now I should add some home runs in there, too." When this happens, even though you're hitting well, it's the beginning of a slump.

First, you take a 1 for 4, and then an 0 for 4. That bounce isn't quite the same in your step, you're not chirping as much as you were three days ago, and you think, "Man, I'm one for my last eight, I gotta get it going again." You begin to worry, just a little about your mechanics — something you should have stayed on top of for the last few days, but you were going great. No need to worry. Today that close call is a strike, and then you guessed fastball but got a curve — you're only another 0 for 4 away from a slump, a slump you thought yourself into because you didn't stay on top of your game when you were on top of your game.

Which brings me to the question I've wanted an answer for during this whole story — Why is it that when you decide to take a strike, just to see what this guy has today, it's always a fastball down the middle?

The more I played, the more I believed that the less you think while hitting, the better off you'll be. No brains, no headaches!

"Get a knock" socks

The one thing every hitter fears is a prolonged slump. And even worse, an 0-for slump. No hits, day after day. Nothing scares a hitter more than that. I had a few prolonged 0-for slumps, but never over 20 at-bats. I ended my rookie year in 1985 with an 0 for 19, until my final at-bat of the season, a home run. My average dropped from .276 to .264 by season's end.

I played with guys who did live through worse slumps. Robin Ventura went 0 for 41 in 1990, Tim Naehring 0 for 39 in 1991, and Scott Hatteburg went 20 at-bats before his first "AAA" hit. All three of these guys handled the bad times far better that I would have — especially Ventura. He was the most calm and collected person in the world during that slump, which may have explained his quick rise to stardom for the White Sox. In 1991, Naehring was pretty calm too, but I got in on the tail end of the slump because I joined the team late. I never saw him get a hit until late 1992, because he had back surgery during the slump of 1991. Hatteberg's 0 for 20 came quickly. He came up because of an injury, and he was a little too scared to be mad about it.

In all three cases, I felt like I wanted to do something to help the guy get a hit, somehow, even though I knew nothing I could do would help directly. For Ventura, I developed the "Get A Knock" sock. I took about 15 sanitary socks, and wrote "Get A Knock" on all of them, then passed them out to everybody on the bench. When Ventura went to bat we all took off our hats and tied the socks around our heads. Three at-bats later, Ventura hit a dribbler to third for a hit, ending the 0 for 41 slump. We tried the same thing in Boston with Naehring, but he went on the disabled list with back problems before the "Get A Knock" sock could work its magic. For Hatteberg I wrote "Hatty" on the socks, but changed after two more hitless at-bats. I figured out that he would be hitting .041 if he got a hit on his next at-bat, so I wrote ".041" on the headbands, and sure enough, Hatty lined one up the middle for a single — 1 for 21.

The scorers

I often wonder where teams get their official scorers for their home games. I wonder if anyone thinks about how much those decisions mean to the players. Scoring a hit or an error is usually pretty clear. But sometimes there are tough plays that don't look all that difficult, or when the scorer sees the slow-motion replay, every ball looks like it should have been caught.

I don't think the scorers themselves realize the potential impact of their tough scoring decisions. For instance, scoring that one-hop liner that glances off the second baseman's glove a hit may have given the player 2 for 5 on the day. Together with yesterday's 0 for 3, the player feels if he just gets off to a good start tomorrow and maybe mixes in a walk, he could be 3 for 10 — .300. If that same play is ruled an error, he's now 1 for 8 going into tomorrow, and the pressing begins: what will an 0 for 4 look like on top of the previous two days? Those decisions can make the difference sometimes between a guy really gaining confidence and going on a 6 for 10 tear, or doubting himself into a 3 for 20 slump.

And for pitchers, it's just as important. With two outs and a guy on first, if that same play gets ruled a hit, the next hitter could hit a home run for three earned runs. But if it's an error and he still gives up a home run to the next hitter, his ERA doesn't jump through the roof.

It seems like I always played on a team with a scorekeeper who would bend over backwards to make sure he wasn't giving out hometown hits. It's well known (to the scorer) that if you hit a questionable ball, and you were playing at home, it would be ruled a hit. However, when I got to Montreal, it seemed like everything was a hit, no matter who hit it — nobody ever made an error! It figures that for the entire two months I played there, when even I could get balls ruled as hits, I only had 13 at-bats.

They don't all even out

One thing that always bugged me about some guys was when they'd say, "Hey, they all even out," right after you hit a shot at the right fielder. BULLSHIT! They don't all even out. I know you shouldn't be too upset when you hit a shot right at a first baseman or shortstop, because they're out there for just that reason — to get you out. And they've been standing in the same places for over 100 years. Obviously, the object is to "hit 'em where they ain't." But when you're considered a great player, if you can do that 3 out of 10 times, it's a little easier said than done.

Let's face it, I was a career .253 hitter with very little power, but my hits were every bit as important to me as anyone else's. In 1989 particularly, I got as many bleeders as anybody in the league. I used to tell people that there had to be at least one 200 pound "Punch and Judy" hitter in this league, and I would gladly accept the role. It always seemed to me that when I hit the ball hard, I was out. If I hit one off the end of my bat or got jammed, I had a good chance to get a hit. As players, we all look for that good grain in our bats, and if you got a knot in the hitting area that was a bonus. Everybody thought the knots were harder wood and better to hit with — so I'd always check for knots in the handle of my bat, figuring that's the part I'd be using to hit, anyway.

I always told people that I didn't want to lift weights in the off-season, because I might get strong enough to hit the ball to the outfielders. But no matter how many duck farts I got for hits, I know I hit more balls hard for outs — so don't tell me they even out. They don't.

Curtain calls

I guess when everyone's career comes to an end, they always reflect and wonder what might have been. My list isn't very long. I did the best I could with limited ability, and feel I proved a lot of people wrong about a nobody from Oregon. I had a good run and a lot of fun. There's really only one thing that sticks out in my mind that I never got the chance to do — a simple curtain call. That one moment when you won the game with a home run, or you had such a great day the fans cheered until you stepped out of the dugout to tip your hat and say "thanks."

I hit a game-winning home run once for the White Sox in Chicago against the Royals. It was the only home run I ever hit at Comiskey Park in four years. It was in the eleventh inning of a cold May night game, so everyone who was still at the game just wanted to go home, and left as soon as the ball was hit.

I can't help but imagine the thrill a curtain call would bring. In fact, I think it would be the single biggest moment a player could have. Everybody in the entire ballpark clapping and hollering, refusing to sit back down until you come back out to acknowledge them. Sometimes, it even holds up the game because the next batter doesn't want the distraction. How great that must feel. Hopping back up to the top step to raise your fist in triumph, first to the fans behind home plate and then again to the outfield fans, knowing that they all had singled you out for that moment of glory.

I consider myself one of very few ballplayers who actually enjoyed the fans and appreciated their presence, and I never got a curtain call, just to publicly thank them all at once.

I remember when Dwight Evans was shamefully let go in 1991 by the Red Sox, and he came back to Fenway with the Orioles. He got a standing ovation for each and every at-bat for the entire three-game series!

His first appearance was something memorable. When public address announcer Sherm Feller announced his name, the Boston crowd went nuts. There were signs and banners all over the place proclaiming the love these fans had for Evans.

Being the true class act that he is, Evans dug himself in at the plate, waited a few seconds, and then succumbed to the cheers of the crowd. He doffed his cap to all corners of the field, raised his arms and visibly said thank you a number of times. He then tried to resume his concentration at the plate, but the fans wouldn't let him.

The onslaught of noise and cheering was something I had never seen in all my years at Fenway. He had to back away from the plate again, and once again the helmet came off. This went on for minutes before he finally got a chance to hit, and at no time during this event was there a player or fan or anyone else saying "Come on, let's get on with the game." Forget his stats, forget his longevity, forget his class, leadership, and gold gloves. If you had never seen any game but that one, those five minutes said everything about Dwight Evans and what kind of player he was.

It's over

In September of 1993, I began to face what every professional athlete must — my career would soon be over. I started thinking about all the time I had spent preparing myself for my playing career and how unprepared I was to give it up. From the little league games to the thousands of balls my dad pitched and hit to me, I had worked to become a ballplayer. It might not be like preparing for any other career, but the preparation is no less important.

I was typical in the sense that I was unprepared for the business world. At 34, with three years of college education and no degree, I wasn't the most employable applicant. But I also knew that I would never apply for an entry-level accounting position. I wanted to get into broadcasting or something baseball related.

In January of 1994, I had exhausted all of my playing options. My agent had contacted every major league team to see if there was any interest in me. There was none. He also contacted every minor league director in every organization and got the same result. Over time he continued to make a pitch for me as a player — until he'd been turned down by every team four different times.

I knew my skills had not diminished to the point where I couldn't be at least an insurance policy for some team. I was in good shape, had a nine-year major league career, was never injured, and could play almost any position. I realized how my recent past had caught up with me. Telling two organizations to shove it (Montreal and Chicago Cubs) and having a fairly well-known dislike for my past manager in Boston (Hobson), didn't lend itself to getting another job. Baseball still operates by the old-boy network in terms of dealing with talent. All the General Managers talk on a daily basis about players they're interested in signing or trading — I burned too many bridges.

It was kind of ironic, because for most of my career I was a "yes" man for any team I played for. Anything they wanted me to do, I did it—no questions, no complaints and no problems. I guess I just got to the point where I really started to feel mistreated, and I was finally man enough to stand up and say I didn't like it. In my business, however, if you voiced your opinion, you took a big chance of losing your career.

I knew my baseball career was over, and I knew I'd have a hard time accepting it. I never said I was the best player in baseball, but there were few players who enjoyed it more than I did. I had done it for 30 years. It was my passion. It was my job. It was a big part of my life. But I had to move on, and I wasn't sure where I was going.

I was recently divorced, so my financial worth was cut in half. I took a lot of pride in knowing that I would never be a ballplayer who once made good money and was later broke. I did then, and continue to have an obligation of spousal maintenance and child support, in addition to my own expenses.

I thought about buying or starting a business, but what? What were my interests? It was the first time in my life when my devotion to the game of baseball became a negative. I had enough money to start something, but I didn't have the education or guidance to make an intelligent decision.

I took on a new attitude of confidence bordering on arrogance. I had nothing to lose by asking for jobs that I didn't think I'd get, so why not be cocky? I called ESPN and asked to be considered for the "Baseball Tonight" show. Ray Knight had been used as a baseball analyst on the show, but took a coaching job with the Cincinnati Reds. I told them I'd be perfect for the job, because I knew all the players and had a good understanding of the game.

The executive producer of the show, Eric Shoenfield, seemed impressed and knew who I was. I had done "Baseball Tonight's" plays of the week three times, and he liked what he had seen. The problem was that they were already heavily pursuing someone they thought was the best baseball analyst available. Shoenfield told me that if he didn't sign, I might be considered for the job.

In the meantime, I had to do something to occupy my time. I couldn't accept doing nothing all day, so I took a job at a golf course — in the snack bar! I made $3 an hour, plus tips and free golf when I was through. I didn't know it would become such a big story.

Spring training was beginning, and since I was living in Phoenix, nine teams were in town. Some of the players began showing up to play golf after their workouts, and couldn't believe what they saw. I served hot dogs to Andy Ashby and Andy Benes of the Padres, Chuck Finley and Mark Langston of the Angels. I even asked then-Angels Manager Buck Rogers for one more chance when he saw me there.

I was desperate. I didn't want to let go of the only career I had ever known without a fight. I was entering an uncertain stage of my life and it came with fear and anxiety.

Langston couldn't believe it was me. "What are you doing back there?" he asked, "How come you're not playing?" I was a little embarrassed to say that I couldn't find a baseball job and for now, "This is my job." Those guys were good tippers though, and besides, I always thought I was the best looking snack bar girl they had!

I kept telling myself that I was proud of what I was doing. Imagine, a guy who made $650,000 a year earlier now making $3 an hour. It sounds like a riches-to-rags story doesn't it? That's what the local papers and a Chicago radio station thought. They called me to make fun of me and laugh at my expense, but I was too smart for that. I told them that I was just biding time until I could decide exactly what I wanted to do. I said I should be an example to all the people who would rather collect a welfare check or unemployment rather than accept a $3-an-hour job.

Working hard was never beneath me, and I would continue to do what I had to do to be happy. I'm sure they were looking to poke fun, but how can anyone make fun of someone who's willing to work?

Soon, I got an offer to work for a publishing company interested in producing sports cards. ESPN also called, but it was just to tell me that they hired the man they were after. It turned out to be Jim Kaat, but two weeks later they called me back and asked me to do feature stories for ESPN2 — work I'm still doing for them.

That summer, while working for the publishing company, I found out that one of the more popular sports radio personalities was leaving Chicago for New York Television. Since I happened to be in Chicago, I made an appointment with Greg Solk, the program director of WMVP Sports Radio. The arrogant attitude took over and once again, I went into a meeting asking for a job I never expected to get.

I told Solk that I thought he should hire me, that he needed someone like me. Looking a little startled, he asked why. I told him that I had a flamboyant personality that the station could use, that I was still recognized as a former athlete in Chicago, and that Norm Van Lier was the only other ex-athlete working on-air for them. "Do you have any radio experience?" he asked.

"No," I said, fully expecting the interview to be over in seconds. I wasn't far off, as our meeting came to a quick close after a few more casual questions. I knew I had made an impression, but I didn't know if it was the right one. It didn't take long to find out. Later that afternoon I was asked to come back to talk with Larry Wert, the General Manager of WMVP. Two weeks later, I auditioned for the job and by mid-July, I had a regular show. I am currently co-hosting "SportsWire" with Brian Davis from 7 to 11 every weeknight on Sports Radio 1000 WMVP.

I continue to expect bigger and better things for myself as I move into a new career in broadcasting. Maybe a job as a color analyst for baseball, either for a team or on a national network level. I got another call from ESPN asking me to be the analyst for opening day in 1995 and I will also do some minor league games for them. Maybe someday I'll have my own TV talk show—everyone else does. Or maybe I will open that business. My fiancee, Christa, keeps telling me that whatever it is, I will become more successful than I ever was playing ball. Right now that may be hard for me to believe, but she does, so that's a step in the right direction.

Epilogue

When Steve Lyons told me that Stephen King had agree to write the foreword to this book, I congratulated him by responding, "That's a lot more impressive than 'Foreword by Tom Demakis.'" With that comment, I must have inadvertently inspired Steve, because a couple of weeks later he asked me to write the epilogue. I read a fair amount, and I can't recall seeing an epilogue written by anyone other than the author. However, when the author answers to "Psycho," he can take certain liberties. Besides, Steve is my friend, and I was pleased and honored to be asked.

I first met Steve in the summer of 1982. He was a top prospect playing Double A ball, not yet knowing that he would fulfill his dream of having a successful major league career. I was an attorney and aspiring agent, trying to convince Steve to become my first baseball client. He hired me, and I immediately knew that I was dealing with a man of rare intelligence and judgment.

In the 13 years since, we have shared many successes and some disappointments. Our professional relationship has been terrific, but more importantly, it has evolved into a great friendship that I cherish. I have learned much about, and from Steve. Almost none of what Steve is about is consistent with the "Psycho" nickname and image.

Steve embodies the values that you want your kids to have. He is loyal, responsible, hard working, and generous. One incident captures the essence of Steve Lyons, the man. Over the years, Steve has made numerous speaking and personal appearances, many for free at hospitals, schools, and Little League banquets, none for grand sums of money. Not once did he break an engagement, and only once was he late. That happened on a Saturday night. He was playing for the Red Sox and had agreed to make a free appearance for a charity in a town in Connecticut that is two hours by car from Fenway Park. The Red Sox game on Saturday afternoon was first delayed by rain, then went into extra innings. It ended only a half hour before Steve's scheduled appearance. Almost anyone else would have used the late ending as an excuse to cancel the appearance. Steve called the organizers to say that he would be late, but if they would wait for him, he would be there. They waited, and he went (and, as always, wowed the audience).

As a ballplayer, Steve was quite ordinary if you measure him by statistics. If you measure him as I do, by how he played the game and by what he gave to the fans, he was an All-Star. Steve never took being a major leaguer for granted. He played every game as if it were his first. Not once in nine years did he not run out a ball, not once was he not ready in the field when a pitch was thrown. He mastered the fundamentals and never hesitated to give himself up to help his team win. He learned to play every position. Simply put, he played the game the way it's suppose to be played.

Off, and even on the field, Steve never forgot who paid his salary. I never saw him refuse an autograph. When he and I were out together and a fan whom he had met before approached him, he would remember the fan's name or some fact about the person with amazing frequency, even though the prior meeting might have been years before. He took a personal interest in the fans, and they reciprocated with respect and affection for him.

Even those fans who never met Steve enjoyed and appreciated his play, partly because he played with intelligence and hustle, probably more because he had fun and was entertaining to watch. Whether playing tic-tac-toe in the dirt behind first base or warming up in left field before an inning by playing catch with a youngster in the stands, Steve enjoyed baseball to the fullest and brought the fans along for the ride. He accomplished this without ever compromising his attention to the game or his effort to help his team win. In fact, the more fun he had, the better Steve played. And that's the way it should be. After all, baseball is only a game, and the object of any game is to have fun. No player of his time had more fun, or made the game more fun for the fans. That's why, in my book, Steve Lyons was an All-Star.

Tom Demakis
May 1995

INDEX